catering

A GUIDE TO MANAGING A SUCCESSFUL BUSINESS OPERATION

catering

A GUIDE TO
MANAGING A
SUCCESSFUL
BUSINESS
OPERATION

BRUCE MATTEL ● **THE CULINARY INSTITUTE OF AMERICA**

 JOHN WILEY & SONS, INC.

THE CULINARY INSTITUTE OF AMERICA

President	Dr. Tim Ryan '77
Vice-President, Continuing Education	Mark Erickson '77
Director of Intellectual Property	Nathalie Fischer
Editorial Project Manager	Lisa Lahey '00
Recipe Testing Database Manager	Margaret Wheeler '00
Production Assistant	Patrick Decker '05

The Culinary Institute of America wishes to recognize the contribution of Ben Fink's photography and the pick-up photography from the Patina Restaurant Group.

Banquet kitchen blueprint in the Appendix © Cody Hicks

Published by John Wiley & Sons, Inc., Hoboken, New Jersey
Published simultaneously in Canada

Designed by Debbie Glasserman

LIBRARY OF CONGRESS CATALOGING-IN-PUBLICATION DATA

Mattel, Bruce.

 Catering: a guide to managing a successful business operation / The Culinary Institute of America, Bruce Mattel.

   p. cm.

Includes index.

ISBN 978-0-7645-5798-9 (cloth)

1. Caterers and catering—Management. I. Culinary Institute of America. II. Title.

TX921.M38 2008

642'.4068—dc22

                                  2007011322

PRINTED IN THE UNITED STATES OF AMERICA

10 9 8 7 6 5 4 3 2 1

contents

acknowledgments

An educational or instructional text is rarely the result of a single person's effort. This book is the result of many formal and informal conversations; it is the informal ones that produced the most valuable material. I wish to thank many of my colleagues at The Culinary Institute of America for not brushing me off when I interrupted their thoughts or work for a bit of information that was important to me at that exact point in time. Those individuals are Tom Peer, Theo Roe, Dan Kish, Charles Rascoll, Gerard Viverito, Dan Turgeon, Gerry Fischetti, and Ezra Eichelberger.

I would also like to thank Dr. Tim Ryan, president of The Culinary Institute of America, for connecting me with industry professionals who greatly contributed to this text; Eve Felder, for her professional and personal support throughout this project; and Greg Fatigati, for his honest advice and for sharing his good and bad catering experiences with me.

The Food and Beverage Institute at The Culinary Institute of America was instrumental to the success of this book. The following individuals have been responsible for keeping the project on track, gathering peripherally related information, and most of all, helping me create realistic deadlines: Lisa Lahey, Maggie Wheeler, Kate McBride, Nathalie Fischer, and Sue Cussen.

Additionally, the contributions of the following people and their respective organizations were essential in allowing me to write about the realities of the catering world documented in this text: John Dougherty and the staff of the Waldorf Astoria Hotel; Anna Kasabian; Mark Beaupre of the JW Marriott Orlando, Grande Lakes resort; and Nick Valenti of the Patina Restaurant Group.

A special thank-you goes out to Alison Awerbuch and the staff of Abigail Kirsch Culinary Productions for its continued support of this project and its openness to allowing me to observe several of its spectacularly catered events.

Thanks also to those outside the Institute who helped in the production and publication of the book: to the folks at John Wiley—Pam Chirls, Christine DiComo, Christina Solazzo, and Ava Wilder; to the designer, Debbie Glasserman; and to Ben Fink for his photography.

Lastly, I would like to thank my wife, Denise, and my son, Jason, for their patience during much of the last few years while I spent many hours alone writing this book.

catering | A GUIDE TO MANAGING A SUCCESSFUL BUSINESS OPERATION

1. introduction to catering

henever people gather together for several hours, they're going to require food and beverages. At business meetings, coffee, tea, and bottled water—at the very least—are made available for attendees. Celebratory occasions such as weddings, christenings, birthday parties, bar and bat mitzvahs, and anniversaries call for special food and drink to complete the festivities. These are all prime occasions for catering.

From a meal in a prestigious stadium skybox to a mobile lunch wagon on a movie set, catering can be bone-china elegant or paper-plate casual, but it always means serving good-quality food and drink to many people.

Several things distinguish a catering operation from a restaurant.

Catering is usually done by prearranged contract—food and drink provided at a certain cost to a specific number of people. The menu at a catered event is usually more limited than a restaurant menu and is chosen in advance by the client. The way the food is prepared is different, too. Although both restaurant and catering chefs do the *mise en place,* or prepare the food ahead of time to a certain extent, catering chefs prepare their food so that it only needs brief final cooking, reheating, or assembly prior to service.

There are two main categories of catering.

Institutional: These caterers at hospitals, universities, airlines, large hotels, and retirement centers provide a wide variety of food and drink to a large number of people on an ongoing basis—usually at the institution itself. The institution usually contracts with a catering company to have this service provided.

Social: These caterers provide food and beverage services to civic groups, charities, corporations, businesses, and individuals on-premise at a catering or banquet hall or off-premise at a selected location.

The opportunities for a catering business multiply every year, given the right demographics—individuals, groups, or businesses who are able to pay for the service.

Who Uses Catering Services?

- **Convention centers**
- **Hospitals, universities, retirement centers, nursing homes**
- **The entertainment industry:** musicians on tour, movie sets, plays in production, professional sports events
- **Businesses:** For meetings, openings, special sales events, corpo-

rate retreats, team-building exercises, awards banquets, executive dining, employee meals, galas, and so on

- ○ **Community groups:** For fund-raisers, donor or sponsor lunches, galas, and so on
- ○ **Individuals:** For special in-home dinners, bridal and baby showers, wedding receptions, birthdays, anniversaries, funerals, and so on

Career Outlook for Catering

The catering segment of the hospitality industry continues to grow every year. During the mid-1990s, catering was actually the fastest-growing sector of the food service industry. According to the Bureau of Labor and Statistics (a division of the U.S. Department of Labor), food preparation careers will be in demand through 2012. Institutional catering—to universities, hospitals, nursing homes, and business campuses—is on the upswing. Social catering to civic groups, charities, corporations, businesses, and individuals is the fastest-growing segment, according to the *Restaurant Industry Forecast 2000*, prepared by the National Restaurant Association.

Why? Contract catering allows institutions to keep costs down. And in the case of social catering, a home-building trend that includes large kitchens with upscale appliances inspires owners to entertain more often. The increase of cooking and lifestyle programming on television has led the average person to learn more about food products, wine, and cooking, and thus want a more sophisticated approach to home, business, or community entertaining than ever before.

Profile of a Successful Caterer

According to the *Princeton Review,* over 70 percent of all catering services are owner run. Thus, a successful caterer usually marries the culinary talents of a chef with the business savvy of a CEO.

For anyone who wants to be a caterer, a passion for entertaining is a prerequisite, because without it, the long hours and hard work will seem tiring rather than exciting and rewarding. Many caterers start out as people who simply love to cook and entertain. Their guests are always complimenting them on their abilities and telling them that they should entertain for a living. There are some very successful caterers who have begun their career this way; however, the passion for cooking and entertaining alone is not a recipe for success.

Before starting a catering business, you should attend formal classes on catering and business management or work for one or more caterers until you have a high level of understanding and a sense of the business.

Some people try to turn their hobby into a small catering business from home, in kitchens that are not licensed by the local health department. There is a big risk in operating this way. Home-based caterers may find themselves in trouble with the health department if their guests become ill from their food. In addition, home-based caterers usually do not understand the realities of running a for-profit catering business with many fixed expenses, such as business licenses, separate business phone and fax lines, and a Web site, all of which are necessary for continued business growth.

If you think that catering might be a great career option for you, check your skills against the qualities that a successful caterer ought to have (see sidebar). See how you fit in, or find those areas in which you'll need more education or help.

Some of these qualifications could be a natural part of your personality or education; you might have to learn others. Or you could hire a person or

Qualities of a Successful Caterer

Excellent organizational skills

Time-management skills

The ability to multitask

A friendly, hospitable personality

The ability to manage stress

An extensive knowledge of ingredients

A high level of written and verbal communication skills

Natural leadership and motivational skills

A knowledge of social and religious cultures and customs

Excellent networking skills

Proficiency in basic accounting principles

Basic mechanical skills

Good negotiating skills

Quick thinking and problem-solving skills

company to handle a part of the business that is not your strong suit. Here are several examples:

- If your culinary creativity soars, but your spelling and grammar are not the best, contract with a high school English teacher or a professional food writer to proofread your letters, contracts, and menus on a case-by-case basis. You may have the best-looking and best-tasting food in your city, but if your contracts, letters, and menus have spelling mistakes, that tells your customers that you aren't top-notch.
- If you're a talented chef with a sense of style but you don't have a clue about accounting practices, take a noncredit adult education class at your local community college, hire an accountant, or shadow a restaurant or catering manager to see how the book work is done.
- If your food and business skills are terrific but your style sense suffers, either concentrate on an area of catering in which this doesn't matter as much—institutional or outdoor barbecue catering—or hire an assistant or catering manager with a sense of style.
- If your food sense, style, and business skills are all great, but you can't fix anything, offer a retainer to a full-time (more expensive) or retired (less expensive) handyman or refrigerator and appliance repairperson to be on call. Then pay the hourly rate for any service call. For a major function, include the cost of this person's services as an insurance policy against culinary disaster. If you can't get the blowtorch to work and you need to make crème brûlée for three hundred, his or her services will be worth the extra money—especially if you have already figured the cost into your per person price.

The bottom line: a successful caterer has all the bases covered.

What Do You Want to Do?
Finding Your Catering Identity

Catering is a popular but competitive field. If you develop an identity or a signature style, you can create the competitive edge you'll need to succeed. Most people associate caterers with mainstream events such as weddings and holiday parties. Caterers who seek out a specific group or niche market have the opportunity to become the preferred caterers when that specific style of catering is needed. And caterers who know how to customize their services to appeal to a specific group or type of event usually continue to grow their businesses.

For example, you might decide to specialize in outdoor barbecue catering and market your business accordingly. You would set up your business with the specific equipment needed for this type of catering and create a customized barbecue menu. If you perform well at the initial events that you contract, you'll have good word-of-mouth referrals. You'll earn back your initial investment for the specialized barbecue equipment quickly, making it difficult for other mainstream caterers who need to rent equipment to compete for this type of party.

Here are a few more examples of catering niches:

○ **Party platters:** Whether dropped off by the caterer or picked up by the customer, party platters are a great way to create a buzz. Sales reps find they can get more attention from a medical or editorial staff when they provide a free lunch. Automobile dealers often want finger foods for potential customers coming to their showroom during a special promotion. Real estate agents may provide food and beverages to potential buyers during an open house showcasing a property.

- **Five-star dining at home:** Although popular, this service is still a niche market in large cities. Instead of going to a high-style restaurant, clients want a five-star experience in the comfort (and, usually, elegance) of their own homes, often for a special dinner for either business or pleasure.
- **Special dietary catering:** Your identity might be kosher or weight-loss foods, if the demographics in your area can support it. Vegetarian or even vegan catering is popular with entertainment industry professionals. If your catering operation can travel to movie sets or rock concerts, or deliver meals to customers, so much the better.

How Do You Want to Do It?
Finding the Right Catering Scenario

The big question is: Do you want to be employed as a caterer by a larger organization or start your own catering business?

As an employee of a larger catering organization, you can expect a median yearly salary of $35,000 to $50,000, according to www.payscale.com, a Web site that publishes accurate, real-time salary reports based on job title, location, education, skills, and experience. The benefits of employment are that you do not take the financial risk of starting a business, you have fewer job responsibilities than a catering business owner, and you gain valuable experience. The downside is that your earning potential is more limited.

As a caterer owning your own business, there is no guaranteed salary. You risk the money you use to start your business, your job responsibilities cover all aspects of the business, and any mistakes you make affect you directly. The upside is that your earning potential is virtually unlimited.

A medium-size catering business grossing $500,000 per year (about $10,000 in receipts every week) can realize a profit ranging from 10 to 20 percent, or $50,000 to $100,000. Top caterers can gross $1 million or more with a similar profit margin—about $100,000 to $200,000 per year. Keeping expenses in line and factoring profit into your pricing are the keys to that profit. (See Chapter 3, "Pricing for Profit.")

Whether you want to start your own business or to be employed as a caterer or catering manager, there are many types of catering to consider.

On-Premise Catering

An on-premise catering operation is made up of a food production area (kitchen) and a connected area where people dine. Examples of on-premise catering operations include restaurants, hotel banquet departments, cruise ships, country clubs, catering halls, and even some religious structures. On-premise operations should be located in desirable, safe locations and have ample parking. Whenever possible, the operation should be easily accessible by car and visible from the road. There should be a drop-off area for guests to allow for valet parking and protect the guests in bad weather. The entrance should have wheelchair accessibility and even an automatic door.

The downside to this scenario is that the larger the facility and the closer it is to a downtown area, the more expensive it will be to launch. However, on-premise catering businesses are a great place to gain valuable experience or a steady income as a salaried employee.

Many on-premise caterers start off renovating former movie theater space in a shopping mall, renting space in an existing school or church, adding on a private banquet room to their existing restaurant, or building a catering hall in areas close to a metropolitan area, but far enough away to find good real estate values.

The following are some examples of the many levels and styles of on-premise catering.

RESTAURANTS

Many restaurants have a private area or areas that can be used for parties. Some restaurants cater parties at their establishments on days that they are normally closed. Some operators even book their restaurant for catered events during normal business hours and close the doors to the public. (Restaurant operators should not turn away their regular clientele too often by closing their entire operation for such private parties.) If you already own or run a restaurant, this is a good way to get started in catering, as all the basics—your overhead expenses, kitchen facility, linens, glasses, and wait staff—are already in place.

HOTELS AND RESORTS

Hotels and resorts depend on their banquet departments to achieve profitability for their overall food and beverage operations. Banquet net profits can range from 15 to 40 percent, while hotel room service and restaurants often lose money. Many hotels have a variety of banquet rooms of different sizes and styles. This allows them to market their catering services to corporate clients for meetings and conventions as well as to private clients for social engagements, such as weddings and bar mitzvahs. Most hotels charge for the rental of the banquet rooms as well as for food, beverages, and service. This rental fee is partly responsible for the banquet's profitability.

Most hotels and resorts have large banquet kitchens specifically designed for high-volume catering. There is usually a separate group of cooks and prep people, headed by a banquet chef. The executive chef oversees this department and collaborates with the banquet chef and event- planning personnel when developing banquet menus or planning individual events. While working in such a venue is a good way to get catering experience, establishing one is a difficult and expensive way to start your own business.

CRUISE LINES

Most cruise lines offer catering services aboard their ocean liners. Event planning aboard a cruise liner is similar to that in a hotel. Some additional challenges are providing lodging for all the affair's guests and the inability to receive additional products once at sea. Cruise lines do have wonderful banquet rooms and other spaces that, along with the natural attributes of the environment, make a great venue for parties. Again, this is a good way to get catering experience, but a difficult and expensive way to start your own business—unless you already own a cruise line!

COUNTRY CLUBS

Most country clubs have banquet facilities. While many clubs only allow their members to hold events there, others allow member-sponsored events or even offer their banquet services to the general public. Country clubs often have golf courses and other sports facilities that lure businesses and organizations to host company-wide meetings or conventions where the participants enjoy a day of activities as well as a meal. Working at a country club can be a great way to gain catering experience and develop your identity before you start your own business—or it can simply be a great job.

PRIVATE CLUBS

Private clubs located in urban areas also provide catering opportunities for their members or the public. These "city" clubs have meeting rooms and dining areas that make them viable catering venues, which can provide valuable (and usually upscale) catering experiences. But unless you want to start your own private club, they are not an option for a practicable start-up business.

BANQUET HALLS

The most obvious of all on-premise catering operations is the banquet hall. These businesses specialize in catering social events. Most banquet halls have the capability of producing multiple events simultaneously. This is important, as the banquet hall usually has no other income-producing functions. It is possible, however, for banquet hall operators to do off-premise catering for the same reasons that restaurant operators can. The downside to a banquet hall is that the start-up expenses are very high. The banquet hall needs to be located in an area with good visibility and accessibility. A good location will mean higher rent—or purchase price and taxes—for the facility. Overall operating expenses, or overhead, will also be high due to the large size of the operation.

In order to be profitable, a banquet hall should be large enough to accommodate anywhere from five hundred to one thousand people at any given time. The dining area can be set up as one or two very large banquet rooms with the ability to be partitioned in order to create more banquet rooms for multiple smaller events. Many banquet halls also have outdoor areas where events can be held. This can increase the overall capabilities of the hall and generate higher revenues. The kitchen, therefore, must be set up to accommodate the needs of the banquet hall when all its dining areas are booked. The event planners for the banquet hall should try to sell similar menu items to patrons holding events simultaneously. This helps streamline production in the kitchen and prevent chaos during banquet service.

Many people decide to host their events at a banquet hall because the experience can be like one-stop shopping. Most banquet halls offer all-inclusive pricing that can include food, service, entertainment, photography, floral arrangements, and anything else typically needed for a catered event. It is therefore important to find people or companies that aspire to the same quality standards as your own when subcontracting for services you do not provide.

RELIGIOUS GROUPS

Some churches and synagogues have banquet facilities. They are operated either by members of the congregation, private catering businesses with an exclusive right to work on the property, or an off-premise caterer brought in by a member of the organization on a party-by-party basis. If your style of food and beverage service fits with the religious requirements of the church or synagogue, this can be a great option for a beginning caterer. If you're the kosher caterer with exclusive rights to serve food at synagogue events, for example, it's a win-win situation. If, however, you have clients who want a catered wedding reception dinner with wine and your church forbids alcohol, you won't be able to store the wine, cook with it, or serve it on the premises. And although the rent you pay helps defray the operating expenses of the church or synagogue, you will not own your space and could be subject to the opinions—and criticisms—of church or synagogue members who feel they do.

Off-Premise Catering

An off-premise caterer has a production facility but holds events somewhere else. The caterer transports all required food, beverages, personnel, and equipment for an event to a location usually chosen by the client.

The biggest benefit to an off-premise catering business is that it usually requires significantly less capital to establish. The production facility, or kitchen, does not need to be in a highly visible location. Because no dining facility is attached, minimal parking is needed. Most off-premise caterers conduct their consultations at the event site in order to assess the venue and plan ahead. This eliminates the need for a fancy office or showroom, although some off-premise caterers choose to maintain them anyway in order to enhance their presence in the marketplace.

Some off-premise caterers have retail spaces, such as gourmet shops or delicatessens, that provide additional income, and special products from catering production—your special barbecue sauce or vinaigrette, for example—can be utilized and sold in these spaces. A retail space can further expose your catering business to the public; most off-premise caterers, however, market themselves through word-of-mouth and by advertising in print and on radio and television.

Many restaurant operators also do off-premise catering. They already have a production facility and can easily modify their operation for off-site events. Many restaurateurs get into catering inadvertently by honoring requests from regular customers. After becoming a de facto caterer in this fashion, a restaurateur will often continue to offer this service to other customers.

Of all the challenges to off-premise catering, transporting all food, equipment, and personnel to the event site is the biggest. Physical strength, coordination, and organization are necessary qualities for any off-premise catering crew. Endurance is paramount, as transportation adds many work hours to any given day. Forgetting even the simplest item—such as a corkscrew—can sabotage an event and create chaos. The weather can cause further challenges. Even if an event is scheduled indoors, inclement weather is still an obstacle when transporting goods from an off-site production facility.

A positive aspect to off-premise catering is the potential for handling much larger events—and finding the perfect settings for them. All banquet rooms have occupancy limits set by the local fire marshal, to which the event planner and caterer must adhere. Off-premise caterers often operate in outdoor spaces and on private property, which do not have the same restrictions. The changes in venue from party to party often stimulate creativity. A good caterer will assess the physical attributes of the venue or property and coordinate menu items and decorations accordingly.

Most off-premise caterers, regardless of whether they handle full-service events, offer pickup or drop-off catering. For example, sandwich platters and salads can usually be ordered from delicatessens in bulk for delivery or pickup. Some operators provide their customers with some equipment, such as chafing dishes and paper goods, and even set up the food for the party for an additional charge. By operating at many different price points, however, the caterer may risk being too much of a generalist by not establishing a specific identity and defining a target market.

Off-premise caterers also rent equipment for the majority of their events. (Chapter 4, "Setting Up the Catering Kitchen," discusses rental equipment and other subcontracted services in detail.) It is therefore important for a caterer to establish good relationships with reputable party rental companies to ensure the quality of any rented items. Clients who seek off-premise caterers for a specific venue understand that there will be additional charges for party rental equipment. Typically, the rental company will give a caterer a 10- to 15-percent commission on items rented for a specific event. This commission will increase overall profitability for the caterer and compensate for the time needed to coordinate and order the equipment.

Off-premise caterers need to have vehicles for transporting goods and product to the event site. While most own one or more trucks or vans, many rent additional vehicles for larger, more complicated affairs. The cost of vehicle purchase, rental, and maintenance needs to be accounted for when pricing events.

Institutional Catering or On-Site Catering

With this type of catering business, an institution such as a hospital, nursing home, college, or office building or complex hires a contract feeder or catering corporation to handle its food service needs. Aramark, Compass Group, and Sodexho are examples of contract feeders. For example, a college may build a student cafeteria and employee dining room, and then pay a contract feeder a set amount per month to operate them. It is the contract feeder's responsibility to order and prepare all of the food, hire and manage the staff, and maintain the facilities. The institution pays all bills directly through its accounting department. The contract feeder makes its profit from the monthly fee that it receives for its managerial services or runs it as a profit and loss–based account.

Institutions using contract feeders save money because contract feeders know how to streamline production and purchase product in a very efficient manner. Creative individuals may not enjoy working for contract feeders, as they often have specific operating procedures that must be adhered to. But before you start your own catering business, you can learn some great lessons in food safety management, organization, efficient service, and cost management from a contract feeder or institutional caterer.

Mobile Catering

Mobile catering means taking food to where the market is, and there are many levels of this type of catering. At the low end, there are small trucks that carry breakfast and lunch items to patrons at construction sites or office parks. These trucks usually have a quilted, brushed stainless steel facade and open in the rear to reveal a small refrigerator, display area, and coffee urn. Pastries, coffee, sandwiches, and cold beverages are the typical fare. When operated in premium locations, these vehicles can become very lucrative. A mobile caterer needs permission or a permit to solicit on both private and public property.

At the high end of mobile catering is the film caterer. Mobile caterers hired by film production companies need to be flexible and operate very smoothly. Their units, often large trailers, have state-of-the-art equipment for food preparation and storage. The side of the unit opens up, a canopy is extended, and tables are set up underneath for dining. Because film companies shoot in many locations, a mobile catering unit should be able to pack up and move with them—quickly. Time constraints, changes in schedule, and varied personalities make this niche in catering one of the most stressful, although it can be very lucrative.

The Bottom Line

As in any business, the bottom line in catering is whether you can make money at it. In Chapter 2, you'll learn about starting your catering business the right way, then continuing on the path to success.

2.
starting your
catering business

Once you've determined that you want to open a catering operation, you know you have what it takes to succeed, you have a niche in mind, and you're aware of your financial capabilities, it's time to get started. Now is the time to focus and concentrate on the tasks at hand. Your commitment to your project is paramount and will allow you to change the vision for your business into a reality. Start looking for that perfect location, one where your business will flourish and grow. Make sure that you have reserve funds to sustain you through those first few uncertain months. As you read on in this chapter, you will see that your reserve capital, your personal commitment, and the location of your business make up the foundation for your future success.

Location, Location, Location

Do you want to sell your barbecue to spectators at sports events? Specialize in catering to individuals at galas and formal events? Go after large groups like bus tours and sales meetings? The identity of a catering business is based on its potential customers, and your location needs to fit your catering business's identity.

While an off-premise caterer can have a production facility in a remote area and still target a specific clientele, an on-premise caterer requires more visibility and a desirable location in order to attract customers. The location also needs to fit the demographics and population. Caterers will pull the most business from the area near their facility. The radius of this area depends on how densely populated it is. A caterer in New York City may not have to venture far outside the five boroughs, northern New Jersey, and Long Island to conduct business, while a caterer in rural Montana may target half that state's population.

A formal demographic market survey will produce information about the residents of the area, including its total population, average age, per capita income, ethnicity, religious affiliations, spending habits, mobility, and possibly their professions. You can find these statistics at your local chamber of commerce, county or state offices on statistics, and on local, state, or federal Web sites. A reference librarian can also help you find this information. Online, you can find demographic information at www.census.gov.

Demographic information should not be the only factor in determining if a location for a business is propitious, however. Other considerations include accessibility, visibility, and especially cost. Many businesses start up in an affordable area and change locations after establishing a positive cash flow. But if you move your on-premise business to another location, there is always a risk of losing some or all of your customer base.

COMMITMENT

Because a commitment to providing excellent quality and service at every event is the essential ingredient to a successful business start-up, catering is a very difficult hobby. People who enter the field as hobbyists often either burn out quickly or end up as professional, full-time caterers. A caterer's mind is full of details, and there is always an ever-expanding to-do list. Long hours, high levels of stress, and physical fatigue come with the territory. There are, however, also great rewards. A successfully catered event creates future business from among the attendees—and lucrative profits. And accolades from catering clients have a pleasing effect on the psyche.

CAPITAL

A new catering business may take some time to establish itself. The majority of new business will come from people who have direct experience of a caterer's work from attending a previous function, or from recommendations. While business may be sporadic at first, some expenses will be constant and ongoing, including (but not limited to) rent, utilities, insurance, and labor. A new business should be well capitalized, or it may be forced to shut down before it has a chance to grow. As a general rule, a caterer should have a reserve of funds equal to six months of all fixed expenses plus half of all labor costs. Product cost and some labor cost will be dependent on the amount of contracted business and should be controllable.

LOCATION

Location is a key factor in the success of most businesses. A safe, visible location is essential for on-premise catering businesses to lure patrons but may not be as important for off-premise catering businesses, which can market themselves to specific target areas by using other means of advertising and exposure (see Chapter 6, "Marketing"). However, all catering businesses should be in areas that are easily accessible to their target markets. Customers who must travel a long distance to a catering venue may think twice about rebooking another event at that location. Plus, off-premise caterers whose production facility is a great distance from their usual venues invest too much time traveling to and from sites, thus limiting their ability to do multiple or overlapping events in one day.

KNOW-HOW

A successful catering business depends on its ability to provide food, beverages, and many other services for a catered event in a way that sets them apart from the competition. It is essential to employ a well-trained chef, an experienced service manager or maître d'hôtel, and a competent bookkeeper prior to launching the business, unless the owner possesses expertise in these areas. An examination of extensive demographic research and a compilation of the competition's businesses brochures will create a repertoire of offerings that give the business its own identity and start it down the road to success.

The knowledge of essential equipment for all areas of the operation, including the kitchen, dining rooms, guest rest rooms, office, and storage areas, is essential in order to deliver properly prepared food and unsurpassed service. A visit to a trade show or food service equipment dealer is a good research tool. And legal requirements should be assessed prior to start-up. At the minimum, adherence to zoning laws should be addressed, liability insurance purchased, and the necessary permits obtained from the building, fire, and health departments.

Creating a Business Plan

Once you know the identity of the catering business and have a location in mind, you are ready to create a business plan. Your business plan will be the financial framework for how you run your business. You'll also need a business plan if you want to apply for a loan or a government grant. Venture capital groups also require a written business plan when contemplating their involvement with a project.

You can get help preparing a business plan through the U.S. Small Business Administration (SBA) office near you, online (http://www.sba.gov/starting_business/planning/basic.html), and from the business department at a community college, your bank, or a fellow business owner.

According to the SBA, your formal business plan should contain the following information:

Contents of a Formal Business Plan

A cover sheet

A statement of purpose

A table of contents

Information about your proposed business:

    A. Description of business

    B. Marketing

    C. Competition

    D. Operating procedures

    E. Personnel: principals (owner, chef, sales leader, and so on) and staffing requirements

    F. Business insurance

Financial data

A. Loan applications
B. A capital equipment and supply list, including sample menus and unit cost of each menu item
C. A balance sheet (prepared with spreadsheet software)
D. A breakeven analysis
E. Pro-forma income projections (profit and loss statements) for three years, detailed monthly in the first year and by quarters in the second and third years, stating the assumptions on which these projections are based (e.g., at least 150 booked events per year)
F. Pro-forma cash flow month by month for the first year, quarterly for the second and third years

Appendices

A. Tax returns of the principals for previous three years
B. Personal financial statements (all banks have these forms)
C. Copy of proposed lease or purchase agreement for building space
D. Copies of licenses and other legal documents
E. Copies of resumes of all principals
F. Copies of letters of intent from suppliers, and so on

Catering Business Plan Example

One of the best ways to educate yourself about creating a business plan is to study a good example. It is very helpful if you know of another catering business whose owner is willing to share his or her business plan with you. You can also check out other business plans at www.bplan.com/sample_business_plans/all_plans.cfm.

Below is an example of a business plan from a hypothetical off-premise caterer, Greenfields Catering, Inc.

Business Plan for Greenfields Catering, Inc.

EXECUTIVE SUMMARY

Greenfields Catering, Inc., an exciting new off-premise catering company specializing in farm-fresh, organic foods prepared with contemporary French flair, offers an unparalleled venture capital opportunity for the right investor.

Greenfields gives the continuing popular trend of corporate and social catering a distinctly new spin, appealing to young urban professionals, baby boomers, corporate executives, and people who appreciate fine food.

Our catering business will capitalize on the success of local farmer's markets and organic grocery stores like Wild Oats and Whole Foods by offering meals catered with foods of similar quality.

COMPANY DESCRIPTION

Greenfields Catering, Inc.
645 Albany Road
Boston, MA 02101
Phone: (508) 555-7777
Fax: (508) 555-7776
www.greenfieldscateringinc.com
Greenfields Catering, Inc., is an off-premise catering company specializing in farm-fresh, organic foods prepared with contemporary flair.

Mission Statement

The company's goal is multifaceted success. Our first responsibility is to the financial well-being of the company. We will meet this goal while trying to consider how our customers embrace our concept and the impact that our business practices and choices have on the environment, and while maintaining an attitude of fairness, understanding, and generosity among management, staff, customers, and vendors. Awareness of all these factors and the responsible actions that result will give our efforts a sense of purpose and meaning beyond our basic financial goals.

Development and Status

The company was incorporated in September 2005 and elected subchapter S. The founders are Jack Green and Sarah Fields. Jack is the president and Sarah the vice president. A total of ten thousand shares of common stock have been issued: Sarah and Jack each own three thousand, and the remainder is retained by the company for future distribution. In addition they have lent the company $25,000 of their own money for research and start-up costs.

A suitable site for the first catering kitchen was found in January 2006 and lease negotiations are in the final stages. The location will be on Albany Road, just within the Boston city limits and close to a dense population of the target market. After the lease is signed there will be three months of free rent for construction; during that time, the balance of the start-up funds must be raised. With that phase completed, Greenfields Catering, Inc., can then open and the operations phase of the project can begin.

Future Plans

If the business is meeting its projections by month nine, we will exercise our option on the adjoining space and develop it for on-site functions. Our five-year goal is to offer both on- and off-premise catering with a combined annual profit of between $250,000 and $500,000.

INDUSTRY ANALYSIS

Although the catering industry is very competitive, the lifestyle changes created by modern living continue to fuel its steady growth. More and more people have less and less time to cook and prepare a big event for family and friends or an important business function. Trends are very important, and Greenfields is well positioned for the current interest in lighter, healthier foods at moderate prices.

The Catering Industry Today

The catering segment of the hospitality industry continues to grow every year. During the mid-1990s, catering was actually the fastest-growing sector of the food service group. According to the Bureau of Labor and Statistics, food preparation careers will be in demand through 2012. Institutional catering—to universities, hospitals, nursing homes, and business campuses—is on the upswing. Social catering—to civic groups, charities, corporations, businesses, and individuals—is the fastest-growing segment, according to the *Restaurant Industry Forecast 2000*, prepared by the National Restaurant Association.

Future Trends and Strategic Opportunities

In 1988, the National Restaurant Association released the *Foodservice Industry 2000* report, which forecast how the industry might look in the year 2010. Some highlights from the panel's findings:

- Nutritional concerns will be critical at all types of food service operations, and food flavors will be important.
- Environmental concerns will receive increased attention.

PRODUCTS AND RELATED SERVICES

Greenfields Catering will offer a menu of food and beverages with a distinctive image. There will be three ways to use our catering service: a catered event at a location, carryout from our kitchen, and delivery to home or office.

The Menu

The Greenfields menu (see Appendix) is moderately sized and moderately priced, offering a collection of ethnic and American items with a common theme—healthy (with low-fat, low-cholesterol, natural ingredients), flavorful, and familiar. Our goal is to create the image of light, satisfying, yet still nutritious food, using local and regional producers as often as possible. There has been an increased awareness of nutritional and health concerns in recent years, and a growing market of people now eat this style of cooking regularly.

Production

Food production and assembly will take place in the catering kitchen. Fresh vegetables, meat, and dairy products will be used to create most of the dishes from scratch. The chef will maintain strict standards of sanitation, quality production, and presentation or packaging with the kitchen and service staff.

Service

We will serve our customers in three different ways: on-site for carryout orders, and off-site at a catered event or when we deliver to offices and homes.

Future Opportunities

Once word-of-mouth brings in more clients, we hope to lease the space adjoining our commercial kitchen in order to offer on-site catering and private dining.

THE TARGET MARKET

We are located in a downtown urban setting frequented by tourists—one to which people travel to eat out. It is also an area known for and catering to the demographic group we are targeting.

Market Location and Customers

The Harvard Square area is one of the most desirable retail locations in New England. The Massachusetts Chamber of Commerce rates it as the third-best retail market in the state. There are more than four hundred businesses in a one-quarter-square-mile area, with average sales of $330 per square foot.

The customer base will come from four major segments:

Local population: The city of Cambridge, with a year-round population of 145,000, is centrally located in the Boston area and is within fifteen minutes' drive of eight major suburbs.

Colleges and universities: Harvard University alone has six different schools within walking distance of Harvard Square and a seasonal population of 22,000. In addition, five more colleges near the square have large student bodies.

Tourism: Counting hotels, motels, bed and breakfasts, and inns, there are over 8,500 rooms available. Last year they were at 92 percent occupancy. We can offer catered lunches for bus trips, and hopefully, on-site dining in a year or so.

Local businesses: The Cambridge Chamber of Commerce lists over nine hundred businesses with an average of twelve employees in the Harvard Square area.

The food concept and product image of Greenfields Catering will attract several different customer profiles:

The "green" business professional: More and more young executives have developed healthy lifestyle habits and want to bring them into the workplace. We offer business breakfasts, lunches, and dinners that incorporate organic foods without seeming too hippieish.

The community-minded person: We offer business breakfasts, lunches, and dinners, as well as special catered events (weddings, bar mitzvahs, anniversaries, and so on) that help support local and regional organic food producers.

People who want a taste of the place: We offer some of New England's finest foods from local and regional purveyors, including lobster and oysters from Maine, cob-smoked ham and cheese from Vermont, and local produce.

People who like really good food: That's just about everyone.

Market Trends and the Future

The population and demographics of Harvard Square have remained steady for the last fourteen years. Tourism has increased 24 percent over the last three years and is predicted to keep growing. Local businesses are increasing at a rate of 18 percent annually.

THE COMPETITION

There are two catering companies in a ten-mile radius of the Harvard Square area that sell food at similar prices. Although this presents an obvious challenge in terms of market share, it also indicates the presence of a large, strong potential market. The newest competitors have made their successful entry based on an innovative concept or novelty. Greenfields will offer an innovative product in a familiar style at a competitive price. Our aggressive plans for takeout and delivery will also give us an opportunity to create a good market share before the competition can adjust or similar concepts appear.

Competitors' Profiles

Competing with Greenfields for its target market are these categories of food providers:

- Caterers of similar menu and price structure who also deliver to offices
- Chain restaurants of similar menu and structure with private rooms

Competitive Strategy

There are several ways in which we will create an advantage over our competitors:

- Product identity, quality, and novelty
- High employee motivation and good sales attitude
- Innovative and aggressive service options
- Greenfields will be the only catering company in the area focusing its entire menu on organic, locally or regionally sourced foods. Our identity will be "truly New England's finest."

MARKETING PLAN AND SALES STRATEGY

Market Penetration

Entry into the market will not be a problem. Greenfields already has a successful mix of events on its books: a one-hundred-person Harvard alumni dinner, an art gallery opening for one hundred fifty, a wedding reception for two hundred, and a private Thanksgiving dinner for fifty. In addition, $10,000 has been budgeted for a pre-opening advertising and public relations campaign.

Marketing Strategy

Focusing on the unique aspect of the product theme (healthy, tasty foods), a variety of marketing vehicles will be created to convey our presence, image, and message:

Print: Local newspapers, magazines, and student publications
Broadcast: Local programming and special-interest shows
Hospitality: Hotel guides, concierge relations, chamber of commerce brochures, and so on
Direct mail: Subscriber lists, offices with the potential of ordering food for delivery, and so on
Miscellaneous: Yellow pages and charity events

A public relations firm has been retained to create special events and solicit print and broadcast coverage, especially at start-up. The marketing effort will be split into three phases:

1. **Opening:** An advanced notice, in the form of a press packet, will be sent out by the PR firm to all media; printed announcement ads will be placed in key places. *Budget: $10,000*
2. **Ongoing:** A flexible campaign using the above media will be assessed regularly for its effectiveness. *Budget: $10,000*
3. **Point of sale:** A well-trained staff can increase the average check as well as enhancing the customers' overall experience. Word-of-mouth referral is very important in building a customer base.

Future Plans and Strategic Opportunities

Catering to offices (even outside of our local area) may become a large part of Greenfields's gross sales. At that point a sales agent would be hired to market our products for daily delivery or catered functions.

OPERATIONS

Facilities and Offices

The catering kitchen is also located at 645 Albany Street. It is a 2,400-square-foot space. A former bakery, it needs only minor structural modifications; the license- and code-related issues are all in order. New equipment will be purchased and installed by a general contractor. Offices of the corporation are presently at Jack Green's home but will be moved to the catering kitchen after opening.

Hours of Operation

The catering kitchen will be available for catered events seven days a week. Greenfields will be closed Christmas Day.

Employee Training and Education

Employees will be trained not only in their specific operational duties but in the philosophy and applications of our concept. They will receive extensive information from the chef and be kept informed of the latest information on organic foods, sustainable agriculture, and local producers.

Systems and Controls

A big emphasis is being placed on extensive research into the quality and integrity of our products. They will constantly be tested for conformance to our own high standards of freshness and purity. Food costs and inventory control will be handled by our computer system and checked daily by management.

Food Production

Most food will be prepared on the premises. The kitchen will be designed for high standards of sanitary efficiency and cleaned daily.

Food will be made mostly to order and stored in large coolers in the basement.

Delivery and Catering

Food for delivery may be similar to takeout (prepared to order) or it may be prepared earlier and stocked. Catering will be treated as deliveries.

MANAGEMENT AND ORGANIZATION

Key Employees and Principals

Jack Green, president, is also the owner and manager of the Green Store, a local natural food wholesaler and retail store. Since 1987 his company has created a high-profile, mainstream image for natural foods. In 1992 he opened a small café within the Green Store that became so popular and profitable he decided to expand the concept into a full-service catering operation. Jack brings with him a track record of success in the natural foods industry. His management style is innovative and in keeping with the corporate style outlined in the mission statement.

Sarah Fields owned and operated La Belle Vie restaurant in Boston from 1995 until she sold it last year to Michelle Farrier and Giselle LaBoite for a 200 percent profit. She brings a French flair to New England foods, along with a great sense of style.

Compensation and Incentives

Greenfields will offer competitive wages and salaries to all employees; benefit packages will be available to key personnel only.

Board of Directors

An impressive board of directors has been assembled representing some of the top professionals in the area. They will be a great asset to the development of the company.

Consultants and Professional Support Resources
At present, no outside consultants have been retained, excepting the design department at Best Equipment.

Management to Be Added
We are presently searching for an executive chef, who will be given incentives for performance and remaining with the company as it grows.

Management Structure and Style
Jack Green will be the president and chief operating officer. Sarah Fields will be the general manager and event planner. She and the executive chef will report to him. The assistant manager and sous-chef will report to their respective managers, and all other employees will be subordinate to them.

Ownership
Jack Green, Sarah Fields, and the stockholders will retain ownership; if deemed appropriate, the possibility of offering stock to key employees exists.

LONG-TERM DEVELOPMENT AND EXIT PLAN

Goals
Greenfields is an innovative concept that targets a new, growing market. We assume that the market will respond and grow quickly in the next five years.

Strategies

Our marketing efforts will be concentrated on catered events and delivery, the areas of most promising growth. As the market changes, new products may be added to maintain sales.

Milestones

After the catering business opens, we will keep a close eye on sales and profit. If we are on target at the end of the first year, we will look to expand to a second unit.

Risk Evaluation

Risk is inherent to any new venture. The success of our project hinges on the strength and acceptance of a fairly new market. After year one, we expect some copycat competition in the form of other independent units. Chain competition will come much later.

Exit Plan

Ideally, Greenfields will expand to a larger space in the next ten years. At that time, we will entertain the possibility of a buyout by a larger restaurant concern or actively seek to sell to a new owner.

FINANCIAL DATA AND STATEMENTS

Enclosed are spreadsheets that show our **start-up budget,** as well as monthly **income and expenses, balance sheets,** and **cash flow statements** representing the way we believe the business will grow during its first three years.

Permits, Licenses, and Insurance Policies

Starting your catering business the right way will save you time and trouble down the road. Get the best legal, insurance, and tax advice before you serve your first party platter. Make sure you have the right business structure (sole proprietorship, limited liability company, or S or C corporation), adequate insurance coverage, health and fire department permits and inspections, and are in compliance with Occupational Safety and Health Administration (OSHA) standards. You'll also want to be aware of payroll taxes and workers' compensation payments, which you can hire a professional payroll service to handle.

The following sections discuss issues that all caterers should address.

INCORPORATION

Incorporating protects you from litigation. If a client sues you and your business is a sole proprietorship, you could lose everything—even personal assets. If a client sues you and your business is a corporation, only what the corporation owns is at risk. Similarly, if your catering corporation goes bankrupt, your meat purveyor cannot sue you directly for money that is owed, but must wait for payment through a bankruptcy settlement. There are different ways to incorporate in each state. Before deciding, you should seek professional legal advice.

When you incorporate, you will also apply to the federal government for a federal employer identification number (FEIN). Your FEIN is the tax status identifier that you will use for invoices, federal and state taxes, payroll, and wholesale purchases.

INSURANCE COVERAGE

■ **BUILDING OR PROPERTY INSURANCE**

A caterer should have insurance to compensate a loss of property. Any building and property within it should be covered in case of fire, theft, and so on. The policy should also cover any liability or the loss of potential revenue caused by the inability to provide services. Suppose your catering hall is destroyed in a fire, for example, and you had several parties booked for the weeks that followed the fire. Because they cannot now take place, you have lost business. An insurance company should not only provide funds that repay any deposits that you received, but also compensate your clients for the inconvenience of finding a new venue for their affairs. The policy should also cover the costs of reconstruction, as well as providing income to you during that time.

■ **LIABILITY INSURANCE**

Every caterer should have insurance that covers injury or illness to clients, guests, and employees resulting from negligence on the caterer's part. There are specialized policies that, through a historic evaluation, can provide maximum protection for the caterer. Find a company or agent familiar with the insurance needs of the catering industry.

■ **WORKERS' COMPENSATION INSURANCE**

Federal law requires all employers to provide workers' compensation insurance to their employees free of charge. This insurance will provide income to an employee when he or she is out of work due to an injury or illness that happens at the workplace during work hours. These policies are costly, and premiums increase for each claim that is submitted. Business owners should consider this cost when determining wages for their employees.

LICENSURE

All food preparation areas must be licensed by a local health department. Each state's laws differ, and may be enforced by local health departments run by counties, cities, or towns. An aspiring caterer should learn about and apply for such licenses prior to any construction, renovation, or takeover of a production facility. After any modifications are made, the applicant needs to notify the health department and request an inspection: Before food can be produced, the kitchen or food preparation area must be inspected thoroughly by a health department official.

The official will point out his or her concerns and rate them as either critical or noncritical. Any critical violations will need to be cleared up before a license is issued. Noncritical violations will not prevent issuance but will need to be rectified prior to another inspection, which will likely be scheduled for the near future. Repeated critical violations can result in revocation of a caterer's license and close the doors of the business temporarily or permanently.

INSPECTIONS

◼ **HEALTH DEPARTMENT**
Food-service establishments are inspected periodically. The health department inspector typically arrives unannounced during a busy production time in order to get accurate data for evaluation. He or she investigates refrigeration temperatures, storage techniques, the internal temperature of food items, and many other things. In most states,

someone on staff has to be certified in food safety. The health department, using local colleges or other institutions, usually administers a food safety course. Once certified, recertification is usually required every five years or fewer, depending on the jurisdiction. In addition, a certified food handler is required to be present at any time food is being prepared at the establishment.

◼ FIRE DEPARTMENT

All businesses that have public access require annual inspection by the local fire and safety officials, who check for unobstructed exits and stairways, required width and length of walkways and aisles, and overall building integrity. All exits must be marked with clearly lighted signs. Fire inspectors also check the fire suppression and exhaust systems over cooking equipment. Proper fire extinguishers must be in designated areas.

COMPLIANCE

◼ OCCUPANCY CODES

Fire safety officials will measure any public space and set a maximum occupancy rate for it. Many local fire inspectors do an initial evaluation of a property and make recommendations prior to their inspection so any necessary changes can be made to accommodate larger occupancies. Once the occupancy limit has been set, make sure you don't book a party or event at which the number of attendees might exceed it. This is a public safety rule with which both on- and off-premise caterers must comply.

■ OSHA STANDARDS

OSHA is a federal agency managed by the U.S. Department of Labor. OSHA sets and maintains progressive standards for safety in the workplace. They include proper coving (rounding of corners) of table surfaces, safety valves on oven pilot lights, acceptable forms of flooring, and much more. Although OSHA has the authority to conduct impromptu inspections, it mostly investigates specific complaints or reported violations. OSHA administers many seminars and forums to help businesspeople comply with safety ordinances. Many informative periodicals are also available. By visiting its Web site, www.osha.gov, you can find much of the necessary compliance information.

Depending on the location of your catering business, additional permits, licenses, or insurance policies may be required by law. You or your attorney(s) should conduct a complete investigation of these issues prior to opening to avoid any possible disruption.

Growing Your Business

Once you've started your business, you need to make sure it grows in order to achieve your business goals. There are many ways to make this happen, but it's your individual catering skills and strengths that often determine what drives your business and how it grows.

○ **Culinary-driven caterer:** An experienced chef who begins a catering business will be concerned with offering the best-quality foods and his or her own opportunities for creativity. The chef may limit the volume of the business in order to control quality and provide a higher level of intricacy. Although the resulting product may command a higher price, the market may not provide enough volume to sustain the business.

○ **Sales-driven caterer:** Business-minded caterers may offer average-quality foods and a simpler menu, and drive the business using enhanced services or clever marketing. They don't appeal to the small, affluent market: Their revenues come from the larger mainstream population.

Both styles of operation have their rewards, but it is profitability that is still paramount. Today, a sales-driven catering business with a consistent product is usually more profitable than one with a culinary approach. Individual caterers should concentrate on what will satisfy them most while making the most profit.

STAY THE COURSE THE FIRST YEAR

After your business has opened, it is important to hew to the strategy set forth in your business plan. When initial business is slow to come, many operators change their identity with the intent of appealing to a different market—by switching the menu from very fancy, upscale items to more common ones, for example. Changing the business identity prematurely is usually a mistake. The public usually senses that the business is in trouble, thus reducing its credibility. It is wiser to start with some reserve capital to sustain the business during the first year or so. The catering industry markets itself largely on referrals and recommendations. It may take the execution of multiple events before word spreads to a large market. Use reserve capital when more advertising is needed above what was initially budgeted.

■ HOW TO BUILD YOUR BUSINESS

To build up clientele and to maintain an established identity, people must associate your business with the type of events you cater, so choose your events carefully. The guests attending any affair are potential future clients. If you are marketing yourself as upscale but decide to cater a simple barbecue with hamburgers and frankfurters, it is probable that guests will label you as a caterer who specializes in such an event. This is not to say that barbecues are not worth catering: many profitable companies specialize in this form of catering. Establishing and maintaining an identity as a caterer, however, is important to your success.

Another tactic in building and maintaining a business identity is offering signature menu items. There are many familiar foods that the public associates with catered affairs. A smart caterer offers them but turns them into signature items by adding a simple twist. For example, the pig in a blanket, a common hors d'oeuvre, is a mini-frankfurter wrapped in puff pastry, baked, and usually served with mustard. Most caterers purchase this item fully prepared and frozen. It is very difficult for any caterer to justify a higher selling price for this item than that of the competition unless it is prepared quite differently. When a client requests the pig in a blanket, a smart caterer might say, "We typically don't prepare those, but we can offer you a similar item, such as Italian sausage wrapped in puff pastry served with a creamy parmesan cheese sauce." The caterer thereby both prevents a direct comparison of this item to those of other caterers, and maintains the identity of his or her business.

Some caterers believe they need to accommodate their clients' requests regardless of how these requests may affect their identity or reputation. The reality is that caterers' reputations are shaped by the food and services they provide. As previously mentioned, most future

Sourcing, Purchasing, Receiving, and Storing Food and Beverages

Sourcing food and beverage products is about finding the best quality for the best wholesale price. This is an area in which you'll need tight controls, well-written product specifications, and good working relationships with your suppliers. If you need forty-eight artichokes for an executive lunch but the produce company delivers twelve of them bruised and discolored, you'll want an assurance that you won't be charged for the damaged ones, or that they can deliver a dozen new ones in pristine condition—fast. You'll also want the person receiving the goods to understand your acceptable level of quality. If this person has never even seen an artichoke before, you'll have trouble.

business will come through the referrals and recommendations of hosts and guests of previous events. The caterer who provides the pigs in a blanket for the sake of accommodating a customer's request should be prepared for future requests for that item from attending guests.

Your current clients and the people they refer may share pricing information. Consistent, fair pricing is necessary to the growth of your business and your reputation. You will have the advantage if your products are all a little different from those of the competition. Differences can include variations on popular menu items, methods of decorating, tabletop design, employee uniforms, and innovative services that the competition does not offer. Attention to these elements will make for a more memorable event—and make it more difficult to compare your business with the competition.

In Chapter 3, we'll look at how caterers price their services to both please their clients and make a profit.

3.

pricing for profit

Pricing catering services can be very challenging; it is also the key to the profitability of your business. Caterers who are just starting out must estimate their expenses for all aspects of their operations in order to price their services accordingly, being sure to figure in profit as well. Established caterers will already have a handle on most expenses, but the cost of food, gasoline for vehicles, natural gas for stoves, and so on changes all the time, so costs must be monitored constantly.

Maximizing Profitability

All the services a caterer offers should include profit in their pricing. A caterer who makes a profit on each product or service has more flexibility with overall pricing. Services can include equipment rentals, entertainment, audiovisual equipment, floral services, and valet parking—as well as food, wine, and liquor.

For example, a caterer who has a liquor license can make a good profit on selling wine, beer, and cocktails at a catered event. Based on industry norms, alcoholic beverages are marked up at least double—and often more. A bottle of wine you buy for $10 wholesale will probably cost your client $20. There is also minimal waste with alcoholic beverages. A caterer without a liquor license is working at a disadvantage by having to price menus higher than a caterer who can also make profit by serving alcohol.

A PRICING FORMULA

There are as many pricing formulas as there are caterers. Here is one simple formula to get you started:

$$OVERHEAD + MATERIALS + LABOR + PROFIT = PRICE$$

Suppose Greenfields Catering has booked a Spanish *tapas* party for fifty people; sangria is the main beverage, and various *tapas* appetizers will be passed butler style. First, Greenfields has to know what percentage of its overhead to build into the price of the event.

OVERHEAD

Overhead costs represent the variable and fixed expenses of any catering business. Expenses that can fluctuate include salaries (for the chef, event planner, and others), utility bills, supplies, rental equipment, and vehicle expenses. Fixed expenses include equipment you've purchased, a mortgage, your marketing and advertising budget, and insurance.

Figure out your overhead costs for the entire year, then divide that amount by the number of catering jobs you expect to have—from your business plan, the previous year's tally, or events you've already booked. The resulting number is the overhead expense you need to build into the price of every catering job.

Suppose Greenfields has a yearly overhead of $200,000. Its owners know that they have to take in $200,000, not including food and labor costs, just to break even. They booked 150 catering jobs last year and are on track to do the same this year. Thus, their overhead divided by the number of catering jobs is:

$$\frac{\$200,000}{150} = \textbf{\$1,333} \text{ } \textit{overhead per event}$$

This overhead number also tells them that if they take on smaller catering jobs, for example, under fifty people, they may not be able to incorporate the entire overhead per event amount into the price of that event. The caterer should build a portion of the overhead amount into the price of that event, but that amount should not affect the price in a way that allows the competition to undercut Greenfields and to take away that business. Greenfields should keep a record of the deficit amount and incorporate that amount into larger events where it barely affects the per person price.

$1,333 *(overhead)* + MATERIALS + LABOR + PROFIT = PRICE

MATERIALS

Materials include the cost of food and beverages, plus handling or delivery. Most caterers have a food cost and a per person cost for every menu item. (We will discuss how to figure food cost later in the chapter.)

The following is the per serving food cost breakout on the sangria and *tapas* menu items for Greenfields Catering:

Olé sangria	$1.12
Sizzling shrimp *tapas*	$1.25
Grilled chicken *tapas*	$0.50
Tapas-style potato salad	$0.25
Grilled vegetable *tapas*	$0.75
Egg and potato *torta*	$0.25
House-cured olives and roasted peppers	$1.15
Orange flan and fresh fruit	$1.25
TOTAL FOOD COST PER SERVING	**$6.52**

Greenfields's owners figure each of the fifty guests at the party will have two servings of everything, so they multiply the total per serving by 100 and get $652, their materials cost.

$1,333 *(overhead)* + **$652** *(materials)* + LABOR + PROFIT = PRICE

LABOR

Labor costs include the cost of service, and may include the cost of food preparation as well. Labor costs include Social Security taxes (FICA), vacation time, compensation for personal or sick days taken, and other benefits, such as health or life insurance.

Greenfields Catering counts the cost of its full-time food preparation employees in its overhead, but figures its labor costs for part-time or hourly wait staff and other workers, such as valet parking attendants and coat checkers, as a variable expense directly related to each event.

Because the *tapas* and sangria will be passed butler style, the party of fifty only needs four part-time waitpersons, who will also assist with setup beforehand and cleanup afterward. At $20 per hour (the part-time hourly rate for wait staff in the area), the combined labor cost is $80 per hour. A typical appetizer party lasts for two hours and requires an hour setup time and an hour afterward for cleanup.

The total charge for the wait staff is then 4 (hours) x $80 = $320.

$1,333 *(overhead)* + **$652** *(materials)* + **$320** *(labor)* + PROFIT = PRICE

PROFIT

Greenfields Catering needs to make a profit of $100,000 this year. Its owners divide this profit figure by the estimated number of booked events, the same way they figured their overhead:

$$\frac{\$100,000}{150} = \mathbf{\$666}$$

$1,333 *(overhead)* + **$652** *(materials)* + **$320** *(labor)* + **$666** *(profit)* = PRICE

Now, they can figure the price for the Spanish *tapas* party:

$1,333 *(overhead)* + **$652** *(materials)* + **$320** *(labor)* + **$666** *(profit)* = **$2,971** *(price)*

That number is rounded up to $3,000 and divided by 50 (people), yielding a per person price of $60.

Greenfields Catering uses this equation as a starting point for pricing each event. An event for five hundred guests will require a far greater share of the overhead—and yield a more-than-average profit. Greenfields Catering could decrease these amounts in pricing its Spanish *tapas* party for fifty if it had large events booked to make up for the shortfall. Arriving at a fair, competitive price for a client—and a profitable one for the caterer— is always the goal.

Once Greenfields Catering has priced this party, the event planner can prepare a fact sheet, knowing that the cost of this party is $60 per person for fifty people. For one hundred people, the cost would be $40 per person. The overhead and profit figures would stay the same, but the materials and labor costs would double, and the sum would then be rounded up and divided by one hundred guests:

$1,333 *(overhead)* + (652 x 2) = **$1,304** *(materials)* + (320 x 2) = **$640** *(labor)* + **$666** *(profit)* = **$3,943** *(price)*

The more guests, the lower the per person price for your client.

When the event planner prepares a proposal for a prospective client, the overhead and profit costs need to be built into the room charge or the per person cost of each menu item. The client should never see the behind-the-scenes pricing equation.

When the owners of Greenfields Catering were figuring out costs for the Spanish *tapas* party for fifty people, they knew they had to charge $60 per person to make a profit. All caterers (as well as restaurateurs) mark up each menu item differently to arrive at the target amount. On the proposal to the client, Greenfields Catering might break out the expenses as follows, charging about four to five times the food cost of each item plus a room charge in order to incorporate the overhead and profit expenses:

PROPOSAL: SPANISH *TAPAS* PARTY FOR FIFTY	
Room setup charge	$430.00
Staffing	$320.00
Subtotal	$750.00
MENU (PRICES PER PERSON):	
Olé sangria	$10.00
Sizzling shrimp *tapas*	$10.00
Grilled chicken *tapas*	$ 5.00
Tapas-style potato salad	$ 2.50
Grilled vegetable *tapas*	$ 5.00
Egg and potato *torta*	$ 2.50
House-cured olives, roasted peppers	$ 5.00
Orange flan and fresh fruit	$ 5.00
Total per person	$45.00
x 50 people =	$2,250.00
GRAND TOTAL	**$3,000.00**
	or
	$60 per person, all inclusive

CALCULATING FOOD COST

Food cost refers to the total cost of a food item; food cost does not include utilities, labor, or supplies. Caterers must know the food cost for the food and beverage items they serve in order to price them for clients. Catering menu items should be marked up by the industry norm—three to five times their cost—in order to help cover overhead and profit.

Here is the equation for figuring food cost:

$$\text{COST PER UNIT} = \frac{\text{AS-PURCHASED COST}}{\text{NUMBER OF UNITS}}$$

To cost out one apple pie, you would figure out the cost of each ingredient. If you bought 5 pounds (80 ounces) of flour for $1.00 and you need 8 ounces for the pie crust, your cost per unit would be:

$$\text{Flour} = \frac{\$1.00}{5 \text{ lbs } (80 \text{ oz})} = \$0.20 \text{ per lb } \textit{or } \$0.10 \text{ for 8 oz}$$

Your cost for the flour alone in the apple pie will be $0.10, or ten cents. Then, you figure the unit cost of each of the other ingredients. Your unit cost list for the recipe might look like this:

RECIPE COSTING FORM

MENU ITEM   Greenfields's Apple Pie   DATE   June 2006

NUMBER OF PORTIONS   8   SIZE   approx 4 oz

COST PER PORTION $ .625   SELLING PRICE $ 6.00

FOOD COST   10.4%

ORIGINAL RECIPE EDIBLE PORTION QUANTITY			PURCHASE QTY		TOTAL COST		
INGREDIENT	QTY UNIT	YIELD %	APQ UNIT		APQ	UNIT	TOTAL ITEM COST
Flour	8 oz	100	5 lb		1.00	lb	.10
Butter	8 oz	100	8 oz		4.30	lb	2.15
Apples, Granny Smith	8 ea	75	10 ea		.275	ea	2.20
Sugar	4 oz	100	4 oz		2.00	lb	.50
Cinnamon, Ground	1 tsp	100	1 tsp		9.60	qt	.05
						RECIPE:	$5.00

Greenfields Catering Apple Pie costs $0.625 per serving.

Beverages are figured the same way. If a one-quart (32-ounce) bottle of cider costs $4 wholesale, that is the unit cost. If you figure 8-ounce pours for mulled cider, the cost per serving is $1.

As in restaurants, wines and spirits are often marked up 100 percent or more, especially when served by the glass. Your cost per serving of a 4-ounce glass of Chianti (at $12 wholesale cost) will only be $1.50, but you could charge clients $6 or $7 per person.

Maintaining a consistent food cost is difficult. Arbitrary pricing, waste, theft, and poor supervision can all increase food cost and jeopardize profits. Most caterers monitor their food cost on a monthly basis. The process starts by taking a physical inventory of product the last day of each month, pricing it, then adding to that figure the total food purchases for the following month. Another inventory is taken on the last day of that month. This figure is then subtracted from the previous figure, establishing the cost of food sold for the month. The cost is then divided by the total sales for that month, determining the food cost percentage for that period of time.

	OPENING INVENTORY (DECEMBER 31, 2006)
+	PURCHASES (JANUARY 2007)
−	CLOSING INVENTORY (JANUARY 31, 2007)
=	COST OF FOOD SOLD (JANUARY 2007)
÷	TOTAL SALES (JANUARY 2007)
=	FOOD COST PERCENTAGE

Even the lowest food costs, however, do not guarantee success. The food cost percentage only represents the relationship of cost to sales. If sales targets are not met, food purchases will be low, and the food cost percentage may remain constant. However, the percentage of fixed expenses, such as rent, insurance, utilities, and taxes, will rise when sales figures are not met, bringing the percentage of profits down or even creating a deficit.

◼ AVAILABILITY OF PRODUCT

When pricing a menu for a proposal, the event planner should have up-to-date knowledge of the cost and availability of ingredients. This information is available from kitchen and purchasing personnel or directly from the caterer's purveyors. While many ingredients are readily available in major metropolitan areas, they may not be for a caterer located in a rural area. Many ingredients are available through general food purveyors such as SYSCO or U.S. Foodservice. These full-service companies, and others like them, provide fresh produce, meat, and seafood, as well as dry goods and sundries. They operate internationally and can usually accommodate any caterer regardless of location.

Specialty items such as wild mushrooms, fresh truffles, game, wines, and certain cheeses may need to be purchased through companies that specialize in these products. A caterer must network or use the Internet to find sources for these items. Many companies have Web sites that display their products along with pricing and shipping information. It is usually possible to have these specialty items delivered within days, regardless of your location. Any premiums on these products need to be accounted for and transferred to the client whenever possible.

Certain products vary greatly in price depending on supply. Prices for fresh products such as meats, seafood, fruits, and vegetables vary the most. When the meat industry has production problems or if foreign embargoes of meat have been issued, prices will increase. When there is a surplus of specific cuts or types of animals, prices for meat usually tumble. Seafood prices react to similar circumstances. Other factors, such as migratory patterns, reproductive cycles, and biohazards also affect seafood's availability. Fresh fruits and vegetables are usually at their lowest cost and best quality when in season. Using local produce usually translates into getting fresher and more readily available ingredients.

Anyone responsible for purchasing food should compare various suppliers before buying. The specifications for the various ingredients should be matched, and the price and service evaluated, before making a decision.

Before you open your catering business, you should have a selection of recipes with their costs—both to you and to the client—established. And you should be able to alter some of your recipes without sacrificing quality. For example, if you can offer Recipe A, made with wild chanterelle mushrooms, and a lower-cost version, Recipe A1, made with fresh cultivated oyster mushrooms, you can bring down the unit cost of the recipe (and thus the per person cost of a dish), thereby appealing to a wider range clients.

◼ PORTION CONTROL

Beyond accurate pricing, you have to make sure that the portion amounts called for in the recipe are carried through to what the kitchen serves. Successful caterers use kitchen scales to make sure all guests receive a 6-ounce portion of salmon fillet; they use 2-ounce scoops to portion out sorbet. Accuracy will help keep you on the road to profitability.

◼ OTHER PRICING CONSIDERATIONS

As previously mentioned, fruits and vegetables harvested during their peak growing season will often cost less than at other times of the year. When these products are not in season, they are often imported from other countries or transported longer distances from areas where they are ready for harvesting. Both of these scenarios considerably raise the cost of the product.

Pay attention to the seasonality of items locally produced to obtain the best quality at the best price. But also be aware of the seasonality of items that are imported from elsewhere, as they will be comparatively less expensive at their peak season regardless of where they are produced. If you are unfamiliar with the seasonality of a particular food, consult a source that will give you a breakdown of the seasonality of an item by region. Employ this practice with the use of specialty produce items that are most affected by seasonality. Examples of such items are:

Apricots	Cherries	Kumquats	Pomegranates
Artichokes	Corn	Mandarins	Pumpkins
Asparagus	Currants	Melon	Rhubarb
Beets	Fiddlehead	Mushrooms	Tomatoes,
Berries	ferns	Nectarines	heirloom
Brussels	Figs	Peaches	
sprouts	Herbs	Plums	

Holidays also affect the price of food and beverage products. For example, caviar is much more expensive if purchased the week before New Year's Eve due to increased demand. Frozen turkey prices often drop a week before Thanksgiving due to industry stockpiling. A smart caterer will use suppliers as a resource for information relative to trends in food and beverage costs.

Inflationary costs must also be considered when pricing menu items for future events. For example, a caterer analyzes inflation and determines that food prices have risen an average of 6 percent per year over a three-year period. The caterer can use that figure when pricing an event scheduled a year or more into the future. Better forecasting allows the caterer to ensure a fair profit without having to go back to the customer and renegotiate the price.

In Chapter 4, we'll discuss how to set up a professional and efficient catering kitchen.

4.

setting up the catering kitchen

The design and function of your catering kitchen is key to the success of your catering business. When you set up the physical plan of your kitchen, you will also be setting up systems for food receiving and storage, food preparation and assembly (and, if you're an off-premise caterer, transportation), worker and food safety, and cleanup. The kitchen staff will be able to produce food much more efficiently and safely with the proper equipment and systems in place.

Kitchen Design and Construction

First, the kitchen itself. Most catering entrepreneurs hire an architect with experience planning food-service facilities to create the layout for their facility. If you have ideas for the design of the facility, your architect will be able to tell you whether they are practical and if so, work them into the overall plan—or get you to rethink them if they're not. And an architect will recommend items that you may not have considered, such as special electrical configurations for outlets, task lighting, and ventilation.

After you and your architect agree on a layout for the facility, the local building inspector will need to approve the plans and issue a building permit before construction can begin. When the construction is complete, the building inspector will inspect it before issuing a certificate of occupancy. The local health and fire departments will also need to inspect and license the facility prior to use.

Before any equipment is installed, all the infrastructure—plumbing, HVAC (heating, ventilating, and air-conditioning) and electrical systems—must be in place. These systems will require inspection by local building department officials before they are covered by floors, walls, and ceilings. There will be specific requirements as to the gauge of electrical wires, the diameter and composition of drain lines, and so on. The general contractor and anyone else that is subcontracted need to be aware of and comply with these requirements.

Make sure you have an electrical system that can accommodate the expansion of your business. If you constantly blow a fuse when you're getting ready for an event, you will lose time, money, and those workers who become frustrated with your infrastructure. Make sure you place ample electrical outlets where you will need them.

Designing a kitchen that can be cleaned easily is also very important. Many kitchen walls are made of ceramic tile, which is not porous and cleans well. Kitchen flooring is also commonly tile. Another flooring option is poured epoxy flooring, which has also proved to be safe, sanitary, and easy to maintain. Kitchen floors must have floor drains to allow for them to be hosed down without excessive water buildup.

KITCHEN LAYOUT

Just as your business plan determines how you will run your business, your kitchen layout plan will determine how you run your kitchen, so make sure it is detailed and practical. See the Appendix for an example of a kitchen layout. The layout and size of your production facility will also affect menu design.

The main areas of a commercial kitchen include receiving and storage, cleanup, production, and office space. When you design your kitchen, think about flow. Efficiency of motion will help everyone work smarter— more quickly and efficiently.

Start with the flow of goods. Ideally, storage areas should be located near the delivery and loading area. This will prevent product deliveries from passing through and disrupting the kitchen's production area. For off-premise caterers who transport products from their facility to clients' venues, the loading area should be located near the walk-in coolers where the product will be stored prior to an event.

Production areas for hot and cold foods should be separate. Hot foods should go from prep area to stove to hot box or an area where they're kept hot until assembly and serving time. Ideally, cold food, meat, fish and dessert preparation should be in areas that are air-conditioned or refrigerated. Cold foods flow from prep area to refrigerator, freezer, or walk-in cooler. Rolling racks should be placed near the appropriate prep workspace so food can go from prep table to sheet pan to rack easily, then be wheeled to the oven, tilt skillet, or walk-in box. Some caterers also have a designated baking section with prep tables, industrial-size mixers, multiple ovens (possibly even convection ovens), and all the accoutrements needed for baking bread, pastries, and cakes.

The cleanup and storage areas for pots and other equipment should also be placed in a space that doesn't interfere with production. Dirty pots, pans, and utensils should flow away from the production, cooking, and baking areas.

All caterers need an assembly area. Many plated menu items are best executed in assembly-line fashion. Whenever possible, use stainless steel prep tables on wheels. These tables are easy to clean and can be arranged in many configurations, allowing workers to access all areas of the tables. Using one worker to place each plate component is the quickest way to assemble plates, but this method is rarely cost-effective because it requires so many workers. Intricate plating in a small, ill-equipped area can, however, lead to inconsistent and substandard products and service. In larger operations such as hotel banquet facilities, conveyor belts are sometimes used to move plates down the assembly line, freeing up both of the worker's hands and allowing fewer workers to place multiple items simultaneously. Another common method is cold plating food and then reheating it on the plate in an oven or warmer close to service time.

Equipment that needs to be plugged in should be always be near an electrical outlet; heavy equipment should be on locking casters to make it both easier to move and hold in place.

CATERING OFFICE

An office area is helpful for keeping distractions such as telephones and computers out of the general workspace. An office also serves as a place to have private consultations and conversations with potential clients and employees. (See Appendix, page 339, for layouts for a banquet kitchen.)

Essential Equipment

After the kitchen layout design for the utilities, walls, floors, and ceiling has been completed, the culinary production equipment is ready for installation. Your choices for kitchen equipment should be based on the menu items you plan to offer, your anticipated volume of business, the physical characteristics of the building, local safety and health codes, available fuels, energy efficiency, and, of course, your budget.

Every catering kitchen requires a basic set of equipment necessary to prepare food. Large equipment includes ovens, stoves, exhaust hoods, prep sinks, pot sinks, vertical mixers, rolling racks (tall, stainless steel racks on wheels that hold multiple sheet pans), prep tables (with and without casters), refrigerators, freezers, dry storage, and pot and dish washers. Small equipment includes immersion blenders, tabletop blenders, knives and utensils, china caps and fine-mesh strainers (for straining large quantities of sauces and purées), colanders, food mills, food storage containers, mixing bowls, piping bags and tips, receiving and portion scales, and oven, meat, and instant-read thermometers.

One way to determine your equipment needs is to construct a menu for a potential event for one hundred people. Look over each recipe and create a list detailing every piece of large and small equipment you will need to produce that menu. Then envision the assembly line and how many kitchen personnel will be required to assemble each dish. If one of your recipe components is a piped vegetable purée, for example, how many piping bags and tips will you need for a speedy assembly process? What other equipment will you need? Service equipment, such as steam tables, utensils, ladles, sauce guns, hotel pans, or bain-marie inserts, should be part of your essential equipment.

The following two examples illustrate how to coordinate equipment with a recipe.

 ## DUCK BREAST WITH PORT WINE–PEPPERCORN SAUCE

YIELD: 80 SERVINGS

Reduction

Duck bones, roasted, 10 lb

Fortified demi-glace, 2 gal

Port wine, 1 bottle

Pinot Noir, 1 bottle

Shallots, minced, 12 oz

Peppercorns, crushed, 1 tsp

Butter to finish

Duck

Duck breast, scored, 80

Apple Garnish

Apples, medium dice, 5 lb

Butter, browned, 4 oz

Orange zest, 1 tbsp

Lemon zest, 1 tbsp

Cognac as needed

Brown sugar as needed

Madeira as needed

Method

1. Simmer duck bones in demi-glace for 3 hours. Reduce port wine, Pinot Noir, shallots, and peppercorns to 80 percent and add reduction to sauce. Adjust seasoning and flavor. Strain. *Montez au beurre* (whisk in butter, a tablespoon at a time, until the sauce is glossy) at service time.

2. Carefully brown duck breasts in tilt skillet, skin side down. Invert just to color the undersides. Cool on racks on sheet pans.

3. To serve, roast to temperature and slice to order.

4. For the garnish, dice the apples and cook in brown butter. Add the citrus zest and all other ingredients to taste. Garnish duck by sprinkling around plate.

Equipment List

1 roasting pan to roast the bones

One 20-qt rondeau to prepare the sauce

1 tilt skillet to sear the duck breasts

5 sheet pans with racks to hold the duck breasts

One 10-qt rondeau to cook the apples

1 fine-mesh strainer to strain the sauce

One 5-qt bain-marie insert to hold the sauce

1 pair of 10-in tongs to turn the duck breasts during searing

One 2-oz ladle to skim sauce

1 speed rack for storage

NEW ENGLAND CLAM CHOWDER

YIELD: 100 SERVINGS

Cherrystone clams, washed, 225

Water, 48 fl oz

Salt pork, ground, 24 oz

Onions, fine dice, 36 oz

Celery, fine dice, 36 oz

Flour, 17 oz

Potatoes, medium dice, 7 lb

Heavy cream, hot, 128 fl oz

Salt as needed

Worcestershire sauce as needed

Tabasco sauce as needed

Old Bay Seasoning as needed

Method

1. Combine clams and water. Steam open the clams in covered rondeaus; pick out the clam meat and chop. Decant broth and set aside.
2. Render salt pork.
3. Add onions and celery; sauté.
4. Add flour; make roux.
5. Incorporate broth; simmer for 30 minutes.
6. Add potatoes; simmer until tender.
7. Add cream and clams and season.

Equipment List

Two 20-qt rondeaus with lids to steam open the clams

Prep sink in which to wash the clams

Standard four-burner range top to cook the soup

1 cutting board to prepare the vegetables

1 French knife to cut the vegetables

1 food processor to paste the salt pork

1 fine-mesh strainer to strain the clam juice

1 large sheet of cheesecloth to strain the clam juice

One 20-qt stockpot or small steam kettle to prepare the soup

1 wooden spoon to stir the soup

1 large balloon whip to incorporate the clam broth

One 6-oz ladle

Three 10-qt bain-marie inserts to hold soup

A CATERER'S EQUIPMENT LIST

Catering equipment is designed to produce large quantities of food in a safe and consistent manner. Caterers not only need equipment to prepare and cook or bake foods, but also to hold and then assemble foods at an event site.

◼ EQUIPMENT FOR PREPARING, COOKING, AND BAKING FOOD

Kitchen scales: A large floor scale placed in the receiving area will allow your receiving or purchasing agent to weigh foods as they are delivered: You'll know immediately if your supplier really has given you the fifty pounds of potatoes you ordered. A portion scale is smaller and designed to fit on a work or prep table. It can be used to make sure each salmon fillet for a dinner weighs close to 6 ounces, or whatever weight the recipe dictates.

Blenders, food mills, and fine-mesh strainers: Tabletop blenders and food mills allow you to purée foods, while china caps or fine-mesh strainers let you strain them in a more efficient manner. A handheld immersion blender will allow you to purée a sauce or soup right in the pan.

Mixing bowls: You should have a range of stainless steel mixing bowls, from very small to very, very large. Everyone from the prep cook to the baker will use them.

Knives: While formally trained chefs will have their own sets of knives, you'll still need knives for your catering kitchen, including paring, filleting, serrated, carving, and chef's knives and cleavers. Your kitchen staff should also be able to keep them sharpened.

Thermometers: Oven, refrigerator, and freezer thermometers are necessary to make sure your equipment is operating properly and adhering to health codes. You'll also need meat thermometers and instant-read thermometers to check the temperature of both raw and cooked foods—to make sure food has been cooked to the right temperature, and to make sure food stays at temperatures safe for serving and storage.

Baking and pastry equipment: Baking and pastry equipment comes in all shapes and sizes: sheet pans, loaf pans, cake pans, pie pans, jelly roll pans, cutters, and 2- to 6-inch rounds; piping bags and tips; measuring cups and spoons; whisks, rolling pins, and pastry brushes; and so on. Many caterers store equipment in translucent plastic storage tubs with their contents indicated in marking pen on the lid or the side of the container.

Vertical mixers: A vertical stand mixer is an invaluable tool for baking. You can also use it for whipping butter, finishing mashed potatoes or

This **vertical stand mixer** from Hobart rests on the floor, but tabletop models with smaller bowl capacities are also available. Associated primarily with baking, for which they are equipped with a dough hook, they can also be fitted with other attachments that make them useful for preparing sauces, mashing potatoes, grinding meat, and making pasta. They can even be used to whip up cake frosting.

vegetable purées, and preparing cold sauces and salad dressings. Vertical mixers come in either tabletop or floor models, depending on the bowl capacity. They are equipped with a dough hook, wire whip, and mixing paddle. In addition, most have a shaft on the face of the machine that allows compatible parts such as a grinding unit, cheese grater, sausage stuffer, or pasta roller to be attached. Most manufacturers sell these attachments separately from the main machine.

Food processors, VCMs, and buffalo choppers: Food processors will speed up the preparation of many menu items. They can be used for making mousselines, mayonnaise, and other emulsified cold sauces;

In addition to slicing, dicing, grating, and chopping, a **food processor,** like this one from Robot Coupe, takes the hard labor out of emulsifying mayonnaise, hollandaise, and other cold sauces. Food processors often come with an assortment of (very sharp) blades, and have a pulse setting in addition to an on/off switch.

A **vertical chopper/mixer** (VCM), also called a vertical chopping machine or a vertical cutter mixer, is like a larger, gentler food processor. It is used to knead dough and mix foods that that require more finesse than a food processor can provide. (Because of its size, it can also handle a much larger volume at one time.)

Manually operated **buffalo choppers** have been around professional kitchens for many, many years. Today, their S-shaped blade and shallow bowl make them a favorite for grinding everything from mushrooms for duxelles and mirepoix for tomato sauce to meat for pâté.

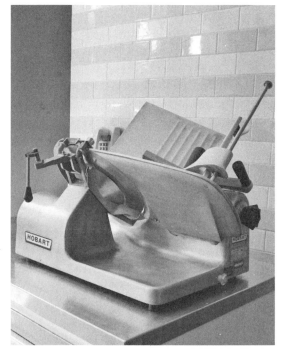

Slicers slice meat and cheese for sandwiches, thin bread for canapés, translucent slivers of Parmesan for salad—and kitchen workers' fingers if they're not careful. Slicers are a dangerous piece of equipment; only appropriately trained employees should be allowed to operate them, and even then only when taking the appropriate precautions.

mincing vegetables; and making spreads. Food processors often have attachments that slice, shred, and grate. A vertical chopper/mixer (VCM) is essentially a large food processor with variable speeds. By interchanging the rotating tool that fits into the bowl, a VCM can be used to prepare dough and blend foods more gently than a conventional food processor. A buffalo chopper has a rotating blade set vertically that remains stationary as the bowl of the unit rotates. Buffalo choppers, like vertical stand mixers, have a shaft that accommodates many attachments such as meat grinders and pasta rollers.

Slicers: Commercial slicers are essential to the catering kitchen. While they are most commonly used to cut sandwich meats and cheeses, a slicer can be used for many other menu items, such as thin bread for canapé preparation and shaved fresh fennel for a salad. Some models can be set to slice automatically, freeing both the food handler's hands to work with the sliced product. In addition, most models come with an attachment that sharpens the rotating blade. The commercial slicer is one of the most dangerous pieces of kitchen equipment, and strict safety measures should be posted in the area where the machine is located.

Machines for peeling or cutting vegetables: Machines such as automatic peelers, deseeders, shredders, slicers, and dicers can take most of the manual labor out of fruit and vegetable preparation. Some technologically advanced models can even create *tourney* (seven-sided football) or *parisienne* (ball) shapes; however, these machines, while ensuring uniformity, can be wasteful. Another option is to find a produce purveyor who sells peeled and precut fresh vegetables. These products sell at a premium price but may be more practical than purchasing an expensive piece of equipment that is only used occasionally.

Deep-fryers: Purchasing a deep-fryer for the catering kitchen is a wise decision, as fried foods are popular with clients. Because deep-fried foods have limited holding times and get soggy rather quickly, off-premise caterers commonly deep-fry menu items in their production kitchens and after transporting them to the catering venue, reheat them in ovens to return their crispness. On-premise caterers, when preparing deep-fried items for a banquet, may fry small amounts at a time and have food runners bring them to the banquet assembly line or buffet in batches.

Deep-fryers range from tabletop models to conveyor units that move food through the hot oil automatically. Most are equipped with filtering systems that allow the oil to be cleaned regularly, thus increasing its shelf life. (Models with automatic filtering systems are also much safer than their predecessors.)

Grills: Many caterers decide to install gas or wood-burning grills as part of their indoor cooking battery. Grilling food for indoor banquet service is very different than for à la carte restaurant service, where each menu item is cooked individually. A caterer will typically grill-mark portion-size menu items on the grill and then finish cooking them closer to service in an oven. This type of handling may be problematic because portion-size items without full surface searing may suffer moisture loss during the final cooking period in the oven.

Outdoor grilling for catered events, especially buffet-style events, is much more practical, because the food is cooked fresh and completely as the guests proceed down the buffet line—and there's a large market for outdoor barbecue-style catering.

Many different models and sizes of grills are available, from portable charcoal to dual-fueled stationary types. Some caterers build their own by cutting steel drums in half, installing legs and casters, and placing an adjustable grate on top. The size and fuel type of the grill you decide on should easily accommodate the events you cater and the grilling style in your area. Gas grilling requires ample propane

The double baskets of this tabletop **deep-fryer** are immersed in the vat of hot oil to create french fries, zucchini fritters, beignets, or any of the other deep-fried foods so popular with catering clients. This model has an automatic filtering system that cleans the oil regularly.

Off-premise caterers may use indoor, gas-powered **grills** like this one to cook menu items partway, transport them to the banquet site, and then finish cooking them in an oven. Outdoor grills, whether fueled by coal, wood, or propane, are used for barbecues and other outdoor events to cook food in one pass.

chapter four: **setting up the catering kitchen** | 75

The **tilt skillet**, also known as a Swiss brazier, can be used to simmer, sauté, sear, stir-fry, and fry large quantities of food. Because it tilts all the way to a vertical position from its horizontal cooking position, it is easy to clean despite its size—its contents or cleaning products can be emptied quickly.

Steam kettles (like the ones pictured here from Groen) release their contents through spigots; tilt kettles tilt to pour out their contents. Both are used to cook stocks, soups, and chowders.

tanks at the ready, but can be an expensive proposition for very large groups. If you're a Texas caterer, mesquite is the wood of choice—in hardwood lump charcoal for grilling or as chips, chunks, or logs for slow smoking. If you fired up a gas grill at a Texas event, guests would be aghast.

Tilt skillets/Swiss braziers: The tilt skillet is one of the most practical pieces of cooking equipment in catering. The tilt skillet has a thermostat that keeps its temperature consistent. The tilt feature allows for easy removal of liquid products, such as soups or stocks, and makes it easy to clean. Its uses include boiling liquids, simmering, sautéing, searing, stir-frying, and shallow or deep frying.

Steam-jacketed or tilt kettles: A steam or tilt kettle is not as versatile as a tilt skillet, but it cooks stocks and soups better. Models will vary in size and capacity, ranging from 10 to 100 gallons. Steam runs through a stainless steel jacket in most models, ensuring even heat over the entire cooking surface. Not only can it boil large amounts of water very

A **convection steamer** without an internal steam generator needs to be connected to a building's steam or water lines so it can produce steam on demand. Chefs like convection steamers because they cook food quickly while retaining its natural color, flavor, and nutritional value.

Caterers often make use of a preplanned system that includes baking sheets and trays, the **rolling racks** or speed racks on which they sit, and the ovens in which they bake, all functioning together as a unit, like this one from Baker's Aid. The sheets and racks are perfect for organizing, storing, and cooling food; the **rack oven** accommodates the sheets and trays in place.

quickly, but it can keep a stock cooking for hours at a perfect simmer. Certain models have spigots that release the product, while others tilt.

Convection steamers: A convection steamer is a tightly sealed compartment, big enough to hold multiple sheets or hotel pans, into which pressurized steam is pumped. If the model does not have an internal steam generator, this type of steamer needs to be connected to steam or water lines. Larger operations may find it practical to have a remote steam generator that operates multiple pieces of equipment. The main advantage of a convection steamer is that it produces steam instantly, reducing the overall preparation time of certain foods.

Rolling racks and rack ovens: Virtually all caterers use rolling racks, sometimes referred to as speed racks, to organize and store food.

These racks hold standard full or half-size sheet pans. It is wise to purchase sturdy models with locking wheels made of aluminum alloy or stainless steel. Special rack ovens are designed to cook foods without removing them from these rolling racks. (Obviously, plastic rolling racks cannot be used with them.) A rack oven system is only practical for operations that consistently execute large catered events. Certain models of rack ovens accommodate a single rolling rack, while others have the capacity for multiple racks that fit over a rotating carousel for easy loading and removal.

Deck ovens: Deck ovens come in many sizes and configurations. Single deck ovens may be stacked to increase capacity. Steel decks can be interchanged with ceramic baking decks, which are ideal for baking bread or pizza. Nonrotating deck ovens may not have a high clearance, making it difficult to roast whole turkeys and other larger items. Rotating deck ovens have multiple decks that can usually accommodate up to three or four full-size sheet pans each. The decks rotate vertically within the oven space, facilitating even cooking. A dial on the front of the oven indicates which shelf is even with the oven door, which helps the cook know where his or her food is at any given time.

Be careful if you choose a single large-capacity oven. If that oven breaks down and requires repairs, it will interrupt production. In addition, it is not energy efficient to operate large-capacity equipment if the volume of business does not warrant it. For these reasons, multiple smaller ovens may be a better choice.

Convection ovens: These ovens come in various sizes and use various kinds of fuel. They have fans that circulate the heated air inside, dispersing heat more evenly and shortening overall cooking time. Most convection ovens hold standard, full-size sheet pans and are equipped with computerized timers and temperature probes.

a

b

These **single deck ovens** (a) from Blodgett—the kind often seen in pizzerias—were stacked to increase capacity, but the clearance may not be high enough for roasting large game. The dial on the front of this **rotating deck oven** (b) is telling the chef that deck 5 is currently even with the oven door. The decks on rotating deck ovens usually have a higher clearance than their nonrotating cousins.

In a conventional oven, cookware can block the heat flow, leading to unevenly cooked food. Because hot air rises, food at the top of the oven often cooks more quickly than food on the bottom rack. **Convection ovens,** like this four-door model from Vulcan, circulate air with a fan, so they can operate at a lower temperature and still cook food more quickly—and more evenly. And because the air in a convection oven is the same temperature throughout, food will cook at the same rate no matter where in the oven it is placed.

Convection ovens are a popular choice for smaller caterers and mobile catering units because they are compact, versatile, and dependable.

Combi ovens: Compact and multifunctional, combi ovens are an excellent choice when space is an issue. These combination ovens heat conventionally as well as with convection, and also have a steam cycle. They have advanced computerized technology that allows the cook to set specific programs for certain menu items. Most are designed to hold food at lower yet safe temperatures without overcooking it or drying it out. Some combi ovens accommodate rolling racks, which make it very easy to move freshly cooked food to a blast chiller or walk-in refrigerator. These ovens are the best choice for caterers who place food on plates while chilled, place the plates on a rolling rack, and then reheat the plated food in the combi oven at service time.

Refrigerators: Proper, practical refrigeration is one of the most important aspects of food production. When designing the kitchen layout, the choice among walk-in, reach-in, or lowboy refrigeration should be carefully considered. Walk-in refrigeration is necessary for storing larger items like raw cuts of meat, cases of fruits and vegetables, and of course, prepared items for events. Many options of each type of refrigeration exist. Size considerations are the most important: hot or even warm food placed in a refrigerator that is too small will dramatically raise its overall temperature, causing it to work harder and posing food safety hazards.

For the catering kitchen, walk-in refrigeration is necessary to

A **combi oven,** like this one from Rational, combines several modes of cooking: conventional, steam, circulated hot air (like a convection oven), or a combination thereof. The combi mode can be up to 50 percent faster than a convection oven, and is also used to reheat foods and hold them at temperature until they are ready to serve.

accommodate rolling racks of prepared food. These refrigerators should be equipped with powerful condensers and high-moisture coils to keep the prepared food as fresh as possible. Separate low-moisture, reach-in refrigeration is best for storing baking and pastry products to help prevent the accumulation of condensation. Lowboy or undercounter refrigeration is helpful for keeping products for assembly chilled and conveniently located.

Blast chillers are important to many caterers who specialize in high-volume events. A blast chiller may resemble a conventional reach-in unit; however, through the use of a higher horsepower compressor and greater air circulation, it brings down the temperature of food in a fraction of the time. Most blast chillers will also print out information necessary for HACCP compliance, such as the temperature of the product when it first was placed in the chiller and the length of time in the chiller before it reached the target internal temperature.

Self-contained, air-cooled refrigerators located in an area where the temperature is high usually have a shorter lifespan than those with condenser units that are remotely located, because they have to work harder to maintain their internal temperature. Another benefit to remotely located condenser units is that the noise and heat that they give off is away from production areas.

Most refrigerators can be equipped with an alarm that goes off when the temperature rises to an unsafe level. During down times, the alarm system can alert a central monitoring station, which in turn will notify you by phone. You will then be able to call for emergency maintenance or move product to another refrigeration unit—and thus prevent a catastrophe.

Shelving: Proper shelving in work and storage spaces contributes greatly to the overall efficiency of a catering kitchen. Shelving should mitigate the need for employees to leave their workspace for commonly used equipment or ingredients. Shelving in refrigerators should be ample, labeled, and easy to clean. When purchasing shelving, look for the logo of the National Safety Foundation (NSF). Shelving certified by the NSF will have specific safety characteristics, such as rounded corners and rust-proof seams. Locking casters on portable shelving units help when it is necessary to move them in order to clean the walls and floors that surround them.

Prep tables: Most prep tables are made from stainless steel and are available in many different lengths and widths. Some models have overhead or undercounter shelving and can be put on casters. Because the configuration of prep tables in a catering kitchen changes according to the menu or style of service, rolling prep tables are advantageous. Like shelving units, tables that are NSF certified will have rounded corners and sealed seams. Their legs will be adjustable so that the table can be stabilized and not wobble. Wooden worktables still exist; however, most health agencies do not allow them because they are porous and difficult to sanitize.

Cutting boards: Cutting boards are available in a variety of materials. Wooden ones, although easy on the knife, are not recommended because they are porous and difficult to maintain. Rubberized or plastic cutting boards are most commonly used in food-service facilities. They can be cleaned much more easily than wooden ones and can be sanitized by running them through a commercial dishwasher, although they sometimes warp. All cutting boards require periodic replacement because through excessive use, the gouges and crevices created by chopping and slicing become excellent habitats for bacteria and other food-related pathogens.

The stainless steel **prep table** has undercounter shelving (upper right) on casters and an extra shelf that slides out when needed.

The marble top provides a nonporous cutting surface.

This stainless steel table comes with lowboy refrigerated storage.

In addition to lowboys, the **prep tables** have cold center storage as well.

Wooden **cutting boards,** like wooden prep tables, are porous and difficult to sanitize. Glass cutting boards are more hygienic, but breakable. Rubberized or plastic cutting boards are sturdy and can be run through a dishwasher. Although this will warp them, they should be replaced from time to time anyway: the gouges and crevices created by chopping and slicing become habitats for pathogens.

◼ EQUIPMENT FOR FOOD HOLDING, ASSEMBLING, AND SERVING

Cook-and-hold cabinets: Alto-Shaam, as well as other food service equipment companies, manufactures cook-and-hold cabinets, which cook foods at low temperatures and then hold the food safely until service time. This equipment is mobile and usually does not require overhead ventilation due to the lower cooking temperatures. Many caterers roast meats in this fashion as the low temperature cooking, coupled with the state-of-the-art technology, increases product yield and allows the food to retain more moisture.

Holding cabinets or hot boxes: Portable holding cabinets or "hot boxes" are used extensively by most caterers. These units are best used short term to hold food just prior to service. Prolonged hot-food holding can lead to quality deterioration and possible contamination.

Some catering operations plate up chilled or room-temperature food for a banquet, cover each plate, and stack it in a holding cabinet or hot box until it reaches serving temperature. To bring cold-plated food up to a hot serving temperature (re-therm) and avoid danger-zone temperatures, it's better to move it directly from refrigeration to a combi oven, let it come to a proper serving temperature, and then move it to portable holding cabinets. The cabinets can be moved to strategically located areas, which will help facilitate service.

Thermo-insulated equipment: Thermo-insulated holding units are used for the same purpose as hot boxes or portable refrigerated units. These portable units are available in many different designs. Some are designed to transport and hold food items on sheet or hotel pans, while others are designed to hold and dispense liquids. Smaller units have double handles to make them easier to carry; larger ones are usually on wheels. One advantage of thermo-insulated equipment is that food can be transported easily in it, and later on it can be used for either hot or cold short-term holding.

These units are well insulated and will gain or lose only one degree per hour if unopened. (They cannot recover lost degrees because they do not have a power source.) Off-premise caterers benefit most from the use of these products; on-premise caterers will benefit more from the use of hot or refrigerated boxes.

Plate trees: Plate trees enable caterers to assemble and store prepared plated food in a compact and secure way. Most plate trees have vertical rows of rubberized pegs that fit plates snugly between them. Plate trees adjust in order to keep the plates level and secure. All plate trees have locking casters for easy storage and transfer to and from the plating area. Some plate trees are designed to be placed in a special oven for reheating the plated food.

Plate caddies: Some plate caddies simply hold stacked plates securely,

This **plate tree's** vertical rows of rubberized pegs hold plated food snugly in place, allowing many plates to be moved from the kitchen to a service area by one person.

allowing a kitchen worker to move them from place to place without much effort. Other units can store plates and refrigerate or heat them for service. These units have several sleeves and are often spring loaded, making them practical to use for a banquet assembly line.

Steam tables: Most caterers use steam tables while plating hot food at an event. Often referred to as bains-marie, steam tables come in many designs but virtually all work by thermostatically heating several inches of water within the bay of the unit. Some are open areas that allow kitchen workers to hold hot food in many different vessels, such as hotel pans, bain-marie inserts, pitchers, and even heavy-gauge plastic containers. Others have lids with openings designed for standard-size hotel pans or specific stainless steel inserts. Many models are double-sided, allowing plates to be assembled more quickly. Some even have variable-speed conveyor belts that move the plate down an assembly line, allowing each worker to place two food items on each plate. This function keeps the plates cleaner and can cut down on labor costs.

Off-premise caterers often rent steam tables for their events from party rental suppliers. Some caterers substitute chafing dishes, but these do not perform as well because they use canned fuel, which does not heat as effectively as gas or electricity.

Steam tables are only meant to hold food, not cook it. There is a high risk of contamination associated with foods that are brought from a chilled to hot state using only a steam table.

Conveyor units: Many caterers use conveyor units to move plates through an assembly line of plated food. The height of these units can

The bay of this **steam table,** or bain-marie, holds several inches of heated water, into which several hotel pans are then inserted. Steam tables are good for keeping food hot, but not for bringing cold food up to temperature.

be adjusted to become level with any work surface. The speed of the belt can be changed depending on the amount of time necessary for each item to be placed on the plate.

Sauce guns and squeeze bottles: Sauce guns are conical and gravity fed; caterers use them to eliminate the mess caused by the use of ladles or pitchers to sauce food. Most sauce guns come with stands that hold them upright when they're not in use. Food handlers use plastic squeeze bottles for liquid plate components. Squeeze bottles work poorly with hot sauces because the pressure created by heat causes the liquid to dispense erratically, but they are excellent for cold sauces, syrups, and glazes.

Utensils and portion scoops: Plating food for banquets should be done with speed and consistency, and that requires special tools. Using a measured serving utensil such as a portion scoop or disher standardizes the number and size of portions served. Solid, slotted, or perforated serving spoons can also be used but make it more difficult to measure precisely.

Additional equipment: Depending on the identity of your catering operation, you may also need special equipment, such as delivery vans, vehicles equipped with cooking equipment and refrigeration, barbecue grills and smokers, or cooking equipment beyond the basics.

As your catering business evolves, there will be an ongoing need to update menus, and thus your equipment. Anticipate this by reserving a percentage of profits for the maintenance of existing equipment and the purchase of new equipment.

Organizing and Managing
Kitchen Receiving and Storage

Once your kitchen layout and equipment is designed for efficient food preparation and handling, you must establish procedures for receiving and storage, recipe development and costing, worker safety, and food safety. Each of these requires its own manual, which can be as simple as a three-ring binder, each page protected by a plastic sheet protector (so any food spills can be cleaned off easily).

RECEIVING

There should be a process in place for receiving all goods: foodstuffs, beverages, and office supplies. The catering business owner, the chef, or a trusted employee should check over each delivery. Look at the invoice enclosed with the delivery; check the invoice against the delivered order to make sure the order is complete. Then, check for quality. If everything is acceptable, initial the invoice and take it to the office to be processed and paid. Then, store the delivered items. If the delivery is incomplete for any reason, make a notation on the invoice and call your supplier immediately.

Keeping good records is an essential business practice. Order and inventory forms, whether blank or completed, should be kept in appropriate files. The receiving and storage manual should have instructions for receiving, sample order and inventory forms, your business tax number information, a map of storage areas in your catering facility and what they contain, and a yearly inventory of all equipment.

STORAGE

Your kitchen will have four basic storage areas: secure storage for wines and spirits, dry storage for products that are shelf stable, cold storage for foods that need refrigeration, and frozen storage. To prevent loss, only your most trusted employees should have access to secure storage. If a prep cook or other employee needs to check the wines and spirits inventory, a trusted employee should open the storage area and be present while inventory is taken. Many caterers keep periodic inventories of food, beverages, paper goods, and so on easily accessible on a hanging clipboard.

Dry storage materials such as containers of olive oil, spices, herbs, rice, grains, and pasta can simply be stored on open shelving. If you use different types of pasta, you might want to keep them in large, clear plastic containers with their contents marked on the outside. Flours and sugars can be kept in covered tubs, also marked—as all-purpose or cake flour, granulated or confectioners' sugar, and so on.

Your walk-in refrigerator should have a preset arrangement, so products are easy to find: eggs and milk products on one side, produce on the other—whatever works for your operation. Label large, plain white commercial containers with black marker so you can see at a glance what they contain without having to open them. Keep products that need to be used first at the front of the refrigerator.

When possible, keep raw and prepared foods separate to decrease aroma absorption from one to the other. In addition, all refrigerated storage must be in accordance with health department standards. For example, most health departments require raw poultry to be stored on the bottom shelves of a refrigerator to prevent cross-contaminating products that may be stored below them.

Anything kept in the freezer should be labeled with the food name and the date it was frozen, so you can use products before they start to deteriorate. Some caterers keep a list of freezer contents with dates and amounts on a clipboard attached to the freezer. When a sous-chef takes out a container of frozen raspberries, he or she marks off the amount on the freezer list. This method cuts down on how often the freezer is opened to check on inventory.

Utensil storage areas should also be labeled. If your operation does a lot of baking, you will have a variety of cake and tart pans, cake decorating paraphernalia, and so on. When possible, keep the equipment in labeled plastic containers so dishwashers can see at a glance where to put things away.

HOW TO BUY OR LEASE EQUIPMENT

After the kitchen plans are drawn up, the equipment and storage is planned, and the systems are in place, you have to decide whether to purchase or lease the equipment you need. If you purchase new or used equipment, you will own it and be able to deduct the depreciated costs on your business tax return. If you lease equipment, you will spend less up front. This could be costlier in the long run, however, if you need to buy to keep up with business demand. Your accountant can run the numbers and suggest which option is more beneficial.

■ BUYING

The best place to view the latest developments in commercial kitchen equipment is at a trade show for the hospitality industry. Manufacturers rent space on the show floor to exhibit and demonstrate their line of commercial kitchen products. Their representatives are on hand to answer any questions regarding the equipment and can tell prospective buyers where to purchase the items on display. It is sometimes possible to purchase the

Your catering kitchen should be built with growth in mind. Make room in your design plans for future extra workspace, storage space, electrical capabilities for additional equipment and easily accessible entrances and exits. When you set up your catering kitchen, buy the largest capacity ovens, refrigerators, and sinks your budget permits. Large volumes of food prepared in small spaces usually suffer quality loss or may become unsafe for consumption. Inadequate refrigeration, for example, can lead to health hazards: If large amounts of warm food are put into a small refrigerator, the temperature of the refrigerator increases, causing the food to cool too slowly and become potentially dangerous. In addition, food that is crammed into an oven too tightly will bake or roast unevenly.

If your business grows beyond the capabilities of your facility, you may have to move to another location or expand the existing one. Both of these options can prove much more costly than initially choosing and designing a facility that can accommodate future growth.

showroom models directly from the manufacturer at a discounted rate. Some caterers attend these shows to view the latest technology in commercial kitchen equipment, record make and model numbers of specific equipment that interests them, and then shop for them at auctions or online auction sites.

There are also many restaurant equipment dealers who sell comparable used or reconditioned equipment at much lower prices than new. New equipment can also be ordered at any local restaurant equipment dealer.

These dealers have catalogs from many manufacturers that you can check out. Another possibility for finding used equipment for sale is through food-service operations that are shutting their doors. The owners of these failing businesses may want to liquidate some of their physical assets in order to pay down some of their debt. Anyone buying this equipment should, however, be very cautious: If another party has a lien on the equipment, it can be repossessed, leaving the buyer at a loss.

■ LEASING

Leasing is another way to get the commercial kitchen equipment you need. Leasing equipment is similar to renting it, but includes an option to purchase the equipment at the end of the lease. The leasing company sets a monthly payment, which is spread over a term of anywhere from twelve to sixty months. At the end of the term, the equipment can be purchased, usually for a nominal sum. While leasing may be more affordable in the short term, the overall price of the equipment ends up considerably higher than if it is purchased outright.

Most caterers also buy service contracts through the manufacturer, leasing agent, or an outside mechanical company. The caterer pays a monthly, yearly, or one-time premium to cover any necessary labor that may result from equipment failure or routine maintenance. Most often, replacement parts are not covered by the service contract, unless the repair falls within the warranty period.

■ RENTING

Many catered events require the caterer to rent supplies and equipment from a party rental service. An on-premise caterer may use such a service when the size of the party requires supplemental equipment to be brought in or a client requests a specific service item that the caterer does not own.

For example, suppose a client books a New Year's Eve event, but after seeing all the plates you own, requests that the food be served on black plates—which you do not have. You believe it's unwise for you to purchase black plates because you would rarely use them in the future, so you decide to rent them (and, of course, pass the extra cost on to the client). Or a client might ask you to provide a martini bar. You may not own enough martini glasses to stock it sufficiently. Renting the glasses is a better option than purchasing them if you get such a request only occasionally. (If you decide to offer this service on a regular basis, however, purchasing the glasses would be a good choice.)

Off-premise caterers use party rental services for most or all of the events they execute. Off-premise catering usually requires customized planning, and the caterer needs all of the options for equipment customarily offered by a party rental company. Although off-premise caterers have a production facility, they may or may not have a lot of storage space for extra equipment. In addition, off-premise catering requires the transportation of all food, beverages, and equipment to the chosen venue. Party rental companies offer delivery and pickup of their equipment, which reduces the caterer's workload.

Off-premise caterers will usually stock samples of service ware, platters, glassware, and flatware to show their clients during the initial or subsequent consultations. These caterers also show clients dimensions and photos of tables, chairs, tents, and tabletop setups, as well as linen swatches and napkin samples. Determining rental needs early in the event-planning process will help the caterer estimate costs more accurately and expedite a written proposal. The fees for any rented equipment are passed on to the customer, usually in an itemized format. The caterer usually charges the client the retail price as written in the product list supplied by the rental company. The caterer will usually receive a discount ranging from 10 to 20 percent from the rental company, which will contribute to the overall profit made on the event.

Off-premise caterers often purchase certain items they need for most events that they would otherwise have to rent, such as serving platters, chafing dishes, coffee urns, pitchers, and serving utensils, because they do not vary greatly in style from party to party. It is not unusual for an off-premise caterer to then include these items as part of the rental list and charge the client the same price for these items as the rental company would. (This is not unethical, as this is still "renting" from the caterer.)

Party rental companies usually require their rented equipment to be rinsed, dried, and packed up before they pick it up. Failing to do so can lead to extra charges for excessive handling, which are assessed to the caterer. The caterer may also need to compensate the rental company if any of the equipment is broken or stolen. The caterer should do an opening and a closing inventory of the equipment and check to avoid such additional charges. Rental equipment may be delivered a day or two before the event and should be stored securely. The equipment will usually be picked up the day after the event and should be stored safely until it is.

Creating a Worker Safety Manual

KITCHEN SAFETY

Your catering facility should be safe and secure for both you and your employees. Inadequately maintained kitchens are dangerous places. It is the responsibility of all personnel to be observant and report any potential hazards to management, and it is management's responsibility to attend to them promptly to avoid accident and injury. Workers' compensation insurance premiums will increase, and productivity and morale will decrease, as a result of any accidents. You may also accrue overtime costs from covering the shifts of any injured worker.

To minimize the risk of accidents and injury, implement a comprehensive training program to educate all staffers on the health and safety hazards that are commonly present in a catering facility. Some of this information is available from the Occupational Safety and Health Administration (OSHA) at www.osha.gov, and can be downloaded, printed, and placed in a worker safety manual. In addition, you will want emergency preparedness information— what to do in case of a fire, severe weather, burglary, power outage, and so on—at the ready. Police, ambulance, fire department, and other contact numbers should be posted prominently, and a flashlight with fresh batteries kept nearby. You will also want to adapt worker safety guidelines to the realities of your catering kitchen, your delivery vehicles, and your event sites.

The following checklists may be posted conspicuously in work areas and included in an employee handbook or worker safety manual.

General Kitchen

- Instruct kitchen workers to clarify instructions for a given task with a supervisor.
- Review any written warning on equipment and verify its proper assembly.
- Lift heavy objects by crouching down and using leg muscles to bear the weight.
- Keep floors free of liquids, oils, and debris.
- Wear long-sleeved shirts or jackets, long pants, and closed-toe shoes. Shoes should have grease-resistant soles.
- Keep first-aid kits stocked and accessible.
- Report malfunctioning equipment immediately.

Storage Area

- Keep all shelving free of protruding material and the items on the shelves stacked neatly.
- Use hand trucks when moving heavy cases.
- Keep floors dry and swept.
- Do not stack food items directly on the floor. Use skids or crates to create a space between the food and the floor.

Cleanup Area

- Do not operate automatic dishwashers unless you are properly trained.
- Do not put any breakable objects near pot sinks.
- Do not pull dish racks out of an automatic dishwasher prematurely.
- Do not place hot cookware at pot-washing station without warning the pot washer.

Production Areas

- Check to see if any machine is plugged in before turning it on.
- Do not wear hanging earrings or other jewelry that can become entangled in any kitchen machine.
- Do not wear loose clothing.
- Use any supplied safety guards when operating a kitchen machine.
- Concentrate on the task at hand. Distraction is the cause of most kitchen accidents.
- Do not feed food into a grinder without using the proper plunger.
- Always cover blenders before turning them on.
- Never take your eyes off your work when operating a meat slicer.
- Never clean the blade while the machine is plugged in.
- Allow steam to escape slowly while opening a pressurized steamer after use.

- Always check to see if the attachments are properly fitted before operating a vertical mixing machine. Never put your hands in the bowl while in operation.
- Check all power cords for damage and do not operate any machine if bare wires are exposed.
- Do not use any equipment if you are unsure of its operation until receiving direction from someone who knows how to use it.
- Keep knives sharp. Dull knives can slip off food items and cause lacerations.
- Keep floors dry and grease free.

Creating a Food Safety Manual

FOOD SAFETY

In addition to worker safety, you'll also have to practice food safety. In the catering business, large quantities of food are generally prepared in a central kitchen and distributed to clients. Proper cooling and hot-holding techniques are critical for preventing the growth of possible food-borne pathogens.

The outbreak of a food-borne illness stemming from one of your catered events would likely destroy your reputation and business. Food-borne illness can be avoided if you and your employees follow safe food-handling practices. Provide safe food for your clients by following food safety guidelines. When you set up your catering kitchen, you should also set up food safety procedures.

Make sure that you and your employees are current with state and local regulatory requirements for food-service establishments to ensure that the food you provide to your clients is safe and wholesome. Usually, one of those requirements is that a key employee on your kitchen staff—or you as the catering owner—pass a food safety course (usually offered at a community college) and be certified by the appropriate health authority. This person becomes responsible for making sure that all kitchen and serving staff adhere to food safety requirements—especially and critically, washing their hands before, during, and after handling foods.

Food safety begins with the safe handling of food as soon as it enters the catering kitchen and ends with the proper handling of leftovers and cleanup after the catered event. Food safety information needs to be included in an operation manual so that your kitchen staff can refer to it easily in case they have questions or concerns. Much of this information is available from your local and state health departments. You can simply photocopy that information to include in your manual. But you, as a caterer, will also have food safety systems that you want to spell out or to be executed in a unique manner. This information you'll have to create yourself.

Here are some basic food safety tips that you can adapt for your own food safety manual:

Tips for Purchasing and Storing Food Safely
   ○ Purchase high-quality foods from a reliable vendor. The food should be in good condition (with the packaging intact), fresh (not beyond its expiration date), and stored at the proper temperature.
   ○ Store potentially hazardous foods, such as meat, poultry, eggs, milk, and fish, immediately in the refrigerator (33° to 40°F) or the freezer (−10° to 0°F).
   ○ Store dry staples at 50° to 70°F.
   ○ Practice first-in-first-out (FIFO) to ensure the safety and quality of your menu items. Labeling foods by type and date lets you know which were stored first so you can use them first.

○ Thaw frozen foods in the refrigerator eighteen to twenty-four hours prior to preparation. Thawing them under cold running water (< 70°F), in the microwave, or extending their cooking time are all acceptable methods for thawing food if quicker thaw is necessary. If the cooking time is extended, be sure that the recommended internal cook temperature for the food is reached.

○ Discard foods that have been in the freezer longer than four months.

Personal Hygiene Food Safety Tips

○ Practice good personal hygiene when preparing and handling food. Wash hands before food preparation, after handling raw foods, after using the rest room, or at any time they become soiled. Gloves may be worn when handling and preparing food; however, gloves can become soiled as easily as hands and should be changed often.

○ Wear clean clothes and aprons when preparing food.

Food Preparation Safety Tips

○ Take measures to prevent cross-contamination of food. Use separate cutting boards and prep areas for vegetables; raw meats, chicken, and fish; and cooked foods.

○ Clean and sanitize food contact surfaces such as countertops, cutting boards, equipment, and utensils. One tablespoon of bleach per gallon of water is an effective sanitizing agent.

○ Wash fresh fruits and vegetables thoroughly under cold running water. When they are stored in the refrigerator, make sure fresh fruits and vegetables are wrapped or stored in containers separately from raw meats.

○ Do not use the same towel that you use for wiping hands to wipe food contact surfaces.

○ Discard any marinade after it has flavored raw fish, poultry, meat, or game.

○ Reheat all potentially hazardous foods, including leftovers, to 165 °F. Gravy or *jus* should be heated to a boil (212 °F).

○ Cook food thoroughly to the recommended internal temperature for the appropriate amount of time. Use a meat thermometer to measure internal cook temperatures.

Hot and Cold Food Safety Tips

○ Keep cold foods cold. Keep them refrigerated or on beds of ice to maintain their temperature below 41 °F.

○ Keep hot foods hot. Hot food for distribution and holding should be kept at a minimum temperature of 140 °F.

○ Discard food if its temperature enters the danger zone (41° to 140 °F) and remains there for two or more hours.

○ Cool hot foods properly. Hot food may be prepared and distributed to the client in temperature-holding equipment, or the food may need to be cooled below 41 °F, distributed cold, and reheated. To cool food properly, portion the food into clean, sanitized shallow containers and place them in a blast chiller until a safe holding temperature is reached, 40° to 50 °F. Transfer to a conventional refrigerator for extended storage. If a blast chiller is not available, separate the food into smaller amounts so that it cools to at least 70 °F within 20 minutes or so and then place in the refrigerator. Make sure the food is covered, dated, and drops below 41 °F within a four-hour period. Also, liquid food may be cooled by placing it in a clean container and then submerging it in a sink or tub of ice and water. Stir the food every fifteen minutes to accelerate the process.

Leftover Food Safety Tip

○ Discard food if its temperature enters the danger zone (41° to 140°F) and remains there for two or more hours. This can happen if foods have remained on a buffet table or a kitchen prep area after an event.

Housekeeping Safety Tips

○ Clean storage and kitchen areas regularly.

○ Implement a pest-control program to prevent the spread of disease.

When your commercial facility is complete, you'll need staff to operate it. Just what kind of staff does a catering operation need? You'll see in Chapter 5.

5.

staffing

Employees are essential; a business cannot grow without them. The quality of a catering company's staff can determine whether the business will survive and grow or fail. Excellent food prepared by competent cooks but served by poorly trained or inexperienced wait staff can spoil an event. Similarly, poorly prepared food cannot be overcome even by the most competent servers. An event planner who forgets even one minor detail for a function is putting the catering business's success at risk. These examples show the importance of hiring, training, and retaining the best employees possible. Finding and managing staff can be the greatest challenge of running a catering business.

If you're just getting started and have the minimum six-months' reserve capital behind you, you may be the owner, function as the event planner or salesperson, and be the executive chef as well, with a few full-time and some part-time workers that you hire hourly as needed. But to really function well, a catering business needs many different types of employees.

It may surprise you to learn that when you're opening a new catering business, you should err on the side of too many, not too few, employees. The reason? You will save time and money by training a group of new employees in the way you want to run your catering business, rather than doing so one at a time. Even though you'll most likely lose some workers in the first few trial-and-error weeks, you'll still be prepared for the onslaught of customers you're hoping for. It's much more efficient to have trained staff ready to handle the growth of the business instead of scrambling to find and train additional employees when the increase demands it.

Top Twelve Characteristics of a Model Employee

1. **Punctual:** Ready to work at the assigned time, not merely arriving at that time
2. **Even-tempered:** Able to work well with other employees
3. **Clean:** Exhibiting good personal hygiene
4. **Flexible:** Able to switch gears when the job demands it
5. **Proactive:** Not reactive to change of procedures or policies
6. **Communicative:** Able to express and articulate ideas and feelings well
7. **Trustworthy:** Honest
8. **Ambitious:** Hungry for a challenge, ready to be promoted to positions slightly beyond current capabilities
9. **Organized:** Able to maintain a neat and clean workstation
10. **Compassionate:** Nonjudgmental of others before getting all of the facts
11. **Innovative:** Demonstrates good problem-solving skills

12. **Creative:** Able to find new and valuable ways to implement the business's mission and vision

Finding and Hiring Staff

A typical catering operation will need a variety of staff positions to operate efficiently. The number of necessary positions is based on the size and complexity of the business and is divided between the front and back of the house. The back of the house consists of kitchen personnel and those in purchasing and receiving. The front of the house consists of the dining room, planning, and administrative staff (see charts a and b on page 110).

Depending on the size and type of your business, you may need some or all of the following staffers:

Back of House

Head or executive chef: In charge of all kitchen activities. Plans menus, develops and tests recipes, creates recipe manual, orders foods and sometimes beverages, trains kitchen staff, and interacts with event planner. Reports to business owner.

Sous-chef: Responsible for the physical condition of the kitchen. Supervises kitchen personnel. Reports to the executive chef.

Prep cooks: Prepare foods and assemble dishes on the banquet line. Take weekly inventory of all foods. Report to the sous-chef.

Pot and dish washers: Wash pots and dishes and put them away.

Purchasing/receiving agent: Sources quality products from purveyors, handles the ordering, then checks the original order against the invoice to ensure the delivered goods are correct and of good quality.

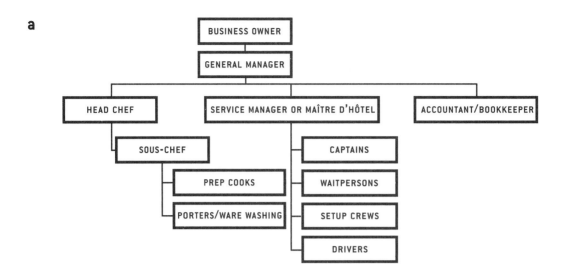

a

These **organizational charts** for a small off-premise caterer (a) and a large on-premise caterer (b) show some of the differences in structure between small- and large-scale businesses. Notice that the large business has full-time employees dedicated to sales; at the small business, the owner, general manager, and perhaps even the head chef perform that function.

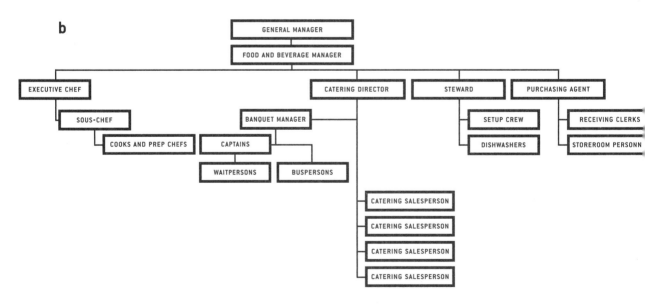

b

Steward: May also function as the purchasing/receiving agent. In some catering businesses, the steward is the front-of-the-house sommelier in charge of inventorying, ordering, and serving wine and alcoholic beverages in the dining area.

Pastry chef or baker: Makes all cakes, cookies, pies, pastries, and other dessert items, including ice cream, mousses, and flans.

Front of House

Event-planning personnel: Sell and plan events. Interface directly with the executive chef and maître d'hôtel.

Banquet manager: Makes sure that banquets run smoothly. May also function as the event planner.

Catering sales representative: Sells the events. May also function as the event planner.

Maître d'hôtel: The head waitperson in charge of service in all dining areas. Hires and trains all wait staff and supervises the setup of the dining area. Works closely with the executive chef and event planner.

Captain: Waitperson in charge of a section of the dining room. Carries out the orders of the maître d'hôtel.

Wait staff: Serve food and beverages to guests. Must be trained in a variety of serving styles, from American and Russian to English and butler style.

Buspersons: Assist in setting up the dining room; serve water, clear, and clean up.

Bartenders: Set up the bar area and serve beverages, including wine, beer, and cocktails.

Valet parking attendants: For catering businesses without parking facilities or at off-premise events, valets park guests' cars in a safe area during the event, then return the vehicles when the guests request them. They are paid an hourly fee but can expect guests to tip them as well.

Coat checkers: Take the coats, briefcases, umbrellas, and so on from guests for safekeeping, then return them as guests leave.

These employees will need specific training about how your operation runs and how you like to handle things.

All employees need to possess certain traits conducive to working in the hospitality industry: enthusiasm, flexibility, adaptability, neatness, cleanliness, congeniality, assertiveness, the ability to work hard as a team player and to think quickly in a crisis situation. While applicants with prior experience or knowledge may request higher salaries, they usually require less training.

Written applications and face-to-face interviews will help you distinguish between poor and viable applicants. Still, it may be difficult to determine if applicants possess any or all of these traits prior to hiring them and seeing them in action. That's another reason to hire more people than you need in the beginning.

Start by determining what specific positions you need to fill. Examine the staffing budget on your business plan, then decide which positions you can fill and the wages you can offer for each. Write specific job descriptions for each position. These descriptions will help prospective applicants determine if they are qualified and should pursue the job. (The descriptions will also be helpful in the development of training materials later on.) See a sample job description at right.

The next steps are to network and advertise to attract a pool of applicants. You'll need to have an application form for prospective employees to fill out. Office supply stores usually stock generic employment applications, or you can find them online at places like www.employment-application-forms.com or www.findlegalforms.com. If you want an application specific

Job Title: Food Preparer, Entry Level

Job Description: In conjunction with management supervision, prepare meals and keep work area orderly and sanitary. Prepare food items according to standardized recipes. Inspect food for quality and safety. Prepare, store, and reheat foods to the proper temperatures and follow Hazard Analysis and Critical Control Point (HACCP) guidelines. Assist in training new food preparers. Coordinate and confer with manager about all advanced food preparation.

Job Requirements

Education: Equivalent to one to three years' trade training at either the secondary or postsecondary level

Experience: Nine to twelve months' effective experience

to your business, consult with culinary colleagues or have your attorney draw one up to your specifications.

ADVERTISING FOR STAFF

There are generally two ways to acquire staff for a catering business: by advertising and networking or by using a staffing agency. Both ways of staffing have their advantages and disadvantages.

Most caterers "advertise" using word-of-mouth networking and referrals from respected culinary colleagues; newspaper ads are a close second. For part-time workers, you can place ads in high school and college periodicals and on bulletin boards. Some caterers network through related businesses in the food-service industry. If you hire a former restaurant manager, steward, waiter, or chef who is well connected (and respected), he or she can recommend many good employees, as turnover in restaurants is a constant. You can also tap into adult workers who want to supplement their incomes or indulge a love of food and entertaining by working a part-time catering job. Firefighters, nurses, and actors often work long consecutive shifts and have several days off per week that leave them time for secondary employment. Simple ads placed at hospitals, fire stations, or actors' guilds may yield positive results. Filing with state employment services may also bring viable applicants forward.

HELP WANTED AD

PAPER: *The New York Times*
DATE: Sunday, September 16, 2007

CATEGORY: Hotel

GREENFIELDS CATERING, INC.
General Manager

Exciting opportunity to join a growing and prestigious organization! Must have prior general management experience in high-end food service and private dining environment. Responsible for full P&L financials and general management of operation. Excellent hospitality and leadership skills required. Must be flexible to work weekends. Competitive benefits and salary. EOE

E-mail resume with salary history to hr@greenfieldscateringinc.com or fax to (508) 555-7776. www.greenfieldscateringinc.com

CROSS REFERENCE: Restaurants

Use these **sample help wanted ads** as guides if you need to advertise for a general manager (at left) or chefs (above). Newspapers' classified ads can often be run on their Web sites for a small additional fee.

FINDING PART-TIME HELP

Most caterers, especially those who operate in populous areas, create and develop a database of people who want supplemental income by working catered events. The database should indicate for what position each person is appropriate—waitperson, bartender, captain, and so on. Such a database can be made up of college students, hospital workers, restaurant workers, artists, musicians, or anyone else who likes to moonlight in catering. The larger the pool of these people, the easier it will be for you to find personnel for each event. Have anyone interested send resumes, fill out applications, and conduct interviews in the same manner as for full-time employees.

After hiring people once or twice, highlight the best performers. The next time you need workers for an event, the planners will know whom to call first. It is common for part-time catering workers to work for more than one company, making it necessary for event planners to secure the best workers by calling them far in advance. There are some people who have the ability and experience to work in several different capacities for a caterer. A caterer might ask a waiter to fill in as a bartender for an event for which a bartender could not be found, and have him trained by another bartender just prior to the event. If he does a very good job, that waiter will now be included on lists for both waiters *and* bartenders in the caterer's database of part-time employees.

Caterers who are relatively small, are located in a sparsely populated area, or only offer weekend or sporadic work opportunities may find hiring difficult, and may decide to work with a staffing agency to satisfy their needs.

WORKING WITH STAFFING AGENCIES

Although virtually all caterers hire permanent employees for production purposes, many use staffing agencies to provide them with additional cooks and service personnel during busier times or when executing events. These agencies supply waiters, bartenders, cooks, valets, coat checkers, and so forth, and usually charge an hourly rate for each. The agency collects withholding and Social Security taxes from its employees. It may also provide workers' compensation and disability insurance, as well as other, nonmandatory, benefits to the employee. The caterer pays the staffing agency—not the workers.

The upside to using a staffing agency is that it frees you from hiring staff yourself. The downside is that the amount paid to the agency is usually significantly more than if the employee is paid directly by the caterer. Another disadvantage to using staffing agencies is that the catering company cannot usually select specific people for its events, and must rely on the workers the agency sends. Most reputable staffing agencies train their staffers well, but the possibility of personality clashes still looms.

Suppose a caterer uses a staffing agency to hire six waitpersons for a wedding, and one of them does not serve the food in the style that he was instructed to use, instead using a technique he previously learned elsewhere. The caterer may complain to the agency and request that it not send that waiter in the future; however, it is likely that the waiter in question will continue his employment with the staffing agency. If he were employed directly by the caterer, on the other hand, he might lose his job. With this example, the caterer will have to deal with the same waitperson twice instead of rectifying the situation. I prefer to go with the original scenario. Caterers usually encounter more compliance and loyalty from employees whom they hire themselves.

Staffing agencies can usually be found in larger towns and cities and may specialize in serving a specific niche, such as the hospitality industry. It is such agencies that should be contacted first. As with any supplier or purveyor, try to locate multiple agencies using the phone book or Internet or by asking other culinary colleagues. Compare them for price, quality, and service before choosing which one to use.

HOW TO HIRE STAFF

After collecting several résumés, evaluate them and schedule initial interviews with those candidates who seem most qualified. Before the interview, have the prospective employee fill out an application. The information on the application should be compared with that on the résumé for consistency. It may also provide facts that prove helpful during a background check.

Most caterers will not offer a position to anyone without first doing a background check, which includes verifying an applicant's personal and professional references and past employment. Look for consistency in descriptions of behavioral issues when calling an applicant's references or past employers. One past employer who speaks negatively about the applicant may not be enough to rule that person out for the position; however, a pattern of punctuality or attendance problems, insubordination, or substance or alcohol abuse problems may be. The more applications a caterer receives, the more selective the caterer can be in hiring.

It is rare for a caterer to use a background check service or agency; however, such entities do exist, and their use may be necessary when hiring a critical upper-management position or when the caterer does not have the personnel in place to conduct the check personally.

◼ REVIEWING RÉSUMÉS

Reviewing résumés carefully can save a lot of time during the interview process. First, scan the résumé to see that it is formatted in a businesslike manner and that there are no gaps in the employment history timeline. Such gaps may signify problems such as lack of ambition or dependability. If these gaps are the only red flags, an interview may still be worthwhile. Ask job applicants about such issues face-to-face: they may exist for good reasons, such as an illness or becoming a caretaker for someone else who fell ill.

Be mindful of any spelling or grammatical errors on résumés as well. Word processing technology, complete with built-in spelling and grammar checkers, makes it difficult to justify such mistakes, which can indicate a lack of diligence on the applicant's part—an attitude that can spill over into the workplace.

Check the applicant's level of professional experience. Make sure he or she has the proper level of training and on-the-job experience. If you want to hire a catering chef, you should look for someone experienced with volume cooking in the banquet department of a hotel, country club, camp, resort, banquet hall; on a cruise ship; or with other catering companies. Training underqualified applicants may take more time then you can afford, and overqualified applicants may tire easily of the job responsibilities and begin a new job search, leaving you with a vacant position to fill once again.

While it's good for an applicant to have a diverse employment history, length of employment is also a good indicator of his or her level of dedication. In an entry-level position, however, education will probably be more of a factor than experience.

Isabel Smith, John Doe, and Steven Jones all have excellent **résumés** (see pages 120–125) and are the types of job candidates you should bring in to interview.

Isabel Smith

23 First Avenue • Boston, Massachusetts 02215

isabel.smith@issmith.com • (508) 555-1115 (H) • (508) 555-7553 (C)

SENIOR MANAGEMENT PROFILE

Operations Management/Strategic Planning/Business Development

Results-driven, accomplished leader with extensive experience spearheading strategic planning, personnel development, and operations for catering facilities, restaurants, and franchise operations. Expertise optimizing profit within high-growth environments, business turnarounds, and startups. Dynamic and creative leader with proven success cultivating strong rapport with customers, vendors, and subordinates. Talent for developing and building solid sales and service teams to dramatically expand existing customer base. Able to speak intermediate conversational Greek. Willing to travel and relocate.

CORE COMPETENCIES

• Entrepreneurial Leadership	• Market Identification	• Customer Relationship Management
• Startup Operations	• HR Functions	• Inventory Management
• Business Turnarounds	• Contract Negotiation	• Coaching and Team Building

PROFESSIONAL EXPERIENCE

PAVILION CATERING CORP.—Boston, Massachusetts   1996–Present
Full-service catering/banquet company with 75 full-time and part-time staff

Director of Operations

Effectively manage resources to attract corporate and private customers for special events, weddings, fundraisers, sports events, concerts, trade shows, and conferences. Hold complete P&L responsibility to include budget management for the company, marketing efforts, and individual events. Develop and manage inventory system. Select, train, and mentor new employees and management, ensuring complete customer satisfaction. Establish sales objectives and evaluate sales staff performance. Manage physical facilities, including 15,000 sq ft facility and eight acres of property, and equipment, coordinating regular maintenance activities.

➤ Increased profitability by implementing strategies to expand customer base; established aggressive food and labor cost controls; evaluated company weaknesses and developed strong business development plans and operational procedure to increase efficiencies.
➤ Played an integral role in positioning company as a regional leader in special events in Boston area.
➤ Successfully coordinated multiple large events, serving 400 to 10,000 guests, both on and off premises.
➤ Spearheaded event planning for 2000 U.S. presidential visit, which included numerous national dignitaries.

Sales and Banquet Manager and Front-of-House Manager   1990–1995

Introduced services to potential customers, cultivating and maintaining network of community contacts. Developed marketing budgets and advertising campaigns. Negotiated customer and vendor contacts.

➤ Increased corporate revenue by implementing targeted sales strategies to attract upscale weddings and social events.
➤ Successfully expanded sales base to include new corporate accounts.
➤ Enhanced customer awareness of company, services, and quality reputation.

THE ORIGINAL PIG STAND/ENJOIE CANDY SHOPPE—Andover, Massachusetts   1989–1995
Startup barbecue food and specialty dessert products company

Director of Operations

Spearheaded development and execution of business plan to introduce new homemade BBQ products and specialty desserts to regional customer base. Acquired rights to name and recipes of a once-famous regional barbecue company. Directed marketing efforts and handled inventory, budgetary, and accounting functions.

➤ Created regional brand awareness of food products and trade names by rolling out powerful marketing plan.

➤ Increased revenues and dining traffic by showcasing specialty barbecue and dessert items at special events and newly acquired casual dining operation.

TAVANI, INC.—Salem, Massachusetts   1983–1989

High-volume full-service restaurant with 50 employees and $2 million in annual revenues

Director of Restaurant Operations

Held bottom-line responsibility for P&L and the turnaround of troubled restaurant. Developed comprehensive marketing and business redevelopment strategy to increase revenue and decrease operating costs. Promoted company to attract new customers and reintroduce new products and service to previously dissatisfied customers. Collaborated with contractors and tradesmen to redesign interior/exterior physical spaces. Directed renovation of back-of-house to accommodate new menu items and increase food quality. Tracked and analyzed sales and expenses. Recruited and developed management team including one GM and four assistant managers.

➤ Increased gross revenues 20% annually to $2 million in the fifth year by: 1. Securing rights to trade names, 2. Implementing new menu designs and products, and 3. Establishing aggressive budgetary requirements to regain stability and control costs.

➤ Promoted MAS Lottery to increase lottery sales by 40% to $500K, thereby increasing company commission. Increased lottery traffic also translated into increased customer counts and food sales.

➤ Authored operational training manuals and procedures to enhance and stabilize operational efficiency.

➤ Negotiated new contracts and pricing structures with vendors and instituted new inventory controls and security measures.

➤ Cultivated strong employee dedication to customer service.

➤ Successfully operated business for six profitable years, then successfully sold company in 2002.

EDUCATION AND CREDENTIALS

Bachelor of Science in Management, 1986 • Binghamton University (State University of N.Y.), Binghamton, NY

Professional Affiliations / Boards:

– Member • Park and Recreation Commission, Suffolk County (1999–Present)
– Festival Chairman • Suffolk County Grecian Festival (1991–Present)
– Metropolitan/Parish Liaison • Greek Orthodox Metropolis of Boston (1993–Present)
– Chairman • Pastoral and Finance Committees, Greek Orthodox Metropolis of Boston (1993–Present)
– Comptroller and Finance Director • Annunciation Greek Orthodox Parish Council (1990–Present)
– Chairman • Building Fund Committee, Annunciation Greek Orthodox Parish Council (1990–Present)
– Chairman • Greek Invitational Gold Tournament (1990–Present)
– Coach and Sponsor • Massachusetts Special Olympics (2001–2002)
– Member • Massachusetts Restaurant Association (1996–2002)

Technical Background: Proficient with MSWord, Excel, PowerPoint, Access, Publisher, Outlook, QuickBooks, and Micros POS

John R. Doe
114 Main Street • New York, NY 10001
(212) 555-8120 (home) • (646) 555-2070 (mobile)
john.r.doe@johnrdoe.com

Objective:
Financial management position that utilizes my computer, analytical, and forecasting skills

Business Experience:

Asset Manager, Grey Lodging Services, New York, NY   **February 2001 to present**

Privately held management company for 70-plus property hotel portfolio. Represent ownership position to hotel operators. Manage capital budgeting and spending, perform quarterly financial analysis of properties in portfolio, for purpose of identifying risks and opportunities. Report findings to ownership and follow up with operators.

- Implemented flexible budgeting process to monitor performance and adjust to changing business volumes.
- Developed working financial analysis and reporting tools using Hyperion products.
- Assisted VP of development in analysis of potential acquisitions and development projects.
- Managed real estate tax appeal process, resulting in initial annual savings of $325,000 for ten properties in portfolio.

Manager of Financial Reporting and Treasury
Saccord North America, New York, NY   **July 1995 to September 2000**

North American subsidiary of 2,500-property hotel and service company based in France. Prepared monthly consolidated GAAP and IASC financial reporting package for New York and Paris office. Directed internal audit process of hotel properties located in USA and Canada. Researched and prepared pro-forma forecasts for development projects. Directed staff of four and delegated responsibility for 18 hotel and four regional controllers.

- Designed and implemented central cash consolidation system, providing daily position balancing and saving $1 million in annual interest costs.
- Researched tax consolidation and merger process that allowed for tax savings of over $6 million in US, and $7 million in Canada.
- Streamlined GAAP consolidation process of multiple companies cutting full reporting time from one month to 7 days.
- Headed PC task force that set up NT network and email system in hotel properties to North American office and France.
- Organized and led project team for installation of Oracle financial system in all hotels and head office.
- Implemented standard internal audit process for hotel properties throughout North America using Generally Accepted Auditing Standards.
- Developed comprehensive pro-forma models for ongoing development projects.

Controller, Development Assets Investment Managers, Inc., Philadelphia, PA   **July 1994 to April 1995**

Managed complete accounting function for real estate investment/management company with two hotels and two residential buildings in Philadelphia, PA.

- Simplified accounting process by installing accounting software, including payroll, timekeeping, general ledgers, and payables, thus allowing for more timely presentation of financial statements.
- Worked with external accountant on tax matters.
- Streamlined banking and treasury process by setting up one central banking relationship.

Controller, Gotham East Suite Hotels, New York, NY   **December 1989 to July 1994**

Managed accounting function for two all-suite hotels with a combined suite count of 685 and combined sales in excess of $25 million. Hotels are part of nine-property all-suite hotel company based in Manhattan.

- Reduced company-wide payroll by $400,000 by centralizing accounting department.
- Developed standardized accounting policies and procedures that allowed for more timely and consistent presentation of financial statements.
- Trained controllers of other properties in use of new systems.
- Installed POS and inventory/menu management system in F&B operations.
- Developed expense control by implementing budgets and variance analysis.

Senior Internal Auditor, Hennely Enterprises, New York, NY   **May to December 1989**

Worked under direction of CPA. Managed staff of four on audits of hotel division of major real estate company.

- Developed comprehensive audit programs to accommodate existing hotel accounting systems.
- Evaluated efficiency of food purchasing systems of NYC properties.
- Wrote standardized policies and procedures to correct points noted in course of audits.

Staff Auditor - Intern, Cornell University, Ithaca, NY   **Summer 1998**

- Worked under direction of CPA, responsible for performing detail audit fieldwork. Duties included internal control evaluations, flow-charting, and complete audit test procedures for various university operating units.

Planning Assistant, Lexpaz Group, Long Beach, CA   **December 1986 to September 1987**

Temporary position working with highly entrepreneurial CEO of export company developing floating trade show concept. Set up business plan of hotel operation on converted cruise-ship. Also set up accounting system for company.

Credit Manager, Peyton Regency Hilton Head, Hilton Head, SC   **April 1985 to December 1986**

Assistant Front Office Manager, Quaint Inn Tallahassee, Tallahassee, FL   **1983 to 1985**

Sous-Chef, Some Thyme, Inc., Media, PA   **1976 to 1983**

Education:
Cornell University School of Hotel Administration, Masters of Management   **May 1989**

- Concentrated in financial management
- Completed all academic requirements of New York State CPA exam
- Researched and wrote monograph project on preparing and optimizing forecasts.
- Held graduate teaching assistantship in School of Hotel Administration. Assisted in development of interactive tutorial programs on Apple Macintosh network.

Florida State University, Bachelor of Arts degree in Hospitality Administration   **April 1985**

- Attended European Summer study program in Leysin, Switzerland
- Achieved Minor in French language

Skills and Interests:
Highly proficient with Microsoft Office–related products. Proficient with Lawson, Oracle, Solomon, Quicken, and Maxwell computer accounting applications. Also proficient with many property management and point of sale systems.

Hobbies include golf, sailing, cooking, and bicycling.

STEVEN JONES

727 Sun Court
Apt. 327
New York, NY 11377

Home: (718) 555-0721
Office: (718) 555-0714
s.jones@sjones.com

SUMMARY

A dynamic financial management professional with keen business acumen and proven ability to focus on the overall business strategy and financial objectives of the operation. Highly skilled in educating and guiding departmental managers to ensure financial and operational goals are achieved.

Specific expertise in the following areas:

- Financial management
- Forecasting and budgeting
- Acquisitions
- Renovation accounting
- Revenue management
- Presentation and communication skills

EMPLOYMENT

FINE HOTEL CORPORATION, Stamford, CT   **January 1999 to Present**

Area Director of Finance

Function as the Controller of the Stamford Fine Hotel and oversee the accounting and financial operations of eight other hotels. Responsible for the production of annual budgets, review of property results and the analysis and presentation of all financial forecasts within the region. Specific duties include:

- Supervision and mentoring of property level hotel controllers.
- Ensure appropriate communications and owner relations for the various properties.
- Active participation in pricing strategy and revenue management decisions.
- Ensure systems of audit and internal controls are maintained.
- Assist in the takeover of new hotels by completing due diligence and implementation of company systems and controls.

DIAMOND REGENCY HOTEL, New York, NY November 1993 to January 1999

Controller
Supervised the accounting function in this 367-room luxury hotel with $37 million in revenue. Major responsibilities include:

- Preparation and presentation of annual financial and capital budgets.
- Production of monthly financial statements.
- Oversaw the accounting for a $35 million property renovation project ensuring project was completed on budget.

- Member of the task force that set up newly acquired hotel's operating budgets and systems of internal controls.
- Active participation in revenue management.

RADIANT HOTELS, Stamford, CT   **January 1992 to November 1993**

Controller

Direct the accounting operations and supervise leased office space business unit of a 467-room property with $18 million in sales.

- Oversaw the conversion of 90 guest rooms into leased executive office suites.
- Responsible for the start-up and management of this new business unit.
- Implemented cost controls that yielded a 5 -percentage point increase in profit over a two-year period.
- Prepared all financial statements and annual budget.

GREAT PARK HOTELS, New York, NY   **May 1988 to January 1992**

Controller   September 1989 to January 1992
Hotel Plaza Apollo

Property controller of a 154-room luxury hotel. Responsible for:

- Preparation of financial statements.
- Preparation of operating and capital budgets.
- Streamlined operations during a period of business recession.

Assistant Controller   May 1988 to September 1989
Salisbury Hotel

Responsible for the accounting function during a $20 million property renovation.

CONTINENTAL HOTELS, New York, NY   **September 1982 to May 1988**

Supervisor of Corporate Accounting
Staff Accountant

- Supervise staff of six in the corporate financial consolidation group.
- Member of a financial reporting team that prepared consolidated financial statements for 100 hotels worldwide.

EDUCATION

BS, Accounting
State University of New York, Oneonta, NY

MBA, 36 Credits completed
Sacred Heart University, Fairfield, CT

◼ INTERVIEWING APPLICANTS

For a potential employee, the interview process can be intimidating. An interviewer who allows the candidate to relax a little will probably get more honest information from the applicant. Start interviews with lighthearted conversation by asking questions such as, "Did you find our establishment easily?" or by offering a glass of water or a cup of coffee. Once an applicant is noticeably focused and relaxed you can ask other, more relevant questions:

1. What do you know about the company?
2. Why do you want to work here?
3. What characteristics do you possess that make you a good candidate for this position?
4. Where do you see yourself professionally five years from now?
5. What challenges have you encountered during your previous employment?
6. What are your greatest overall assets?
7. What are some areas in your professional life that you would like to improve upon?

◼ SCREENING APPLICANTS

Many businesses require mandatory drug testing for potential employees. People who abuse drugs or alcohol are poor candidates for employment in catering. The work environment of those employed in catering is the party environment of those for whom they work and there is often easy access to alcoholic beverages. This may prove too problematic for an active addict or too tempting for someone trying to stop drinking.

Testing for drugs does not, however, reveal alcohol abuse problems, and it may be difficult to detect such a problem during a job interview. Hopefully, a background check will reveal an applicant's alcohol-related problems. There are numerous Web sites that sell kits approved by either the Food and Drug Administration (FDA) or the Substance Abuse and Mental Health Services Administration (SAMHSA), a branch of the US Department of Health and Human Services, that can be used to screen applicants for both drugs and alcohol. The least expensive kits test either urine or saliva, although the samples must be sent to a laboratory for testing at an additional expense. Hair and blood testing, although more reliable, is more intrusive, and has to be overseen by a health-care professional.

While holding short-term positions is not uncommon in the food-service industry, if many of an applicant's past employment experiences were short-term, it's important to determine whether the applicant resigned from those positions or was terminated. An applicant fired from many jobs is probably not worth taking a chance on.

Although you can refuse to hire someone based on employment history, drug test results, and lack of education or experience, Title VII of the Civil Rights Act of 1964 prohibits discrimination in hiring based on race, color, religion, sex, or national origin. Some states and localities also prohibit discrimination based on marital status, sexual orientation, and gender identity. Violations of these labor laws can result in substantial fines and possible jail time. In addition, there are minimum age requirement for employees, some of which are related to the position's responsibilities. For example, in New York State, you must be at least eighteen years of age to serve alcoholic beverages. These laws can be reviewed by visiting the Web site of the US Department of Labor at www.dol.gov, as well as the Web site of the department of labor in your own state and city.

TAX ISSUES INVOLVED IN HIRING WORKERS

As far as the IRS is concerned, there are two types of workers—employees and independent contractors. Employees will need to fill out a W-4 form so you can pay their wages and withhold their Social Security payments and federal taxes (as well as their state and local taxes, if any). At the end of the calendar year, you will need to provide employees with a W-2 form, a statement totaling their wages and the Social Security, FICA, and state and local taxes (if any) that have been withheld.

■ STAFF

Most caterers regard their staff as employees, not independent contractors. This distinction is important, as it determines if the caterer is responsible for paying and collecting income tax on the workers' behalf. The IRS considers workers, regardless of how often they work, as employees if they are given specific behavioral guidelines to follow, such as:

- They are expected to dress according to management specifications
- They work specific hours as determined by management
- They are asked not to smoke on the job

■ FREELANCERS

Independent contractors, also known as freelancers, are hired on a per job basis and are given guidelines and deadlines. They are usually not continually supervised as employees are. Workers being paid only on commission may also qualify for independent contractor status. An independent contractor takes care of his or her own Social Security payments and taxes; however, you will need to send each one a 1099 statement enumerating the total payments you have made to him or her during that year if that amount is more than $600. Your accountant can advise you about tax issues related to employee and independent contractor status.

Regardless of whether employees are hired on a full-time, part-time, or per diem basis, the caterer who hires them is responsible for providing some types of insurance and collecting and paying certain taxes. Most employers must carry workers' compensation and unemployment insurance for all of their employees. (The number of employees varies state to state, but you usually need a certain number of employees to require mandatory workers' compensation insurance.) These costs should be taken into consideration when assessing the affordability of specific salaries.

◼ PAYROLL SERVICES

Many caterers hire a payroll company to take care of all payroll-related issues; such companies eliminate a lot of paperwork. A payroll company will confer with you about the gross amount of pay for each employee; deduct taxes, Social Security, and FICA payments; pay them to the appropriate authorities; and then issue a check to each employee.

Any caterer who pays employees as independent contractors in order to avoid tax and insurance liabilities is taking a big risk. An IRS audit will inevitably uncover this and result in the caterer paying not just the back taxes, but penalties as well. Caterers should also not pay their employees under the table (i.e., with cash that goes unreported to the government). If the caterer is audited, extensive penalties and back taxes will result. And once caught, the caterer can expect routine audits from federal and state authorities for as long as the company remains in business.

UNDOCUMENTED WORKERS

A caterer may be tempted to hire undocumented workers or those without legal residency status and pay them cash for the time they work. Undocumented workers will often work long hours for less pay than legal employees, and a new caterer in certain areas of the country may be inundated with undocumented workers looking for work. It is very important for caterers to resist the temptation to hire these individuals. The Immigration and Naturalization Service (INS) routinely inspects businesses that it suspects of being at high risk of employing such workers—including catering companies. A caterer who is found to employ them is subject to large fines and will be routinely inspected in the future. Multiple violations can result in more serious penalties.

I-9 forms must be filed for any employee hired after November 6, 1986. Protect yourself and your business by requiring some verification of citizenship or legal residency status when they are filed. The National Restaurant Association has posted the process for filling out an I-9 form on its Web site, http://www.restaurant.org/legal/law_immigration.cfm. It is important to note that severe penalties, both monetary and criminal, can be incurred if an employer knowingly hires or continues to employ an undocumented worker, or if the employer fails to fill out the required paperwork. For example, monetary fines can range from $250 to $10,000 for each unauthorized worker on staff; criminal sentences can last up to six months. Paperwork violators can be fined between $100 and $1,000 per employee. This can add up to several thousand dollars per undocumented worker and can potentially break a business.

Staff Training

Your staff must first be oriented and then trained to the specific requirements of your business. Your executive chef is in charge of training kitchen staff (see Chapter 4, "Setting Up the Catering Kitchen"); your maître d'hôtel should train your wait staff (see Chapter 8, "How Can We Serve You?"); and your event planner/sales manager, your sales and event-planning staff (see Chapter 7, "Event Planning"). All training should be positive and highlight the benefits of such training to the employee, while accomplishing the goals of the business.

CREATE AN EMPLOYEE HANDBOOK

Many caterers have an employee handbook that details the job descriptions for each position and the expectations the employer has for all employees. In this handbook, the caterer can also detail things like workplace behavior (employees may not chew gum or use toothpicks while on duty), dress code (employees must be in a clean uniform at the start of each shift), and hygiene (employees must wash their hands thoroughly before and after handling food). An employee handbook should also include worker safety and food safety guidelines (see Chapter 4, "Setting Up the Catering Kitchen"), as well as an explanation of laws regarding sexual harassment in the workplace.

SEXUAL HARASSMENT

There are two types of sexual harassment. If a supervisor asks for sexual favors from a subordinate and threatens that person with dismissal if he or she does not comply, it is considered quid pro quo harassment. The display of repeated, unwanted sexually oriented behavior, including off-color jokes and intimidating behavior, is considered creating a hostile work environment.

A sexual harassment policy should be regularly communicated to all employees and managers and should be written with:

- A statement that sexual harassment will not be tolerated (a zero-tolerance policy)
- A definition of harassment
- A guide to help employees lodge a complaint

A signed statement acknowledging that they have read and understand the policy should be collected from all employees and managers. Most larger businesses have set up confidential hotlines to deal with these issues.

TRAINING

The objective of formal training is to give employees information and tools to be successful at assigned tasks *before* they are given the actual responsibilities, in hopes of preventing costly mistakes. Such training can be conducted outside the workplace in a classroom setting, or by an existing employee who then becomes the new employee's mentor. Formal training is especially important for those employees who sell or book catering events, have direct contact with guests—such as wait staff and maîtres d'hôtel—or who prepare food. Positions with minimal responsibility and good supervision—like valet parking attendant, coat check, pot and dish washer, and busperson—may only require on-the-job training.

All training programs should have a checklist of objectives or competencies that must be met before an employee is ready to assume his or her position. These objectives should directly correlate with the employee's job description. The following is a job description for a prep cook followed by the necessary training steps to be conducted by the sous-chef.

Prep Cook Job Description

1. When no events are taking place, working hours will be from 9:00 A.M. to 5:00 P.M., Monday through Friday. On days when events are being held, work hours will vary. Overtime pay will go into effect when more than forty hours are worked during a normal workweek.

2. All prep cooks are required to wear a uniform that will be provided by the employer. Black work shoes, socks, and a baseball-type cap must be worn and will be provided by the employee. Long hair below the upper neck line and beards must be restrained by a hair net. Ear and hand jewelry is not allowed, with the exception of one wedding ring.

3. Prep cooks will check a designated clipboard for a daily list of items to be prepared. The specifications for each item are listed in the manual available from the sous-chef. Prep cooks must not deviate from these specifications unless told to do so by the sous-chef or executive chef.

4. Prep cooks will work safely and adhere to all food safety guidelines as provided in the employee manual.

5. Prep cooks will clean all hand tools and knives that they use. All other pots, containers, and utensils will be cleaned by the stewarding personnel.

6. Prep cooks will assist with general cleaning, maintenance, and sanitation of the kitchen.

7. Prep cooks must assist the sous-chef with menu development and new recipe testing.

8. Prep cooks must inform the sous-chef if the level of any ingredient falls below 25 percent of the standard amount kept on hand.

Training Steps for Prep Cooks

Conducted by the Sous-Chef

1. The sous-chef will give the prep cook a copy of the work schedule for the week and go over the times that the prep cook will need to be on-site and working. The prep cook will sign the document, signifying that he or she has read and understood the schedule.

2. The sous-chef will give the prep cook a copy of the dress code and go over it with the prep cook. The prep cook will sign the document, signifying that he or she has read and understood the dress code.

3. The sous-chef will show the prep cook the designated clipboard with the daily list of items to be prepared, and the manual in which the specifications for each item are listed. Prep cooks must not deviate from these specifications unless told to do so by the sous-chef or executive chef. The sous-chef will check to make sure the prep cook has prepared each item according to specifications.

4. The sous-chef will make the prep cook aware of all food safety guidelines from the employee manual and make sure the prep cook complies with them.

5. The sous-chef will make sure the prep cook cleans all hand tools and knives that are used. All other pots, containers, and utensils will be cleaned by the stewarding personnel.

6. The sous-chef will make sure the prep cook assists with general cleaning, maintenance, and sanitation of the kitchen.

7. The sous-chef will include the prep cook in menu development meetings and new recipe testing.

8. The sous-chef will give the prep cook an overview of the inventory in the pantry, walk-in refrigerator, and freezer, and explain that the prep cook must inform the sous-chef when the level of any ingredient falls below 25 percent of the standard amount kept on hand.

9. At the end of the week, the sous-chef will give a report to the chef on the progress of the prep cook's training.

Managing Staff

Many caterers claim that the hardest part of running their business is managing their staff. Personality clashes, excessive absences from work, tardiness, insubordination, and lack of compliance with a dress code are some of the common complaints. It may seem logical for a caterer to terminate an employee who keeps violating the rules of the business. In truth, it is not always that easy.

A trained employee is difficult and expensive to replace. Training new employees usually requires the assistance of someone on staff and may result in overtime pay for that staff member. Often, terminated employees file for unemployment insurance benefits whether they deserve them or not. If the employer has not adequately documented the behavior that led to dismissal, the former employee may be successful in his or her claim for benefits, which will increase the employer's insurance rates.

A progressive discipline policy can help resolve most employee issues. Such a policy is designed to improve employees' performance by first explaining why certain behavior is inappropriate and then offering ways to improve. The discipline policy should be explained in the employee handbook.

The most important aspect of a progressive discipline system is that it allows the employer to document any pertinent information about the employee in an organized fashion. This documentation is often necessary when an employee challenges the reasons for his or her termination and starts legal action against the employer. If you can prove through documentation that a terminated employee was warned numerous times and produce employee-signed documents substantiating your claim, you will have an excellent chance of winning any legal action brought against you. Through trial and error, however, most caterers are able to maintain an efficient staff that for the most part works in harmony.

How to Get the Best from Your Staff
- Provide monetary incentives, commissions, or bonuses for extra effort and seniority.
- Offer health insurance benefits.
- Create some flexible shifts during slower times of the year.
- Increase salaries periodically.
- Lead by example: Get into the trenches with your staff during crunch times.
- Develop multiple management styles: One approach may be good for some and bad for others.
- Implement a strict anti-harassment policy.
- Research establishments that provide the type of food and service that you expect from your employees and pay for your employees to visit them.
- Feed employees well, especially before or after catering events; a good family meal shows concern for your staff's health and emotional well-being.
- Treat all employees with respect and do not get caught up in your own ego.

PROBATIONARY PERIODS

Probationary periods for new employees are an effective way to determine if an employee will work out long term. During such periods, new employees can be terminated for any reason, at the caterer's discretion. While the length of probationary times varies among caterers, most are three or six months. Some employers choose longer probationary periods and do not provide benefits to employees during that time. A probationary period can also be shortened at the caterer's discretion in the case of a promising employee. One disadvantage to a probationary period is that it may discourage some qualified applicants from accepting a job.

A written probationary period contract may prove useful. Such a contract should be signed by the employee and supervisor prior to the first day of employment, and include:

- The start and completion date of the probationary period
- Possible reasons for termination
- Designated work days and hours
- Information about periodic meetings to discuss progress
- Information about wages upon successful completion of the probationary period, whether or not they change

Probationary periods can also be used in conjunction with progressive discipline. Employees performing poorly may be put on probation with the stipulation that if they do not improve during that time, they will be terminated.

PERFORMANCE REVIEWS

Performance reviews are usually conducted after a probationary period and annually thereafter. To conduct a performance review, you must first have criteria and information for evaluation. Maintain a file on each employee containing information on his or her employment history (dates of hire, promotion, etc.) and job description. Include written notes about the employee you take during staff meetings, positive or negative letters or feedback from clients, certificates from trainings the employee completes, peer evaluations after events, or any other information needed to assess the employee's performance.

During a performance review, management evaluates whether the employee is fulfilling the requirements of the job description and meeting expectations for dress code, hygiene, and behavior. Many caterers also set goals for the employee for the coming year—perhaps learning a new culinary skill or taking management training. An employee found unsatisfactory can be put on probation again, demoted, or fired. An employee with a very positive performance review might be offered a better position, a raise, or other benefits, such as more vacation time.

RETAINING STAFF

The strength and growth of your business depends on keeping good staff. Turnover and training cost your business money—not to mention the impact on your own stress level. There are many ways you can retain staff.

Pay your employees what the business can afford without sacrificing profit. Offer incentives based on superior performance, extra hours worked, and reliability. (Do not, however, promise short-term increases that are unrealistic.) Develop training programs that decrease the need for employees with prior experience. Pay employees promptly. Try to include other benefits (health and life insurance, 401K contributions, paid vacations, etc.) as the business allows.

When your business is just getting started and you can't yet afford long-term paid benefits, you may still be able to offer paid personal and sick days, merit-based bonuses, flexible hours, or tuition reimbursement for professional or personal development classes to key employees. The people who sell your events and services will usually make a commission directly related to the revenues they generate. When you provide them with training to make them successful at selling, everyone prospers.

When your business is ready to offer a benefits package to its employees, check with them first to determine what their needs and desires are. Then consult with a benefits company so you can offer what your employees want and need—and your business can afford. Payments for benefits can be handled directly through your payroll—and your payroll company.

How to Research and Set Salaries

1. Find out what industry leaders pay people for comparable positions, making sure to get a multiregional sampling of information.
2. Find out if those companies offer other incentives, such as health insurance benefits, commissions, or paid sick and personal days, in order to get a sense of overall compensation.
3. Establish an amount that your company can afford for each position.
4. If offering competitive salaries jeopardizes overall profitability, find other incentives to lure good job candidates, such as more vacation time, abridged and flexible work hours, day care for young children, and the possibility of working from home.

In Chapter 6, you'll learn how to attract customers to your new business.

6.marketing

When you develop a business plan for your catering enterprise, you decide on your catering identity, whether it be mobile barbecue, on-premise fine dining, or off-premise casual food. A marketing strategy—which is also part of your business plan—describes how you're going to get the word out about your new venture.

Marketing essentially means showcasing your business and all it has to offer in appealing ways in order to attract the maximum amount of viable customers to it. A caterer's marketing program should communicate to targeted potential clients that the food, beverages, and services provided by that caterer will be of the highest quality and a step above the competition's.

Most caterers start marketing their business prior to opening. It is very important to have sufficient funds in place to continue the marketing campaign after the business has opened. In fact, advertising after the business has opened is more effective because the customer now has a physical entity to attach to the images of the business conveyed through advertising. There are many different ways to market a catering business, and a savvy businessperson will use a variety of methods.

The Four Ps of Marketing

There are four basic categories that affect marketing decisions. Their integration has been termed a "marketing mix," a phrase coined by Neil H. Borden in his 1964 article, "The Concept of the Marketing Mix," which was published that year in the *Journal of Advertising Research*. The basic components of this mix are:

1. Product
2. Price
3. Place (distribution)
4. Promotion

These four areas are considered controllable and can be changed according to the constraints that arise in the marketplace, including new trends and product availability.

> **Product:** Product refers to both specific products *and* services. Marketing decisions on products should be based on quality, style, safety, functionality, and uniqueness.

Price: Marketing decisions in this area can be affected by seasonality, availability, volume discounts, wholesale versus retail pricing, and the pricing strategy of competitors.

Distribution: Distribution involves how products or services get to the customer. Marketing decisions about distribution can be affected by transportation considerations, perishability, packaging, inventory management, and order processing.

Promotion: Promotion is the communication of information about the business to customers with a positive end result. Decisions in this area are affected by marketing budget, the availability of advertising vehicles, sales personnel, and publicity.

This framework can be used to formulate and organize even the simplest of marketing campaigns; use it as a checklist to ensure that each area is considered before you invest advertising dollars.

Brand Your Business

Everything people see is a potential marketing tool—the sign in front of your banquet hall or catering kitchen, your catering vehicle, your business cards and letterhead, even the uniform worn by your kitchen and wait staff. It makes sense, then, for everything associated with your business to display your catering company's logo. It will communicate your brand through a unified message.

Have a graphic artist (if you have a big budget) or even a college art student (if you don't) create special artwork or a logo you can use for marketing. This logo will go on your business cards, stationery, the side panel of your catering vehicle, all print media ads, and the sign in front of your business.

For example, Greenfields Catering, our hypothetical off-premise Boston caterer, decided to use a digital color photograph of one of its colorful entrées on a white plate in a green field. With this photo, the owners communicate their image—contemporary, high-style catering with a French flair using organic or "green" ingredients—all in one picture. Greenfields uses this digital photo on its business cards, catering menus, brochures, delivery vehicle, print media ads, and the sign outside its catering kitchen.

YOUR MARKETING PLAN

Your initial marketing plan should target the market outlined in your business plan. Greenfields Catering has a marketing budget of $20,000 for the first year and a target market of young urban professionals. It spends 75 percent of its budget on the digital photo, business cards, brochures, stationery, vehicle signs, a yellow pages ad, a Web site, and a scheduled tasting for corporate marketing and event-planning executives during its first month of business. From this push, its owners hope to start booking corporate events, and from word-of-mouth generated from the business events, book social events like engagement parties and weddings when these young urban professionals make a life change.

After Greenfields's owners see how their initial marketing efforts pay off, they will also consider spending the rest of the budget by placing some monthly ads in a Boston city magazine whose emphasis is on what's trendy and hip in the area. They also hope to have an event featured in the society column of a Boston lifestyle magazine.

How you want to use your catering business artwork depends on who your target market is. People who live and work close to your banquet hall? Society mavens who read local, upscale magazines and society rags? Corporate marketing managers who frequent certain trade shows and read the daily newspaper or a local business magazine? Young families who listen to a certain radio station? Brides-to-be who love spa treatments?

The two general markets that caterers target are public and private corporations or companies, and individuals. (It's rare for a caterer to only work with one and not the other.) Corporations and companies require catering for events such as employee holiday or retirement parties, business meetings, seminars and symposia, and employee retreats. Individuals hire caterers for social events such as weddings, anniversaries, housewarmings, and so on.

A marketing budget should be divided between these two areas—social and corporate—because each needs to be marketed differently. But whatever advertising vehicles are used for each, it is a caterer's specialized services that will set the company apart from its competition. A catering company that conducts simple research on its corporate clients and designs creative and practical menus specifically for business meetings, with items that are healthier and less messy to eat, may create a competitive edge for itself. The research may come as a result of a simple survey administered via e-mail (with permission) containing questions about eating habits or desires.

Here are some of the ways to spend your marketing dollars:

◼ SIGNAGE

Signs identify a business but also serve as a primary marketing tool. An on-premise caterer's large, legible signs make it easy for the public to locate its facility. An off-premise caterer that does not need a large, decorative sign near its production facility might invest in premium signage for its vehicles instead. Signs should be attention grabbing. Avoid crowding too much information or multiple logos and catchphrases onto a sign; this can confuse the public.

Vehicle signage is a marketing tool. A truck owned by Abigail Kirsch has the company's logo displayed prominently on its side, and its name and address—also in the company's corporate typeface—on the door.

Before purchasing signage, find out what kind of signs the local building code permits. Any professional sign company will be aware of area building codes. (You can also find out at the local building inspector's office.) Many caterers use magnetic signs, which can be affixed to the side of a car, van, or truck and then easily removed. The advantage to magnetic signs is that they can be transferred to any vehicle; the disadvantage is that they can fall off in inclement weather. Having multiple magnetic signs ensure that you always have something on hand in case one gets lost or if you need multiple vehicles for an event.

◼ BROCHURES, BUSINESS CARDS, AND STATIONERY

Business cards, brochures, and business forms such as proposals, contracts, and statements all make a statement about the quality of your business. In addition to the logo and contact information, you might want to include a catchphrase (such as "Catering for All Occasions") on all your promotional materials and correspondence. Other useful information to include in a brochure is a list of sample menu items, photos of a past event, a brief list of notable clients, and some positive quotes about the company from past clients.

Use concise, easy-to-read print on quality paper stock. Embossing and multiple colors will also enhance printed materials. Unless you have a computer with cutting-edge graphic design software and high-quality printing capabilities, it's better to have a professional printer handle the creation of all business documents that contain graphics. Cost-cutting techniques, such as the use of cheap paper or clip art, can create a negative impression with potential clients. After all, clients want catered events to be clean, organized, and professional: Your promotional materials must communicate these traits about your business. A cheap or flimsy brochure will communicate exactly the opposite.

■ ADVERTISING IN PRINT AND ELECTRONIC MEDIA

Advertising on television and radio, and in magazines and newspapers, will bring in new business and give your catering business a presence in the marketplace. Although such advertising will bring more exposure and name recognition, you won't get nearly as much business this way as through word of mouth.

Choosing specific advertising media is difficult for a caterer, especially when the business has recently opened. Ask any media salespeople who contact you about their demographics. If you are interesting in attracting brides-to-be or society mavens, you'll want to know if a lifestyle magazine is geared toward baby boomers or young families with babies, or if the free monthly women's magazine is placed primarily at doctors' offices or upscale hair salons with spa services.

Advertisements that run only once are not very effective, even if they reach a large audience, because people need to hear or see something several times before they will remember it. Advertisements targeted to a smaller population—especially your target market—and that run repeatedly will be more successful.

Yellow Pages or Phone Book Ads

When you establish telephone service for your business, it is automatically listed in the white pages of the telephone directory published by the provider. Any additional listing, whether in the white or yellow pages of that directory, carries an additional charge. The telephone directories published by the telephone companies—as opposed to the smaller neighborhood versions that have abridged listings—are usually the best ones in which to advertise: They are the most comprehensive and complete.

Many catering businesses have dramatically increased inquiries and sales by advertising in the yellow pages. The drawback to this type of advertising is that potential customers are likely to call several caterers and compare their prices and services. Because these customers do not yet know anything about the quality of any caterer's food, the caterer with the lowest cost may have the advantage. To combat this, it is important to train personnel responsible for fielding inquiries from phone directory advertisements to accentuate your company's unique qualities and products. In addition, these employees should make it a priority to up personal consultations between the potential client and an event planner.

Yellow pages ads are expensive compared to those in many other local periodicals. One advantage of yellow pages advertising is that virtually every business and household will have a telephone directory: other periodicals usually require the customer to subscribe, purchase, or at least decide to pick up a free copy.

When you're deciding on the design and size of your ad, look at past or existing ads by other caterers; potential customers will call caterers with larger ads first. For a very upscale catering company, however, a sophisticated design, even in a smaller space, may appeal to a more desirable clientele and help weed out other inquiries by people looking solely for the company with the lowest price.

Most telephone directory advertisements run annually and can either be paid for in advance, in installments, or even tacked on to the business's telephone bill. Advertising sales representatives from the publishing companies will often call business owners not just to sell them ad space, but to help them choose the size and design that best represents their businesses as well. Ads that are placed in more visible areas of the publication, such as the front or rear cover, cost significantly more than ads placed in a specific section. Multiple listings are more costly but can be very effective. Caterers that advertise in the "Caterers" section as well as in the "Party Planning Services" section, for example, may receive more inquiries than competitors who advertise in only one area.

Trade and Lifestyle Magazines

Newspapers and magazines provide a lot of viable advertising opportunities for caterers. Some target a specific profession—such as *Specialty Coffee Retailer, Architectural Digest, National Real Estate Investor*— while others appeal to people with specific interests or hobbies—such as bridal or wedding magazines, food service industry publications, and city guides designed for tourists. If you are interested in advertising in any periodical, ask first about its circulation and the frequency of publication. A one-time shot to a relatively small number of subscribers may have little or no impact. Other important information to know is the average per capita income of its subscribers, the average amount subscribers spend on entertainment, the area of its distribution, and where in the magazine your ad would do best. The sales representative should be able to answer all these questions. Ask for discounts for a long-term contract or running your ad more frequently. Or inquire about a free test ad to see if the publication's readership responds (it never hurts to ask). Some companies might "trade out," or offer an ad in exchange for catering services valued at the same amount.

Radio

Radio advertising is very effective for catering businesses. Ask the radio sales representative questions about the station's demographics—such as the times and days of the largest listening audience; and the age, per capita income, area of residence, and primary professions of its listening audience—and make sure they jibe with your own target market. The radio station will usually help with the production of the ad or refer you to a company who specializes in designing commercials made for radio.

Radio ads should also be run repetitively. Unlike print ads, radio ads are ephemeral. They are usually only effective when broadcast during the same time period of the day—over and over again. Potential catering clients hearing a radio ad for the first time may not be in the position to record the information and may tune in at the same time the next day in hopes of hearing the ad again. Many radio ads have a jingle, catchphrase, or accompanying music that becomes familiar to the frequent listener. Caterers should consider these options and consult with station personnel in order to make good choices that best represent the business.

Web Sites

The Internet is probably the most commonly used business marketing tool. For a relatively low investment, a caterer can construct a Web site and establish e-mail communication, allowing potential clients to browse its offerings and contact an event planner to set up a consultation. Careful planning must go into the design of the site, however. Web design companies can provide the graphics and programming needed and strategically "locate" the site so that a simple keyword search, such as "caterer," causes a search engine to list it at the beginning of the search results. Opportunities exist to become a sponsored site on various search engines, an arrangement similar to paying for advertising space in magazines or newspapers.

Update your Web site often—especially your client list. Showcase seasonal and holiday menus. And always provide an e-mail link to an event planner.

DVDs as Business Cards

Some caterers copy their Web sites onto DVDs, which they then hand out as business cards. An interactive DVD allows potential clients to visit the catering company virtually on their computer without using the Internet.

Direct Mail

Direct mail is a great way to target corporate accounts and potential customers in your demographic or your geographic area. A direct mail company can sell you lists of addresses that are sorted by zip code or other demographic information, such as per capita income, age, gender, or personal interests. You can then print and package the mailing yourself or hire a company to do so. Direct mail companies will design the graphics, write the copy, choose the paper stock and packaging, and mail the material to a targeted audience.

The disadvantage of direct mail is that a targeted mailing from a caterer is often considered junk mail and tossed in the trash without much thought. A professional direct mail marketing company may be able to package the product in an innovative way, causing it to stand out from other mail and, hopefully, be opened by the recipient. Overall, direct mail marketing is statistically more effective when sent to companies at which employees are instructed to open every piece of mail delivered.

Show and Tell

There are many other ways, sometimes much less costly, to promote a catering business. Some caterers will discount their services when asked to cater events for nonprofit or charitable organizations. In exchange for the discount, the host organization promotes the catering company by listing its name on all correspondence for the event, including mailings, brochures, and menus. In addition, the organization persuades the media covering the event to mention the caterer by name. Guests of the event then often hire the caterer for their future private events. Depending on the type of organization, discounts and donations may even be tax deductible.

You should be careful when choosing any type of event to which your business will be linked in a public way. If you cater a political party's fundraiser, for example, you may be labeled as a supporter of that party— even if you're not.

Scheduled Tastings

Potential clients can be invited to open houses or scheduled tastings to sample food, view banquet rooms, and get a sense of how a caterer operates. Such tastings are yet another way to market your product. Quality caterers include a sample table complete with linens, floral pieces, and dinnerware in their displays. Most will also have uniformed service personnel help staff the tasting and serve samples of recommended menu items.

At such events, always have portfolios with photographs of past events your business has produced, as well as business cards, brochures, and client lists for prospective clients to take with them.

Bridal and Trade Shows

Bridal and trade shows are another great way to get your name out there. Although it is rare for a caterer to book a wedding at a bridal show, you can give out brochures and business cards along with a small sample of a signature dish. Attendees are there to gather information and usually make contact with a caterer at a later date.

Hotel and restaurant trade shows, retail food shows, and even street fairs are also opportunities for caterers to display and market their goods. Many chambers of commerce host expos designed to showcase local businesses. These are excellent marketing venues as well as opportunities to network with other local businesses, which commonly recommend each other to their customers.

Piggybacking

Some caterers piggyback on another business's marketing campaign. For example, a car dealership having a big sale might allow a local caterer to hand out food samples and promotional materials to the customers that come into its showroom. The car dealer is happy because the food samples help enhance its customers' experience in the showroom; the caterer is happy because he or she is able to get brochures and business cards into the hands of many potential future customers.

Similarly, a realtor who specializes in upscale residential properties may want to make an open house more alluring. A smart caterer will offer elegant, butler-style hors d'oeuvre and beverages—at cost—and serve them during the open house in exchange for being allowed to hand out his or her own promotional materials. Quite often, it's a win-win situation: The entertaining potential of the property gets underscored, and the caterer acquires new business.

Word of Mouth: The Best Kind of Marketing

The best form of advertising for a catering business is word-of-mouth advertising. In fact, the majority of your incoming business will be the result of referrals or recommendations from satisfied clients or from a guest at one of your events. An inquiry that originates this way should be considered serious, and you should feel confident that the time spent consulting with the potential client will be well worth it.

Why is word-of-mouth advertising so valuable? Most people who decide to host a catered event fear poor-quality food, service, or décor will embarrass them in front of their guests. Hosts are also concerned about appearing cheap or tacky. These fears compel most potential catering clients to ask family, friends, and acquaintances for referrals to caterers. Potential customers that result from yellow pages ads usually contact several caterers and compare them according to what they promise on paper. But getting a referral from someone who has experienced a caterer's product—and whom the client trusts—carries enormous influence.

Word-of-mouth advertising will continue perpetually as long as the quality of each event is very high and customers have a good perception of the value of your services. Making your business cards available after an event is a subtle but valuable marketing tool and helps guests promote your catering business via word-of-mouth.

In Chapter 7, we'll get started with the basics of event planning, from the initial contact to adding all the bells and whistles a client could want.

7.

event planning

Planning a profitable event that meets or exceeds your clients' expectations is the cornerstone of catering success. It is how you grow your business as well as your reputation, because, as we discussed in Chapter 6, word of mouth is the most effective marketing tool you have. When you plan and execute a successful event, it creates a buzz that no amount of advertising can buy.

What the Catering Client Wants

All catering clients want:

- Great food, beverages, and service for their guests
- The appropriate entertainment
- An event their guests will enjoy and remember
- A virtually mistake-free, stress-free event
- An event that appears lavish—never cheap
- Great weather

While the weather is out of everyone's control, an event planner can help the client achieve all of these other objectives.

The Role of the Event Planner

A profitable event that pleases the client starts with the event planner, sometimes also called the function manager. If you have a small operation, you are probably the owner, event planner, and chef all rolled into one. If you own a larger business, then you will probably employ an event planner. Large hotels, banquet halls, and convention centers might give event planners different titles, such as catering manager, catering sales manager, catering sales representative, convention or conference service manager, or banquet manager. Whatever the title, the event planner is essentially in charge of making sure the event is a success from start to finish.

Depending on the type of business you have, other employees may function as event planners from time to time. For on-premise operations such as hotels, country clubs, banquet halls, and large restaurants, event planning is typically the responsibility of the banquet manager. In many cases the banquet manager will be the only contact person for the client. After the client agrees to the plans, the banquet manager will communicate specific functions for the event to the appropriate people, often using a banquet event order (BEO). Most larger, off-premise catering operations

What Event Planners Do

Visualize the event based on the initial conversation with the client. A photo album showing past events, complete with pictures of menu items and of tabletop and room setups, can help clients articulate their needs.

Suggest practical and seasonal foods and beverages. Periodic meetings with the chef(s) and purchasing agent can help bring the planner up to speed on what products are readily available for the date of the booking. Product guides are also available through industry Web sites.

Recommend sources for a variety of services, such as bands, DJs, photographers, limousines, decorators, and other ancillary providers. All planners should compile a portfolio of ancillary provider information, complete with photos or samples of each provider's work.

Accommodate clients' budgetary restrictions without requiring them to forego quality. A good caterer will offer tiered menus that, although their raw ingredients may differ, reflect similar creativity and appeal.

Staff an event properly to ensure it runs smoothly.

The panoramic view supplied by the wall of windows gives this indoor banquet room a more spacious feel even when it is set for maximum capacity.

also have an event planner or banquet manager who meets with clients. While the functions of these positions are similar, the off-premise event planner might travel to the site of the event to conduct the initial consultation with the client.

Some event planners work independently. These planners act as general contractors for their clients, subcontracting all required services—including catering—for the event. The event planner gets the client's approval for each detail for the party. The customer usually pays the independent event planner a flat fee for services. The companies hired by an independent event planner will sometimes be required to give the planner a commission in exchange for the business. The fee will vary from person to person (it may sometimes be a flat fee).

Sometimes a chef acts as an event planner, especially if the food is going to be the star of the show. Chefs have the most experience determining the seasonality of menu items. Providing direct access to a competent chef also lends credibility to the catering business itself, so even if your business has an event planner, your clients should be allowed to meet with its chef at least once. There are sometimes technical questions about food that only the chef can answer, and he or she can also suggest viable menu substitutions to meet budget or dietary constraints.

The chef is also aware of menu items associated with other events your company is catering around the same time as the one being planned. By selling more of those same menu items to a potential client, you can trim food and labor costs (purchasing more of the same ingredients can result in volume discounts from purveyors), and your kitchen staff can work more efficiently while preparing a volume of one menu item than when preparing multiple items.

An event planner is warm and energetic, diplomatic, discreet, patient, and charming—and is always well groomed. He or she has stellar problem-solving skills, the ability to remember names and faces, and a genuine love of the hospitality business. Event planners should be experienced in all aspects of kitchen and serving operations. A planner should also have extensive resources for the other services that will be necessary for events, such as floral arranging, party rentals, and entertainment.

WHAT THE EVENT PLANNER NEEDS TO SUCCEED: AN EVENT-PLANNING MANUAL

To be effective, an event planner needs information—and lots of it. An event-planning manual keeps it organized, accessible, and easy to use.

Whether kept in a binder or stored in a computer file, such a manual should contain:

- A calendar or planner for recording client contact information and the times and dates of all bookings made by anyone at the company
- Catering menus for food and beverages, complete with photos of a large sampling of menu items
- Initial contact forms that include notes about preliminary conversations with the client
- Proposal forms
- Contracts and receipts for deposits
- A portfolio of ancillary service providers, such as bands, photographers, and florists
- Banquet event orders
- Final billing forms
- Follow-up correspondence, thank-you cards, and the like

Event planners at off-premise caterers often consult with clients at the site of the event, and carry with them a digital camera, a tape measure, graph paper, and a pencil in order to evaluate the site. Successful event planners will also maintain files on every catering client, so they can anticipate their tastes and desires the next time they want to book an event.

FOUR QUESTIONS WITH WHICH TO START THE EVENT-PLANNING PROCESS

The event-planning process starts when a potential client makes contact with your catering company. This might happen with a phone call, a fax, or an e-mail triggered by an advertisement, a recommendation or a referral from a former client, or as a result of the client attending an event your company catered.

GREENFIELDS CATERING, INC.

645 Albany Road • Boston, MA 02101

Phone (508) 555-7777 • Fax (508) 555-7776

www.greenfieldscateringinc.com

Farm-Fresh Foods with a French Flair

June 28, 2007

Ms. Eva March
218 Hollow Road
Staatsburg, NY 12580

Dear Ms. March,

Thank you for allowing Greenfields Catering, Inc. to cater your daughter Doris's wedding last Saturday. It was a pleasure working with you and your husband. I hope that all of your guests enjoyed themselves and got home safely.

Please consider us in the future for any occasions that may require catering services. If you have any feedback that will help us in our ongoing goal to be the premier caterer in the area, please get in touch with us—and please tell your guests they should feel free to call or write to us as well.

We are most grateful for your business.

Sincerely,

Jack Green
Sarah Fields

Thank-you letters can be a subtle means of soliciting new business from current clients, and from their guests.

The first contact with a potential client is critical. Your event planner should exhibit the highest level of hospitality, courtesy, and most of all, patience. During the first phone call, your event planner needs to ask the potential client a few questions, with the planning book at the ready. If the client's proposed event "passes" these four test questions, then it is business worth pursuing.

1. **Do you have a date in mind for the event?** When your event planner checks the planning manual, he or she will know if your business is

Outdoor elements can often be brought "indoors" with a little ingenuity. Caterers should not contract for outdoor events that cannot be protected from the weather, which can be unpredictable.

already booked on the date in question. Many successful caterers are fully booked weeks, months, or even years in advance. If you're already booked, ask the client if there is any flexibility in the date of the event. If the date does not work out, refer the client to another reputable caterer you know.

2. **How did you hear about us?** Clients who make contact with a caterer as a result of a personal experience or a referral from a friend or colleague are usually serious. A potential client who has found out about your business via the yellow pages is probably contacting multiple caterers and is not aware of the qualities that make you compare favorably to your competition. Although menu items from caterer to caterer may be labeled similarly, they can be at opposite ends of the tasting and presentation spectrum. A good planner will seize every opportunity to cite the special qualities associated with each menu item.

3. **Have you selected a location for the event?** For off-premise caterers, this question can determine budget and feasibility. The location may be inaccessible by truck or simply too far away.

4. **How many guests are you inviting?** The room capacities set for on-premise caterers must be observed. Make sure that you can handle the number of guests before meeting with the client and writing a proposal.

THE INITIAL CONSULTATION

Once these questions have been answered satisfactorily, your event planner can schedule an initial consultation—usually a face-to-face meeting — to discuss the details of the event, such as menu design, beverage service, event personnel, ancillary services, and budget. On-premise catering businesses will have this meeting on-site, while off-premise businesses will meet at the intended location of the event. Wherever the consultation takes place, the event planner must be sure to obtain certain pertinent information by asking more questions.

- ○ **What is the occasion?** Knowing the occasion will help in the selection of the menu, style of service, and decorations.
- ○ **Is the affair planned for the daytime or evening?** Menu items and pricing vary based on this information. Smaller portions of food are more appropriate for daytime affairs. Guests attending events during the evening usually consume more alcoholic beverages.
- ○ **What is your budget?** Although this is important, it may be beneficial to wait until the planner has described some or all of the services offered before soliciting this information. The client usually has a target amount of money in mind; however, that figure may increase if the event planner earns the confidence of the client. Most people are usually prepared to spend more money to meet their complete vision for their affair.

VISITING THE OFF-PREMISE SITE

Many customers are not aware of the limitations—or of the potential—of their chosen venue. As the expert, the event planner should be able to identify them.

For example, a couple planning their daughter's wedding may want to have a sit-down dinner under a tent on their own property for 150 people. After visiting the site, however, the event planner determines that no more than 80 people will fit comfortably in the area the client has in mind. The event planner should then suggest alternate plans—for example, changing the format to an elaborate cocktail party without assigned seating, or using an alternate venue.

A different couple might be planning a similar wedding. In their case, the

All the information about an off-premise event is collected on **off-premise site visit sheets** like the following, which can then be used to prepare for the event and to book any necessary subcontractors.

ANALYSIS AND KEY INFORMATION SHEET

NAME: _____ DAY: _____ DATE: _____

PHONE (home): _____ (business): _____ (fax): _____

CELL PHONE: _____ E-MAIL: _____

PARTY ADDRESS: _____

BILLING ADDRESS: _____

FACILITY CONTACT/ADDRESS: _____

PARTY AT A GLANCE:

        HOME / TENT / TEMPLE / OFFICE / OTHER: _____

        PLATED / HORS D'OEUVRE—STATION—DESSERT / FRENCH SERVICE

        BUFFET: ALL—/ SOME SEATED / LAP SERVICE   **TABLE SETTING:** FULL / FLATWARE ON BUFFET

WEDDING / BAR-BAT MITZVAH / ANNIVERSARY / BIRTHDAY

OTHER: _____

IN HONOR OF: _____

ESTIMATED # OF GUESTS: _____ ADULTS: _____ CHILDREN: _____

CEREMONY LOCATION: SAME AS RECEPTION / OTHER: _____

RECEPTION LOCATION: HOME / FACILITY: _____

DRESS: **Guests:**   [ ] Black Tie   **Staff:**   [ ] Tuxedo
                             [ ] Casual   [ ] Bistro Apron
                             [ ] Business   [ ] White Jacket
                                                     [ ] Khaki Pants/White Polo Shirt

TIMING	TIME	NOTES
Truck departure time	A.M. P.M.	
Truck arrival time	A.M. P.M.	
Staff at party	A.M. P.M.	
Set-up time allowed on floor	A.M. P.M.	
Invitation call time for guests	A.M. P.M.	
Ceremony starts	A.M. P.M.	
Ceremony ends	A.M. P.M.	
Cocktails and hors d'oeuvre	A.M. P.M.	
First course	A.M. P.M.	
Salad	A.M. P.M.	
Entrée	A.M. P.M.	
Post-entrée	A.M. P.M.	
Dessert	A.M. P.M.	
Party concludes	A.M. P.M.	
Staff departure	A.M. P.M.	

	BAR	SERVICE BAR	APPETIZER	ENTRÉE	POST ENTRÉE	DESSERT
Liquor						
Red wine						
White wine						
Champagne						
Beer						
Cordials						

LIQUOR LOCATION: _____

BUTLER ONLY: YES / NO   IF YES—SERVICE BAR LOCATION: _____ **SPECIAL:** _____

COCKTAIL NAPKINS: HOST / FLORIST / RENT   **AK HANG COATS:** YES / NO   **COAT CHECK #'S:** YES / NO **RACKS:** RENT # ____

WEDDING EQUIPMENT:

CHUPPAH: FLORIST / OTHER: _____ _____
CEREMONY TABLE: HOST / FLORIST / RENTAL
KIDDUSH CUP: HOST / OTHER
KOSHER WINE: HOST / OTHER   WINE: RED / WHITE
GLASS OR WRAPPED BULB TO BREAK: HOST / OTHER
MICROPHONE: BAND / OTHER

CEREMONY:

OFFICIATED BY: _____
LENGTH: _____   GUESTS: SEATED / STANDING
RECEIVING LINE: YES / NO   IF YES: CHURCH / TEMPLE / HOME

TRADITIONS:

WELCOME TOAST / FIRST COURSE:	YES / NO BY_____	TABLE #: _____
CHALLAH BLESSING:	YES / NO BY_____	TABLE #: _____
FIRST DANCE:	YES / NO WHEN_____	TABLE #: _____
TOAST:	YES / NO WHEN_____	TABLE #: _____
CAKE CUTTING:	YES / NO	
BOUQUET TOSS:	YES / NO	

BAR / BAT MITZVAH:

WELCOME TOAST / FIRST COURSE:	YES / NO BY_____	TABLE #: _____
CHALLAH BLESSING:	YES / NO BY_____	TABLE #: _____
SING HAPPY BIRTHDAY:	YES / NO BY_____	TABLE #: _____
CANDLE LIGHTING:	YES / NO BY_____	TABLE #: _____

RENTAL INFORMATION:

STEMWARE:

BAR: MACHINE-BLOWN / HANDBLOWN
ALL-PURPOSE / FLUTE / CORDIAL / PILSNER / SHOT / MARTINI / MARGARITA / OTHER: _____
TABLESET: WATER: MACHINE-BLOWN / HANDBLOWN / OTHER: _____
         WHITE WINE: MACHINE-BLOWN / HANDBLOWN / OTHER: _____
         RED WINE: MACHINE-BLOWN / HANDBLOWN / OTHER: _____
         CHAMPAGNE: FLUTED / MACHINE-BLOWN / HANDBLOWN / OTHER: _____

CHINA	PURPOSE	GLASS	WHITE RIM	OTHER
Station—6" or 8"				
Service plate—10" or 12"				
Appetizer				
Soup				
Salad				
Entrée				
Chop plate				
Post entrée				
Dessert				
Bread-and-butter/cake plate				
Cup and saucer / demitasse				
Cookie plate				

NAPKINS: RENTAL / FLORIST - COLOR_____
SERVICE NAPKINS: RENTAL / FLORIST - COLOR_____
SILVER: Beacon Hill _____ Manhattan _____ Rochelle _____ Other _____
CHAIRS:

	FACILITY	# TO RENT	LACQUER COLOR	RECEPTION FRAME/COLOR	CUSHION COLOR
Ceremony					
Cocktails					
Tablesetting					

RENTAL DELIVERY: DAY: _____   TIME: _____

RENTAL PICK-UP: DAY: _____   TIME: _____

LOCATIONS: <u>KITCHEN AREA:</u> GARAGE / COCKTAIL COOK TENT / DINNER COOK TENT

            <u>EVENT AREA:</u>   COCKTAIL TENT / DINNER TENT / OTHER: _____

ARRANGEMENTS OR SPECIAL CONCERNS:

LATE NIGHT DELIVERY / NIGHT PICKUP?

LONG HAUL / UNUSUAL OR DIFFICULT CARRY?

DOUBLE USE OF TENT OR RENTALS?

SERVICE ENTRANCE: _____

STAFF ENTRANCE: _____

ACCESS TO FREIGHT ELEVATOR: _____

RULES OF BUILDING: _____

OTHER: _____

OUTSIDE SERVICES:

TYPE	RECOMMENDED BY	COMMISSION DUE	ADDRESS / PHONE	COMMENTS
Florist	CATERER /HOST	YES / NO		
Music	CATERER /HOST	YES / NO		
Photographer	CATERER /HOST	YES / NO		
Video	CATERER /HOST	YES / NO		
Lighting	CATERER /HOST	YES / NO		
Entertainment	CATERER /HOST	YES / NO		
Valet parking	CATERER /HOST	YES / NO		
Tenting	CATERER /HOST	YES / NO		
Other services	CATERER /HOST	YES / NO		

TIMES:

CEREMONY: _____ TO _____

COCKTAILS: _____ TO _____

DINNER: _____ TO _____

TENTING DETAILS:

LOCATION	SIZE	FLOORING	CARPETING	DANCE FLOOR	LIGHTS	CANOPY
Ceremony						
Cocktails						
Dinner						
Cook tent						
Bandstand and flyer						

OUTDOORS / FAIR WEATHER:

	SOURCE	EQUIPMENT	LOCATION	LINEN / SOURCE
Coatracks				
Escorts cards				
Challah / ceremony				
Bar 1				
Bar 2				
Bar 3				
Service bar(s)				
Cocktail tables				
Drop tables				
Station 1				
Station 2				
Children's soda bar				
Seating				
Dais / dumbbell				
Dinner buffet				
Dessert buffet				
Cake table				
Sundae bar				
Ceremony location				
Gift table				

INDOORS / BAD WEATHER:

	SOURCE	EQUIPMENT	LOCATION	LINEN / SOURCE
Coatracks				
Escorts cards				
Challah / ceremony				
Bar 1				
Bar 2				
Bar 3				
Service bar(s)				
Cocktail tables				
Drop tables				
Station 1				
Station 2				
Children's soda bar				
Seating				
Dais / dumbbell				
Dinner buffet				
Dessert buffet				
Cake table				
Sundae bar				
Ceremony location				
Gift table				

COOKING INFORMATION:

LOCATION: _____

HOUSE OVENS: SINGLE / DOUBLE / FLOOR / PROFESSIONAL / W/# _____ RACKS

BROILER: YES / NO

KITCHEN: SMALL / MEDIUM / LARGE

OVENS: GAS / ELECTRIC / CORNING

FREEZER SPACE: YES / NO

REFRIGERATOR SPACE: YES / NO

IMMEDIATE ACCESS TO: UTILITY ROOM: YES / NO

GARAGE: YES / NO

BUTLER'S PANTRY: YES / NO

SCREENS NEEDED: YES / NO LOCATION: _____ #'S NEEDED: _____

ROOM FOR RENTED OVENS: YES / NO LOCATION: _____

USE: _____ KITCHEN ONLY

_____ GARAGE ONLY

_____ KITCHEN AND GARAGE

_____ GARAGE AND COOK TENT

_____ COOK TENT

RENT WORK TABLES: YES / NO LOCATION: _____

ADDITIONAL LIGHTING NEEDED? YES / NO

ADDITIONAL ELECTRICAL OUTLETS NEEDED? YES / NO

ROLLS OF PAPER / PLASTIC NEEDED? YES / NO #'S _____

FANS / HEATERS NEEDED? YES / NO #'S _____ SOURCE _____

OTHER COMMENTS: _____

GLATT KOSHER DINNERS: _____ # VEGETARIAN DINNERS: _____

HOST TO DO: | FLORIST ITEMS:

_____ MOVE FURNITURE AS DISCUSSED HORS D'OEUVRE FLOWER: YES / NO

_____ CLEAR KITCHEN COUNTERS CENTERPIECES FOR _____ COCKTAIL TABLES

_____ PROVIDE FREEZER/REFRIGERATOR SPACE CENTERPIECES FOR _____ TABLES

_____ CONNECT HOSE FOR DISHWASHING TABLE #'S: YES / NO #'S _____

_____ EMPTY GARAGE BY CENTERPIECES FOR _____ BUFFETS

_____ CLEAR DRIVEWAY BY NOSEGAY CAKE TOP _____

_____ SEPTIC TANK CLEANED CANDLES _____

_____ SPRAY FOR BUGS EASEL _____

_____ CUT GRASS SCREENS _____

_____ INDICATE CIRCUIT BREAKER LOCATIONS COCKTAIL NAPKINS _____

_____ INDICATE PHONE LOCATIONS LINEN / NAPKINS _____

ESCORT CARDS / PLACECARDS _____

WATER SOURCE: _____

STAFF CHANGING AREA: _____ RENT RACKS #'s _____

GUEST BATHROOMS: #'s _____ LOCATION(S): _____

GARBAGE LEFT WHERE? _____

PARKING LOCATIONS:

STAFF VAN: _____

CATERER'S TRUCK: _____

STAFF CARS: _____

SPECIAL NOTES AND DIAGRAMS

PARTY:		Guests		ADDRESS:	
DATE:	Page:				
DELIVERY DATE:				PU DATE:	

TABLES	#	$	Total	GLASSWARE	#	$	Total	CHINA: White Rim	#	$	Total
Rectangle:				All purpose		0.60		Cup & saucer		1.30	
4' x 30"		8.25		Water		0.85		Glass mugs		0.60	
6' x 18"		8.75		White		0.85		Soup plate		0.65	
6' x 30"		8.00		Red		0.85		Soup liner		0.65	
8' x 24"		8.75		Classic flute		0.85		7" plate		0.65	
8' x 30"		8.00		Brandy		1.05		9" apt plate		0.65	
				Glass pitcher		3.00		10" dinner plate		0.65	
				Silver pitcher		10.25		9" salad plate		0.65	
Rounds:				BAR				Dessert		0.65	
24"		7.75		All purpose		0.60		10" set plate		0.65	
30"		7.75		15" gallery trays		7.95		Chop		2.75	
36"		8.00		Glass pitcher		3.00		Cookie plate		0.65	
54"		8.25		Silver pitcher		10.25		Charger gold		7.70	
60"		8.50		Ice scoop		3.00		SILVER			
66"		10.50		Silver ice bucket		6.75		Soup spoon		0.60	
72"		10.50		Bar carpet		6.95		Fish fork		0.60	
60 1/2		8.50		Champg bucket		10.75		Fish knife		0.60	
24" x 42"		15.00		Ice tub		8.50		Dinner fork		0.60	
LINENS				COFFEE				Dinner knife		0.60	
Square:				50 c coffeemaker		15.00		Salad fork		0.60	
54"		8.75		100 c urn		18.75		Salad knife		0.60	
60"		9.75		50 c Farberware		27.50		Cheese knife		0.60	
72"		10.75		Samovar 25 c w/tray		60.50		Butter fork		0.60	
84"		11.75		Samovar 50 c w/tray		66.00		Dessert spoon		0.60	
90"		12.50		Samovar 100c w/tray		71.50		Dessert fork		0.60	
Banquet 136"		17.50		Silver coffee pourer		7.25		Teaspoon		0.60	
				16" round trays		7.25		Demi spoon		2.15	
				Silver creamer set		6.30		Oyster fork		2.15	
Rounds:				Glass creamer set		3.85		Silver set		7.50	
84"		13.50		Lg. glass creamer set		4.25		Silver fork		3.25	
90"		13.75		Silver creamer tray		4.95		Silver spoon		3.25	
96"		14.75		Sugar tongs		2.15		Salad tongs		3.55	
102"		16.00		TRAYS				Ladies petite		3.00	
108"		16.00		Silver: round 12"		6.85		Cake server		3.55	
114"		17.00		Round 16"		7.25		MISCELLANEOUS			
120"		19.50		Round 18"		7.35		Extension cords		35.00	
126"		24.75		Round 15" gallery		7.95		Garbage can		8.25	
132"		25.00		Rectangular 18"		8.00		Broom/ dust pan		22.00	
Work linen		14.50		Oval 18"		8.00		Hand truck		75.00	
				Insert		14.00		Ashtrays/glass		0.60	
				Oval 23"		8.25		Votives		1.35	
Napkin:				Beaded rnd		10.75		Silent butler		7.50	
Service		0.70		Beaded sq		10.70		Coat rack w/40hangers		24.75	
Cocktail: pkg 100		7.40		Beaded oval		17.25		Perforated Lexon		7.75	
Cotton		0.95		Plain square		10.50		Numbers/100 (1–200)		7.75	
Linen		1.65		Plain oval		10.50		Screens blackout- 6'		30.00	
Bar mops		1.25		Black laquer round		10.15		KITCHEN			
Liners SIZE:		4.10		Chelsea round		6.00		Cook tops		52.00	
		4.10		Cake stand silver		6.50		Butane		11.00	
CHAIRS				Cake stand glass		6.00		Half sheet		2.25	
Folding		3.00		Ceramic large		14.00		Sheet trays		2.25	
Black wood		3.50		Porcelain oval		21.75		Jack stack		82.50	
Natural		4.10		Silver bread tray		5.45		Chef apron		6.30	
Gold/silver		5.50		Silver wire basket		7.95		Cutting boards		7.40	
Reception gold		7.40		Copper réchaud		125.00		Open racks		60.50	
White		7.75		Copper pan		60.00		Stove w/tank		100.00	
Black		7.75		CHAIRS				Proofer		110.00	
Natural		7.95		8-qt silver chafe		60.00		BOWLS			
Fruitwood		7.95		Chafe insert		9.75		Silver 4"		4.65	
				8-qt stainless chafe		20.00		Silver 5"		6.00	
				F/S x 22" oval		8.25		Silver 8"		7.20	
				5" revere		6.50		Glass V 4"		0.75	
				Gravy ladle (small)		3.00		Glass V 5"		0.75	
				SV set		6.50		Silver-footed mint bowl		3.75	
				16" silver		7.25		Square 4"		0.75	
				Salt & pepper		2.50		LINERS FOR V		0.75	
				Pepper mill		6.50		Additional charges		375	
				Table stands/#/tall		5.25		TOTAL RENTALS			
								TOTAL COST PP			

property *is* large enough for 150 people; the event planner notices a group of trees arranged beautifully on the property and suggests that hors d'oeuvre be served in that area.

There are many other reasons to inspect an off-premise site prior to an event. Possible hazards such as broken stairs or pathways can be dangerous. Proper lighting is necessary for evening events. Auxiliary lighting, heating, or cooling may be necessary for safety reasons and should be arranged in advance so that the cost can be passed on to the client. Lack of foresight can jeopardize the safety of guests and employees and even damage the reputation of the caterer.

Brainstorming about menu items, decorations, table appointments, and service can also be enhanced by consulting at the site. The physical characteristics of the location alone often stimulate the event planner's creativity. There may be a fountain on the property that can be used as the centerpiece for a buffet simply by arranging tables around it, for example.

MENU DESIGN

Designing a menu for a catered event is not a simple process. There are many variables to consider, such as budget, food and beverage availability, and style of service. Food served buffet style may differ from the food served during a sit-down meal, even if the occasion is the same. Menu items served outdoors usually differ from those served at an indoor venue. Cultural and dietary restrictions also need to be accomodated based on the client's wishes and needs.

A potential customer may request menu items that are not practical, based on the event planner's opinion and experience. The planner must know how to suggest more realistic alternatives without implying that the client's suggestions were ridiculous. The event planner usually consults the chef, maître d'hôtel, or beverage manager prior to planning an event, although this may not be necessary if there are proven menu packages in place; however, each catered event is a little different and such packages often need to be modified.

If a client requests menu items or services that are outside your company's areas of expertise, either try to sell the client alternate menu items that you feel confident executing or collaborate with someone who can provide the special item or service requested. For example, if a client requests a buffet with a sushi station, hire a sushi chef for the evening, or contact a Japanese restaurant that can set up such a station in a professional manner. A caterer can usually subcontract such services and mark up the price.

An event planner needs to be conscious of how the client is reacting to any suggestions. Certain facial gestures and repetitive questions may be signs that the client is confused or uncomfortable. A good planner will recognize these signs and either clarify what he or she is saying or offer alternate suggestions.

◼ SOMETHING ON THE MENU FOR EVERYONE

The event planner should find out the age group, cultural background, and medical concerns of the guests in order to accommodate their needs. While the majority of catering clients will ask for specific menu items when they expect children to attend an event, they may not automatically consider the needs of elderly guests or those with specific dietary restrictions. Many elderly people stay away from foods that are hot and spicy. A caterer providing kosher foods has to pay a rabbi to oversee production and usually pays more for its food products than non-kosher caterers, which is why kosher catering is more expensive. (Non-kosher caterers can have a kosher meal brought in from an outside source for observant Jews attending a non-kosher event. Many full-service food purveyors carry kosher meals, which usually come frozen.) Vegetarianism is gaining in popularity and must be accommodated accordingly. Many people have certain food allergies. Guests may or may not notify their host about their special food needs prior to an event, so an event planner should inquire about these concerns if the client does not bring them up during the consultation.

Some menu choices may not be appropriate simply because they will not appeal to a majority of guests. Many people have aversions to foods such as game, certain mushrooms, and other, more obscure food items. When planning a catered event, the event planner should suggest menu items that will not intimidate guests and are fairly mainstream.

Dealing with Money and Contracts

MENU PRICING

When an event planner uses the proper tools to determine menu pricing, there is less risk of losing the client to the competition. The planner should also know the specifications of the ingredients so that a fair comparison can be made among proposals. For example, a caterer who makes guacamole from fresh Haas avocados usually has higher costs for that item than one who makes it with canned avocado. But the item on both menus will read "guacamole"; it is up to the event planner to explain the difference and to justify any higher price (see Chapter 3, "Pricing for Profit").

This is not an easy task. Some clients do not have an extensive understanding of food and are only comparing price. This is an unfortunate reality of event planning. Caterers should not lower their standards or sacrifice profitability in order to earn an account. Substitutions may be suggested, but by lowering the price, the client may come to distrust the caterer: When a price is lowered without modifying the menu item, it may appear to the client that the price was inflated to begin with. Modifications can include substituting prepared ingredients (like frozen spinach) for raw ingredients (like fresh spinach). By making such a substitution, enough labor may be saved to allow for a decrease in the price of that menu item.

The question that must always be asked is, "How does this change affect quality?" Depending on the application, a difference in quality may not be perceptible to the client. The caterer should not compromise quality in any observable way in order to accommodate a client's budget. There are many convenience food products, however, that save on labor and that do not affect quality, including prepeeled garlic and prewashed lettuce mixes. These foods should be tasted and applied to test menu items before using them.

BUDGETING

The event planner works with the client to determine the budget for an event. Written proposals should separate this amount into food, beverages, services, rentals, other ancillary services, tax, and possibly gratuities. Some caterers give their customers an all-inclusive package price for an event that encompasses all of these costs. Whichever the case, the event planner must determine how much of the total budget is available for designing the menu while still allowing for profit.

Some of the play in the cost of an event is in the overall cost of its menu. Suppose a client requests a carved ice bowl containing extra-large poached shrimp with cocktail sauce to be served as an hors d'oeuvre, wanting their guests to help themselves to the shrimp while admiring the ice sculpture. Yet this one menu item represents the highest cost to the caterer. Because the shrimp are self-service—and a very popular food—the caterer knows from experience that a lot of them must be provided, at

A sparsely laid four-top in a **private dining room.**

least four to six shrimp per person. The event planner prices this item and includes it in the proposal. The client then feels that the overall menu price is too high and needs some adjustment.

A savvy event planner will suggest changing the higher-priced self-serve shrimp bowl to shrimp passed on trays by servers. Caterers know that most people will take only one or two hors d'oeuvre when they are served butler style—so two smaller, less expensive shrimp can be budgeted per person, rather than five larger ones. Shrimp could remain on the menu, but at a lower price point; or the client could still choose to spend the extra money on the shrimp bowl. Most important, whatever the client ultimately chooses, by suggesting a substitute or modified menu item, the event planner has demonstrated the catering company's expertise and flexibility.

An event planner must also remember not to cut corners in the wrong place. If a planner suggests an upscale menu and subsequently serves the food on utility china, the guests' overall experience will be cheapened. Decreasing the number of personnel needed for proper service in order to budget more money for food is another bad decision. Excellent food that is poorly served will result in a negative experience for guests. Any services that are subcontracted, such as entertainment, photography, and equipment rentals, should also be of similar or higher quality than the services the caterer provides.

All caterers have fixed and operational expenses that they must consider when pricing an event. Sometimes, a caterer cannot provide services because the client's budget is simply too low (see Chapter 3, "Pricing for Profit"). After you have considered all the options, there are times when you must simply refer a client to another caterer. Sending away business is always a difficult decision, but working hard and not making any money is worse. Hopefully, the client will understand your perspective, respect it, and call you again for a future event whose budget is not as financially restrictive.

WHEN TO CHARGE MORE, WHEN TO CHARGE LESS

A caterer who can customize services to a customer's specific requests is entitled to mark up those services higher than other, more routine services: The extra conceptualizing, planning, and execution justify the higher cost. Generally speaking, off-premise catering is more expensive than catering at a banquet hall. The additional planning, transportation issues, and more customized approach result in additional costs.

But there are several reasons you might consider offering a discount to a client: repeat business from corporate clients, the third wedding reception you've catered for a valued social client, or a very large party at which the per person cost will be much less than for a smaller party, for example. A discount should equal a decrease in net profit for the caterer, never a financial loss. All discounted prices must be described in the contract in a clear, detailed manner. If not, referrals from customers who have received discounts in the past may expect the same deal, even if the circumstances are different.

WRITING A PROPOSAL

Within a week after the initial face-to-face consultation, a planner should write a formal proposal detailing estimated costs for the event. Whether an itemized or inclusive proposal is used, the proposal should be written clearly, look professional, and be well organized. Each page should bear the caterer's logo and contact information.

The first page should be a cover letter written by the event planner thanking the client for the potential business. The second page should contain all of the pertinent information about the event. The date, time, number of expected guests, location, and type of event are usually listed first. The schedule of events, including any ceremony or meeting, cocktail hour, the main meal period, and after-meal festivities, is then discussed. Incorporated within this list may be all of the menu choices and activities taking place in conjunction with each item. The costs for the event usually follow and should be listed clearly. A short paragraph stating deposit requirements and contract information can follow the costs or be included in the cover letter.

The cost for an on-premise event at a hotel, country club, or banquet hall is often arranged as a package deal. This type of proposal will list all of

GREENFIELDS CATERING, INC.

645 Albany Road • Boston, MA 02101
Phone (508) 555-7777 • Fax (508) 555-7776
www.greenfieldscateringinc.com

Farm-Fresh Foods with a French Flair

EVENT PLANNING WORKSHEET

Client contact info:
: Cook's Software
2991 Paul Revere Way
Boston, MA 02102
(508) 555-6787 phone
(508) 555-4551 fax
Contact: John Espinall
jespinall@cookssoftware.com
Cell phone: (508) 555-4768

Day and date:
: Saturday, March 17, 2007

Time:
: Lunch 11:30 AM to 1:30 PM

Venue:
: Patriot Golf Club
The John Adams Room
156 Patriot Parkway
Boston, MA 02102
(508) 555-4557
Contact: Patrice Mitchell, general manager
Cell phone: (508) 555-4995

Number of guests:
: 100

Guaranteed number:
: 90

Special arrangements:
: Herbal tea bar. This is a planning meeting, so there will be a binder of materials on the chair at every place setting. Clients want a high-protein lunch. There will be chilled sushi (and chopsticks) at each place when guests arrive.

Coat room:
: Outside Longfellow Room.

Parking:
: At club.

Centerpieces:	Low, oblong arrangement on each table from Eden Floral. Contact: Adam Kennedy, (508) 555-3221. Florist to deliver.
Orchestra:	None.
A/V request:	Three large flat-screen TV monitors for PowerPoint presentations. Microphone, sound system, and lectern. A/V equipment and setup through Cook's Software—John Espinall will organize.
House count:	Check with John Espinall, cell phone (508) 555-4768.
Head table:	Twelve guests at long banquet table: CEO and executives plus board members. Table to be dressed in pale blue and black, the colors of the company's logo. Chopsticks.
Dining room:	Diagram and seating plan attached. Banquet table for head table, round eight-tops for remaining guests.
Lunch:	11:30 A.M. sharp. White tablecloths, black napkins. Chopsticks.
Menu:	Chilled sushi (three pieces) Grilled grass-fed beef and seasonal vegetables Grilled johnnycake Assorted Vermont cheeses, including cob-smoked cheddar, fresh chèvre, and blue cheese Apples, pears, and grapes Herbal teas, coffee, and bottled water
General directions:	Kickoff of strategic planning conference. The client wants noise kept to a minimum, so clear dishes quickly: no talking. Following the cheese course, put bottled water, pots of hot water, and coffee carafes on the table for self-service. Lunch meeting ends at 1:30, then clear tables and remove linens, but leave tables up for a second function later on. Golf club's housekeeping department will vacuum and empty trash.

The **event planning worksheet** is an internal form of correspondence that does not go to the client; it gives instructions to the event manager.

the services to be provided by the caterer. There will be a per person price for these services: This type of proposal does not break down the costs for food, beverages, service, and other ancillary costs, making it simpler for the client to comprehend. Service charges or gratuities may be included in the per person price or be listed separately. Any applicable taxes should be listed as a separate entity.

Most off-premise caterers itemize costs on their proposals. An off-premise event is often more costly because time is needed to set up and clean up, and some equipment rental is usually required. It is easier for the caterer to justify these costs to the client by itemizing them on the proposal.

You will want a prospective client to book the event with a deposit as soon as possible after receiving the bid. Otherwise, you could lose other business for that date while waiting. Many caterers indicate a "please respond by" date on their proposals and instruct their event planners to make follow-up phone calls to answer any questions or hasten a decision.

DOWN PAYMENT AND CONTRACT SIGNING

After a client accepts a proposal (perhaps after some modifications), the caterer should send a copy of the finished proposal and two copies of the catering contract to the client. The client should sign both copies of the contract and send them back to the caterer along with a down payment. The actual amount or percentage will vary from caterer to caterer, but is usually between 25 and 50 percent of the value of the total contract. At the very least, you will want it to cover your food costs in case your client has to cancel the event at the last minute.

The event planner and anyone else that may be contacted by the client concerning the event should retain copies of the proposal and contract for reference.

You can draw up your own contracts or have your attorney do so for you. Either way, a contract should be as specific as possible and include at least the following information:

- Names, addresses, and telephone numbers of the parties involved (buyer and seller)
- Date of the agreement and date and time of the event
- Location of the event
- The specifications for the room setup, decorations, tablecloths, and so on
- The menu
- The estimated and guaranteed attendance
- All service arrangements
- The duration of the event (e.g., open bar from 6 P.M. to 7 P.M.)
- A description of the entertainment, if applicable
- Pricing arrangements and conditions under which prices will increase
- The deposit required
- Any discount for full payment at the time contract is signed
- Cancellation provisions, specifying circumstances under which a cancellation will be accepted (e.g., illness, broken engagement, death) and how much of the deposit will be retained under such circumstances
- Applicable taxes
- Space for signatures at the bottom of the contract form

Carefully consider contract terms, write them in simple language, and print them in a size that is easy to read to ensure that everyone understands them. The contract legally binds the client's down payment with the caterer's future services. A caterer who accepts a down payment must be responsible with those funds: they must be available to purchase goods

GREENFIELDS CATERING, INC.

645 Albany Road • Boston, MA 02101
Phone (508) 555-7777 • Fax (508) 555-7776
www.greenfieldscateringinc.com

Farm-Fresh Foods with a French Flair

February 9, 2007

Kathryn Jameson
13 Clover Hill Street
Cambridge, MA 02138

Dear Ms. Jameson:

We are delighted to enclose our proposal/contract for the celebration in honor of your wedding.

Please do not hesitate to call us to discuss any aspect of your celebration. While all final details will be resolved at a future meeting, we ask that you sign the last page of the contract and **return the entire original document, together with your reservation fee** to ensure your reservation of the space and date. The enclosed copy is for your records.

After we acknowledge receipt of your reservation fee and signed contract, we will outline the timetable and steps to follow to make sure that every aspect of your wedding celebration will be memorable.

We look forward to sharing this special occasion with you.

Sincerely,

Pamela Brown
Sales Manager

Jeremy Stiles
Director of Sales

:jrc
Enclosure: Contract
File No.: 0205

A **proposal** is like a rough sketch of an event and its costs, created for the client by the catering company, usually by the event planner.

A **contract,** whether for a social (a, pages 184–187) or corporate (b, pages 188–191) client, is like a map of an event; by the time it is finalized and signed, most of the planning is complete, and any potential changes are accounted for in the document itself.

GREENFIELDS CATERING, INC.

645 Albany Road • Boston, MA 02101

Phone (508) 555-7777 • Fax (508) 555-7776

www.greenfieldscateringinc.com

Farm-Fresh Foods with a French Flair

February 9, 2007

PROPOSAL / CONTRACT

WITH: Kathryn Jameson and Phillip Hoffman

LISTING: In honor of Kathryn Jameson and Phillip Hoffman's wedding

DATE: Saturday, December 22, 2007

OCCASION TYPE: Wedding celebration

APPROXIMATE NUMBER OF GUESTS: 100

MINIMUM GUARANTEED GUEST COUNT REQUIRED: 90

OPTION:

IF CEREMONY IS AT A CHURCH/TEMPLE, PLEASE FILL IN THE FOLLOWING:

NAME OF FACILITY:_____TOWN:_____

CEREMONY TIME: FROM_____TO_____   RECEIVING LINE: FROM_____TO_____

DRIVING TIME TO CATERING LOCATION:_____

TIMETABLE

TIME	LOCATION
5:00 P.M.	Dragonfly Inn

THE INVITATION TIME MUST BE AS INDICATED AND NO EARLIER TO ENSURE
THE GRACIOUS RECEPTION OF GUESTS.

	TIME	LOCATION
Ceremony	5:00 P.M.	Garden
Cocktail reception	6:00 P.M.	Garden
Dinner reception	8:00 P.M.	Dining room

MENU AND BEVERAGE ARRANGEMENTS
FROM OUR STANDARD WEDDING PACKAGE

- Choice of eight hors d'oeuvre served butler style
- Choice of two cocktail stations
- Three- or four-course luncheon or dinner (Client to preselect two of the following: poultry, beef, or fish; each guest to choose one entrée once seated)
- Occasion or wedding cake
- Five-hour premium brand open bar
- Champagne toast and champagne throughout
- House wines

Food and beverage enhancements, if desired, will be chosen from the then-current offerings at a menu meeting prior to your event.

Seating is based on ten or twelve guests per table, as space allows.

ALSO INCLUDED

- Ceremony space
- Coat check and restroom attendant
- Valet parking
- Meals for band or DJ, photographer, videographer

Gratuities included for coat checker, restroom attendant, and valet parking attendant(s).

Price per person + 20% service charge	$100.00
x 5% sales tax	$ 5.00
Estimated per person total	$105.00
x minimum guaranteed number of guests	$ 90
MINIMUM TOTAL	**$9,450.00**

Price based on a six-hour event. Overtime will be charged at $6.00 per person per half hour, excluding service charges and tax. All calculations will be based on your final guaranteed guest count or actual attendance, whichever is higher.

CPI clause: The per person price quoted in this contract will be adjusted equal to any change in the latest published Massachusetts Consumer Price Index (CPI). This change will be calculated from the CPI at the date this contract is presented to the latest published CPI at the time payment is due.

Latest published CPI: 223.1

• • •

Reservation fee required

First payment required: $4,725   Date required: February 19, 2007
Second payment required: $4,725   Date required: December 17, 2007

The reservation fee is based on 50% of your estimated total: $9,450*.

*Plus CPI increase

Balance is due no later than five (5) business days before your event in the form of cash, certified check, or wire transfer.

• • •

Please sign below and return the entire original document, together with your payment. If we do not receive the required reservation fee and signed letter when due, we reserve the right to release the space for the date outlined in this agreement.

Accepted by: For Greenfields Catering, Inc.

_____   _____

Date: Date:

_____   _____

:jrc
File No.: 0205
CORPORATION FEDERAL TAX ID#: 12-3456789

b

GREENFIELDS CATERING, INC.

645 Albany Road • Boston, MA 02101

Phone (508) 555-7777 • Fax (508) 555-7776

www.greenfieldscateringinc.com

Farm-Fresh Foods with a French Flair

November 25, 2006

John Espinall
Cook's Software
2991 Paul Revere Way
Boston, MA 02102

Dear Mr. Espinall:

We are delighted to enclose our proposal/contract for your luncheon.

Please do not hesitate to call us to discuss any aspect of your function. While all final details will be resolved at a future meeting, we ask that you sign the last page of the contract and **return the entire original document, together with your reservation fee** to ensure our space is reserved for your event on this date.

After we receive your reservation fee and contract, we will outline the timetable and steps we will follow together to make sure that every aspect of this luncheon will be memorable.

The enclosed copy is for your records.

We look forward to sharing this occasion with you.

Sincerely,

Pamela Brown
Sales Manager

Jeremy Stiles
Director of Sales

:jhw
Enclosure: Contract
File No.: 0116

GREENFIELDS CATERING, INC.

645 Albany Road • Boston, MA 02101
Phone (508) 555-7777 • Fax (508) 555-7776
www.greenfieldscateringinc.com

Farm-Fresh Foods with a French Flair

November 25, 2006

PROPOSAL/CONTRACT

WITH: John Espinall of Cook's Software

LISTING: Cook's Software luncheon

DATE: Saturday, March 17, 2007

OCCASION TYPE: Company luncheon for clients

APPROXIMATE NUMBER OF GUESTS: 100

MINIMUM GUARANTEED GUEST COUNT REQUIRED: 90

Please confirm the following important information as soon as possible:

TIMETABLE

	TIME	LOCATION
Invitation	11:30 A.M.	Patriot Golf Club

(The invitation time must be as indicated and no earlier to ensure the gracious reception of guests.)

Cocktail Reception	n/a	n/a
Luncheon Reception	11:30 A.M.	The John Adams Room

*We reserve the right to charge extra for the room based upon the final guest count
up to five days prior to the event.*

MENU AND BEVERAGE ARRANGEMENTS

- Chilled sushi (three pieces)
- Grilled grass-fed beef and seasonal vegetables
- Grilled johnnycakes

- Assorted Vermont cheeses, including cob-smoked cheddar, fresh chèvre, and blue cheese
- Apples, pears, and grapes
- Herbal teas, coffee, and bottled water

Food and beverage enhancements, if desired, may be chosen from the then-current offerings at a menu meeting prior to your event.

Price per person		
+20% service charge	$	75.00
x 5% sales tax	$	3.75
Estimated per person total	$	78.75
x expected number of guests		90
Food total	$7,087.50	

Food and beverage total*   **$7,087.50**

*Exclusive of the beverage-consumption charges outlined below.

Additional service personnel

Should the expected guest count increase, the service staff will increase accordingly.

Server fee: $65.00 each $ 650.00

Bartending fee: $65.00 for 3 hours
$20.00 per additional hour per bartender
Estimated hours $ 0.00

Valet parking: $130.00 per parker $ 260.00
Coat-check fees: $65.00 per attendant $ 65.00
Service total: **$ 975.00**

Beverages

Additional beverages served after the one-hour open bar will be charged on consumption as follows (all prices exclusive of service charge and tax):

Soft drinks	$2.00 per drink
Imported beer and wine	$4.50 per drink
Name brands	$5.00 per drink
Premium brands	$6.00 per drink
Cordials	$6.50 per drink

Wine selection

Audiovisual equipment n/a

Equipment rental fees

+ 5% sales tax	$ 0.00
Estimated equipment total	$ 0.00
Estimated services total	$ 975.00
Estimated food and beverage total	$ 7,087.50
Estimated grand total	**$8,062.50**

Price based on a two-hour event. Overtime will be charged at $6.00 per person per half hour, excluding service charge and tax. All calculations will be based on your final guaranteed guest count.

Reservation fee required

Payment required: $4,031.25   Date required: December 17, 2007*

* Four months prior to the event date, March 17, 2007

The reservation fee is based on 50% of your estimated total: $8,100*

* Rounded to the nearest hundred.

Balance is due at the conclusion of your event.

Please sign below and return the entire original document together with your payment. If we do not receive the required reservation fee and signed letter when due, we reserve the right to release the space for the date outlined in this agreement

Accepted by: For Greenfields Catering, Inc.

_____   _____

Date: Date:

_____   _____

:jrc
File No.: 0116
CORPORATION FEDERAL TAX ID#: 12-3456789

for the actual event. Smaller caterers with sporadic business should be especially careful with any down payment and probably reserve it for goods needed for the designated affair.

- Is a down payment refundable? This is a complicated issue. There are two reasons to not refund a client's deposit. A caterer usually purchases most products, especially perishable ones, in the week prior to the event. After a caterer has done the actual purchasing of goods for an event, the caterer should be compensated for these costs—through the down payment—in the case of a cancellation. A caterer may also experience a loss of revenue due to a cancellation. When a caterer is fully booked for a specific date, he or she may turn down other business for that date. When a client cancels an event for a date that could have been booked for another event, it is a loss of potential revenue; a contract should guard against this possibility.
- A contract typically lists a timetable for the refund of a down payment; the timetable and the amount refunded will vary from contract to contract. For example, a contract may state that 100 percent of the down payment can be refunded if the client cancels ninety or more days prior to the event, but that the down payment is nonrefundable if cancellation occurs thirty days or fewer before the event is scheduled.
- Hourly charges for services rendered beyond the designated ending time of the event should always be enumerated in a contract. Most on-premise catering contracts also include liability clauses clarifying clients' liability for damages that they or their guests inflict on the caterer's building or equipment. These contracts will also prohibit clients or their guests from bringing food and beverages to the event that were not provided by the caterer.

○ Some caterers even review the contracts of their competitors before writing their own. And if you do create your own contract, always have a lawyer review it before using putting it to use.

SUBCONTRACTING ANCILLARY SERVICES

A successfully catered event requires many kinds of services. While food and beverage preparation and service is the primary function of the caterer, other services, such as entertainment, photography, and decorating, may be provided by outside sources. All services and activities that occur during an event must be coordinated carefully regardless of who provides them. Most caterers subcontract certain services they need at their events. The client or an independent event planner hired by the client may also arrange for certain services for the affair. Whoever hires the subcontractors, each aspect of the catered event must still be executed at the highest level of quality.

When a caterer plans an event that requires outside services, several suppliers for each service should be compared in numerous ways before deciding which one is the best for the job. Price alone should not be the deciding factor.

Start by networking. Using the Internet, yellow pages, industry periodicals, or personal contacts, locate several providers for each required service. A range of providers that offer different levels of a similar service is best. For example, a photographer who takes color or black-and-white prints and compiles them in an album may be priced at one tier. Another photographer who applies special effects such as antiquing to his photos and also compiles a digital slide presentation may command much higher prices. Once you have found multiple sources for each service, compare them for price, service, and quality and then decide which ones you'd like to work with.

Some clients will ask to sample certain menu items or to look at certain table appointments prior to an event. In fact, the event planner may have a lot of contact with the client prior to the actual affair. This is not uncommon and is part of the event planner's job.

Most caterers offer some form of menu sampling to the client, many in scheduled tastings that are part of their marketing plan. For most established caterers, menu sampling usually occurs after the initial proposal has been drafted and accepted by the client. Menu sampling should be a way for a client to finalize the menu selection for an event or for a first-time client to determine whether to book with you. It is also appropriate to provide samples of certain menu items your event planner has suggested that are not familiar to the client. The client may also want to sample the food to experience its quality; this will also help to establish your credibility.

Caterers are professionals and should not allow themselves to be micromanaged by their clients, however. Clients may ask the caterer to provide a sampling of every menu item to be served at the affair. Although caterers should be sensitive to their clients' concerns, such a request is generally unreasonable, and the caterer or event planner must be to careful handle this situation correctly. The caterer may want to accommodate the request at a convenient time for both parties, but should charge a fee for this service. The fee can be simply the cost incurred by the caterer for the food or the per person price as included in the proposal. Caterers should always be compensated for expenses that occur outside the terms of a proposal or contract, and some caterers ask for a down payment prior to any menu sampling.

Some subcontracted service providers need very little management. A wedding photographer, for example, will choreograph photos with the bridal party and guests. The only interaction the photographer will need with the caterer is likely a discussion about the schedule of the event, which will provide him or her with information about specific photo opportunities. Other subcontracted services, such as party rental equipment or staffing through an agency, require a lot of planning and management by the event planner.

Most caterers have an arrangement with their ancillary providers that allows the subcontracted services to be marked up. A photographer may build an extra $200 into his or her price to the client and then give that $200 to the caterer as a finder's fee or referral fee. Remember, it can work the other way around as well. If that photographer refers you to a client who ultimately signs a contract for catering services, he or she may expect a finder's fee from you.

GUARANTEEING THE NUMBER OF GUESTS

All caterers require their clients to guarantee a number of guests sometime before the actual event takes place. The guarantee facilitates the planning process, determining how much food and drink to purchase, staffing requirements, the amount of tables, chairs, and flatware, and so on.

Most caterers require the guaranteed count one to two weeks before the event; other caterers require the count thirty, sixty, or even ninety days before. The reality is that most clients will have the best idea of how many guests they are expecting one week or so prior to the event: It is not uncommon for people to respond to an invitation late or to cancel on the same day. Regardless of these circumstances, once a caterer receives the guaranteed count from the client, that number cannot be reduced. (This stipulation should be included in the contract.)

The client should always be allowed to raise the amount of guests expected—up to whatever point is feasible for the caterer. Most caterers will have a cutoff point forty-eight to seventy-two hours prior to the event before which the client can continue to add guests to the final head count. This number should not be set as a percentage of the total number of guests, but rather as a specific number. The caterer should set the number at something that can be conveniently accommodated without purchasing and preparing additional product at the last minute. (In fact, most caterers already include an overage number in their production forecasts, preparing extra food and beverages in anticipation of overcooking, spillage, and so on.)

The cost of this additional product should always be figured in when pricing the original proposal. If a caterer prepares for fifteen additional covers on a regular basis, for example, he or she should use this figure as the maximum allowable increase of the head count. On the rare occasion that a large amount of people beyond the guaranteed count show up at the event without the caterer being notified in advance, the client can be held liable. In this instance, the caterer's performance is jeopardized by being inadequately prepared to handle the additional people and possibly running out of food and/or providing substandard service. After the event planner gets a guaranteed guest count from the client, the event is ready to be executed. And the majority of the time, things will go as planned.

Executing the Event

The client and event planner will need to communicate often during the planning process to clarify event details. Inevitably, some minor things will change right before or even during the function, but by the time the client

a

b

Specifics about the **banquet room's setup** (e.g., the number of tables and the number of chairs at each; a) and the **tabletops' design** (china pattern, linen color, etc.; b) will be specified in the banquet event order.

submits the guaranteed count, all major pending concerns on both sides hopefully will have been laid to rest.

The event can now take place.

Caterers are responsible for the execution of an event regardless of whether all of their staff shows up or whether a key person is ill. Caterers can never cancel on their clients; this would damage their reputations irrecoverably, quite possibly putting them out of business. All caterers should have contingency plans in place for replacement personnel and products.

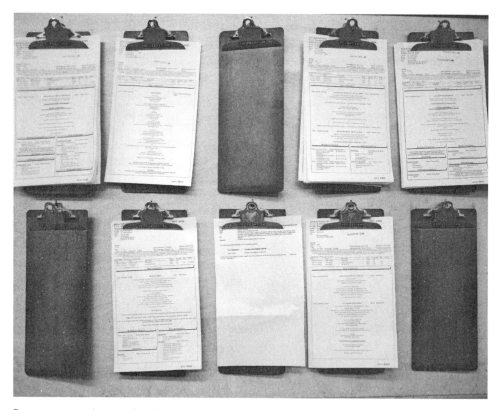

Banquet event orders are often distributed among all catering company employees to streamline communications and make sure everyone gets the same information.

THE BANQUET EVENT ORDER

After all of the details have been discussed and settled, the event planner will construct the banquet event order (BEO), a document that communicates all pertinent information about an event to anyone responsible for providing any of the necessary services for its successful execution.

The banquet event order is usually not given to the client but rather used as an internal tool. Some caterers do choose to use the BEO as a contract and include signed clauses that other caterers include in a more formal contract.

A banquet event order usually starts with basic information: the date and time of the event, the client's contact information, the type of function, its location, and the expected number of guests. The schedule of events then follows and includes menus, wine and beverage choices, and specific information about decorations. Other information, including table configurations, menus for employee and professional meals, dietary restrictions, delivery schedules, and so on, should also be listed. The BEO is then distributed to all personnel involved in the event's planning, including the general manager, catering manager, chef, maître d'hôtel, purchasing agent, housekeeping manager, and possibly others, depending on the size and organization of the specific operation. The BEO may also be sent to outside vendors who are providing a service for the event.

Much of the information on the BEO is consistent with that of the written proposal sent to the client, with the possible exception of prices. Many people in catering management omit the pricing information on copies of the BEO that are distributed to personnel to whom costs are not relevant. There may be many revisions of a BEO prior to the event. The final copy is printed after receiving the guaranteed number of guests from the client.

The purpose of a BEO is to provide consistent and complete information on one document and to prevent miscommunication. The BEO should be

FUNCTION ORDER/CONTRACT

Client name: _____

Day and date of event: _____

Number attending: _____ (Minimum billing is for _____ people)   Final count: _____

Contact person: _____

Address: _____

Home phone: _____ Work phone: _____ Fax: _____

CEREMONY

___Yes ___No   If yes, indicate time and location: _____

RECEPTION

Reception time and location: _____

BAR

Time bar opens:_____ Time bar closes:_____

Bar closed during dinner: ___Yes   ___No   If yes, indicate time:_____

Champagne toast: ___Yes ___No   Wine with dinner: ___Yes   ___No

FOOD

Passed hors d'oeuvre:

Hot: _____   Cold: _____

Hot: _____   Cold: _____

Hot: _____   Cold: _____

Hot: _____   Cold: _____

Hot: _____   Cold: _____

Hot: _____   Cold: _____

Displayed hors d'oeuvre:

_____

_____

Dinner time and location: _____

First course:

Second course:

Banquet event orders, or BEOs, contain highly detailed instructions for an event, although information related to money is often left off those copies for general distribution.

Third course:

Fourth course:

Dietary restrictions:

Dessert:

Coffee, decaf, tea, iced tea:

Beverages: (All beverages are charged on consumption plus % sales tax and % service charge)

Cost per person: $ _____ plus % sales tax and % service charge

Children's meals:
Cost per person: $ _____ plus % sales tax and % service charge

Professional meals:
Cost per person: $ _____ plus % sales tax and % service charge

---

DEPOSIT:

A deposit of $ _____ is required with this signed contract and must be received in our office by _____.

The cost for this event is based on a minimum guaranteed count of _____ people.
Note: If the final count is more than the minimum guaranteed count, the final count is the amount due.

The final guaranteed count and final payment (by bank check, money order, or cash) must be made seventy-two (72) hours prior to the event.

Cancellation policy:

CATERING COMPANY'S NAME agrees to service this event as described above. The designated representative agrees this constitutes the entire booking between the parties above and that any food, drink, or services provided in addition to that described will incur additional charges. Any changes to this agreement after signature must be mutually agreed upon by both parties and documented by an event change form. A copy of the final agreement will be provided to you.

_____   _____
Event manager   Date   Client   Date

CATERING COMPANY NAME

www.yourcompany'swebsite.com

Slogan

Street address
City, State zip

Phone (212) 555-5556
Fax (212) 555-5655

Month day, year

Client name
Street address
City, State zip

Dear Mr/Ms Client Name:

I enjoyed meeting with you and finalizing the plans for your wedding celebration on *day, month date, year.*

I have enclosed two event orders that summarize all the services that *Catering Company Name* will be providing for you. Please take a few moments to review the document, then sign one copy and return it to us.

At our final meeting on *date* and *location*, please bring the following information:

- A seating plan with the number of guests at each table
- A guaranteed number of guests
- Payment, in the form of a certified check, based on the guaranteed number of guests

At that time, any miscellaneous items will be reviewed. In the meantime, do not hesitate to call if you have any questions.

Sincerely,
Name
Event Manager

:PREPARER'S INITIALS
Enclosure: Event Orders
File No.: 0000

Issue Date:

Client: Day: Date:

Contact: Title:

Phones: (H):   (W):

Event: IHO:

Salesperson:

Event Manager:

Est. No. of People: Min. Guar.   Final Guar: No. of Tables:

C E R E M O N Y
Location:

Ceremony: Start: End:

Receiving Line/Kiddush: Start: End:

ACTIVITY		FROM	TO	LOCATION(S)
Bride's room				
Photos				
Rehearsal				
Bridal party waiting:	Women Men			
Invitation time				
Ceremony				
Cocktails and hors d'oeuvre				
Dining and dancing				
Special transportation				
Special				

			TIPS ACCEPTED?	
OTHER SERVICES	YES	NO	YES	NO
Restroom	•			•
Coat check	•			•
Valet parking	•			•

O U T S I D E   S E R V I C E S
FLORIST: Contact: Phone:

	#C/Ps	LINENS	SPECIAL
Cocktail tables			
Dinner tables			

BRIDAL ARCH/CHUPPAH:

MUSIC: Contact: Phone:

FUNCTION	# PIECES	START TIME	SPECIAL
Ceremony			
Cocktails			
Dinner			

SPECIAL:

PHOTOGRAPHER: Contact: Phone:

VIDEO: Contact: Phone:

Host items: Alphabetical place cards
               Kiddush cup
               Favors
               Yarmulkes

               Miscellaneous:

               Light bulb in napkin for ceremony

Linens: Underlay:
               Overlay:
               Special:

Room setup: Dinner dance
               Please note: smoking is prohibited

Place card table: Size: Location:

Black tie: Yes/No

ALCOHOLIC BEVERAGES:

TYPE	OPEN BAR	NUMBER OF HOURS	SPECIAL	$.CHARGE
Liquor: name brands	Yes	5		Included
Beer and soft drink	Yes	5		Included
Cordials				

WINES	HOUSE	SPECIAL	BAR	PASS	MEAL	TOAST	$ CHARGE
White	Yes		Yes	Yes	Yes		Included
Red	Yes		Yes		Yes		Included
Champagne	Yes		Yes		Yes	Yes	Included

Consumption charges will be presented at the conclusion of the event as per prices listed above. (Twenty % service charge and % sales tax additional.

SUMMARY OF CHARGES

CPI as per contract. Today's CPI = Difference of or %

ITEM	ORIGINAL CHARGE AT	PLUS CPI INCREASE	FOOD ENHANCEMENTS	BEVERAGE ENHANCEMENTS	+20% SERVICE CHARGE	% SALES TAX	PER PERSON TOTAL
Food and beverage							

Minimum guaranteed guest count given five (5) days prior to your event cannot be reduced. Price is based on a _____-hour event. Overtime will be charged at $6.00 per guest per half hour excluding service charges and tax. All calculations will be based on the final guest guaranteed count.

ADDITIONAL CHARGES

ITEM	$ CHARGE	+20% SERVICE CHARGE	% SALES TAX	TOTAL

RESERVATION FEE RECEIVED: $

METHOD OF PAYMENT: Certified Check   **PAYMENT DUE:**

BILL TO:

ANY CHARGES INCURRED ON THE EVENING OF THE EVENT MUST BE SETTLED
BY VISA, MASTERCARD, OR AMERICAN EXPRESS.

EVENT MANAGER: _____   **FILE NO:**

ACCEPTED BY: _____   **DATE:**

proofread by the event planner before distribution and compared to the proposal sent to the client for consistency. The physical design of the BEO should be straightforward and easy to read.

DURING THE EVENT

The highest level of hospitality should always be extended to all guests and clients during the event. Service personnel should be encouraged to smile and act professionally. Service should be attentive but not overbearing (see Chapter 8, "How Can We Serve You?"). The client should be approached only as requested or when absolutely necessary.

The caterer should have business cards on hand during the event but should wait until someone requests one before handing them out. The event itself should speak to the quality of your catering business. Too much promotion—placards, posters, business cards at each plate—will undermine that.

The schedule of events as listed on the BEO will guide the catering staff through the function. The catering staff should be prepared for any unforeseen circumstances that may cause a delay in service and always be flexible. The communication between the maître d'hôtel and the chef should always be optimal to prevent premature final preparation or plating of food items.

If the client or any guest creates a delay in service that causes the catering staff to work later than the contract dictates, the client is responsible for paying for that extra time. (In the event that any of the catering staff causes such a delay no additional fees should be added to the bill, and the caterer is responsible for any additional pay that is required.) Either way, the client should never feel rushed or pressured in any way.

THE PSYCHOLOGY OF THE FINAL PAYMENT

Final payment can be made before, during, or after the event. The remaining balance owed is usually collected during or afterward; some clients prefer to pay the balance beforehand to avoid the distraction from their guests. There are also occasions when the person responsible for payment does not attend the affair and may prefer to settle the bill in advance—this is common with corporate functions.

The event planner or caterer should discreetly brief the client on when the final payment is expected. Some caterers collect the balance between service of the entrée and dessert, when the event's momentum slows down somewhat, allowing the host and caterer to meet and settle the bill.

Although rare, there are occasions when a client is unhappy with an aspect of the event and may want not want to be charged. This is always a difficult situation to handle. Perhaps a client did not like the sauce that was served with the lamb; the caterer feels, however, there was nothing wrong with the sauce, nor was it misrepresented to the client in the proposal or contract. Because it is simply a case of opinion or subjectivity, the client is responsible for full payment. (If, however, the caterer feels that there was a legitimate problem with the sauce—or anything else—an adjustment of the final bill should be made.)

If this unfortunate conversation took place while there were still services to be rendered, the client would likely have to concede to the caterer to avoid any interruption during the event. If the caterer waited until all services had been rendered and the event was over before collecting final payment, however, he or she would have less leverage when trying to get the client to pay in full. Ultimately, the caterer might have to accept partial payment and try to collect the balance through legal channels, such as small claims court.

Most caterers' clients retain them on a repeat basis. Once a long-standing relationship has been established with a client, the caterer may find it more suitable to collect final payment after the event has taken place.

The final bill should be written and itemized clearly. When preparing the final bill, the contract and proposal should be cross-referenced to avoid any oversights.

GREENFIELDS CATERING, INC.

645 Albany Road • Boston, MA 02101
Phone (508) 555-7777 • Fax (508) 555-7776
www.greenfieldscateringinc.com

Farm-Fresh Foods with a French Flair

Company Name
Contact
Address
City, State Zip Code

Month Day, Year
File number: 0000

INVOICE

Party Date: Month Day, Year
Event: Name of party

ITEM DESCRIPTION	QUANTITY	UNITS	UNIT AMOUNT	TOTAL

Subtotal: food, beverage, and incidentals $ 00
Service charge $ 00
Subtotal   **$**   **00**
5% sales tax $ 00

Grand total $ 00

Total payments received $ 00

Balance due upon receipt $ 00

_____
Signature

A simple **invoice**, like the sample above, is commonly used by caterers who deliver prepared foods but who may not provide any additional catering services.

GREENFIELDS CATERING, INC.
645 Albany Road • Boston, MA 02101
Phone (508) 555-7777 • Fax (508) 555-7776
www.greenfieldscateringinc.com

Farm-Fresh Foods with a French Flair

Month Day, Year

C a t e r i n g   I n v o i c e

Bill to: Contact:
Name: Name:
Address: Title:
City, State Zip: Telephone:

Bill for:

Date	Description	Amount
	Food x number of people	$
	Beverages x number of people	$
	Bar charge on consumption	$
	Miscellaneous	$
	Rentals	$
	Labor	$
	Subtotal	**$**
	17% service charge	$
	5% tax	$
	Gross billing	**$**
	Deposit	$
	Total due (less deposit)	**$**

_____
Signature

To avoid any misunderstandings, the **final bill** should be written and itemized clearly. It may be presented to the client during the event.

FOLLOW-UP

Most event planners or caterers will follow up an event with a letter or card thanking the client for the business and including an additional business card to use for a referral. Some caterers also enclose a questionnaire about

Tables set for an **outdoor garden wedding** use formal place settings and fresh flowers as centerpieces.

their services so the client can provide constructive criticism or feedback. Like your contract, this is something you can create yourself. It should be very easy for the client to fill out and return to you: A follow-up questionnaire can be as brief as three questions on a self-addressed, stamped postcard—your client can fill this out in a minute and pop it in the mail. Always add some personal touches to such correspondence, such as "Please extend our congratulations to the bride and groom" or "Tell the bat mitzvah girl that we said mazel tov!"

This kind of correspondence should go out a few days after the event, while its memory is still fresh for all concerned.

Some caterers use a **follow-up questionnaire** so the client can provide feedback about the event. It can be lengthier than this one, but it should be easy for the client to fill out and return.

In Chapter 8, we'll learn how to train—and retain—servers so that every event runs smoothly.

8.
how can we
serve you?

Showmanship contributes greatly to the overall success of every catered event. Bands, orchestras, and disc jockeys (DJs) are often responsible for creating an upbeat and enjoyable atmosphere. However, it is a well-trained service staff that really sets the tone for any affair.

Diners enjoy a meal in an unusual setting—the lobby of the famous Metropolitan Opera House in New York City, next to its signature arched windows and underneath the famous retractable Austrian crystal starburst chandeliers.

The Importance of Staff Training

Good training in the efficient execution of service is the responsibility of dining room managers. Upper management must demonstrate—and have their service personnel practice—the type of service a client desires until everyone understands and executes well the style of service. This includes what to say to guests as food and beverages are served. At the very least, clients and guests should be served their food and beverages in an efficient, professional manner.

When a catering business is firing on all cylinders, service personnel can do much, much more than simply serve food to contribute to the wow factor of the event. A parade of servers, each carrying a flaming baked Alaska as they enter the dining room, is an experience that guests will remember for a long time. Chefs or servers at interactive buffet stations—presently the most popular buffet service model—can seem like food television come to life as they chat with guests about what is being prepared for them. French service during which a classic Caesar salad or a flaming dessert is prepared tableside, then plated for each diner, can also be impressive. Synchronized service shows a snappy precision that only the best caterers can achieve. Even the valet parking attendants, running to fetch the vehicles, can be service oriented with a "my-pleasure-to-serve-you" attitude.

From the event planner or function manager to the busperson, all service personnel must act as a team with one goal in mind—to meet or exceed the expectations of the client. This means that everyone from the catering business owner to the event planner to the chef, wait staff, and valet parking attendants should know what those expectations are. How that information flows to each staff member is as different as each catering business. Some caterers have weekly meetings with their event planner, chef, kitchen crew, and other full-time staff to discuss and plan upcoming events. A second meeting is held a few hours before each event to inform part-time staffers of the particulars of that evening's function. For smaller businesses with fewer full-time staffers, one meeting and a few phone calls might suffice.

WHO'S WHO?

The hierarchy of a service team depends on the size of the catering operation as well as the occasion or style of each event. Here are the most common service positions:

Uniforms provide a cohesive identity for a caterer's staff and, if they include the company's logo, can establish its brand. They also lend an air of professionalism.

Event planner or function manager: This is the person who has planned the event with the client, constructed the banquet event order, and has remained the point person throughout the entire event planning process. In large hotels, banquet halls, or convention centers, the event planner might be known by a different title, such as catering manager, catering sales manager, catering sales representative, convention or conference service manager, banquet manager, banquet setup manager, or assistant banquet manager. The event planner is usually present at the event to ensure that every detail is well executed. He or she also collects final payment from the client unless other arrangements have been made.

Expediter or food checker: The line chefs are sometimes too busy preparing multiple dishes to pay close attention to detail; the event planner is in the dining area, not the kitchen. The expediter or food checker, therefore, functions as the quality-control person in a catering kitchen, examining each plate before it is served to a guest, and warning whoever has enough authority to tell the chefs that a dish, plate, or platter needs fixing before it goes out. For efficient food service, the expediter should check cold dishes an hour before service, and hot dishes thirty minutes before.

Maître d'hôtel: This person supervises the setup of the dining room and choreographs the service of food and beverages that follow. In addition, the maître d'hôtel may greet the guests, help them to their seats, and describe the menu items. The maître d'hôtel is also the liaison between kitchen and dining room and communicates with the chef on issues such as the timing of courses, actual guest counts, dietary restrictions, and special requests. Very formal events or events held in banquet halls require a maître d'hôtel.

Captain: The captain manages the service of a specific section of the dining area. He or she usually remains on the floor, attending to the specific needs of the guests and making sure that each table in the section gets served properly. The captain will pour the wine in the absence of a sommelier.

Sommelier: The sommelier or wine steward will recommend specific wines to the client and, during the banquet, serve them with each course. This position is only used for the most formal banquets. Many caterers do not hire sommeliers but rather have their waiters or captains serve the wine.

Waitpersons: They may have various responsibilities, depending on the structure of service, including setting up and breaking down tabletops, passing hors d'oeuvre, bringing food and beverages to guests, clearing place settings, pouring wine, and setting up and dismantling the servers' pantry, an area that contains items such as extra flatware, napkins, ice, hot beverage machines, and many other items that may be necessary during banquet service.

Runners or food handlers: Their main responsibility is to bring food from the kitchen to the dining room. They may also assist with setup and breakdown of the dining room and the maintenance of the servers' pantry.

Buspersons: Responsible for bringing used china, flatware, and glassware from the dining area to the ware-washing area, buspersons will also typically pour water, serve bread, and assist with the clearing of the table between courses. Buspersons also assist with the setup and breakdown of the dining facility.

Bartenders: Bartenders set up the bar, mix cocktails, and pour wine, beer, and soft drinks. It is not uncommon for a bartender to also serve beverages at tables after the cocktail hour of a banquet has concluded and the guests have all been seated. Multiple bartenders are often needed to handle the cocktail portion of the banquet, after which one is left at the bar and the others become wait staff for the remainder of the event.

Setup crew: Large catering operations commonly employ housemen or a setup crew responsible for erecting all tables, chairs, dance floors, podiums, tents, audiovisual equipment, and similar hardware for their events.

The Basics of Table Service

Here are the basic principles of food and beverage service that all wait staff must know and execute well:

○ Serve from the left when a waitperson is placing food from a platter on a guest's plate.
○ Serve from the right when food has been preplated (although modern convention also allows service from the left).

A **place setting** with the standard five-piece flatware, red and white wineglasses and champagne flute, and square dinner, salad, and bread-and-butter plates set one atop the other.

○ Serve all beverages from the right.

○ Serve soup from the right; but if the soup is poured by a waiter from a large tureen into a soup cup, as in French-style service, it is served from the left of the guest.

○ Serve women first and the remaining guests in a clockwise direction.

○ Clear soiled plates and glasses from the table from the right.

○ Place empty crockery and fresh cutlery on the table from the right.

○ Never reach across a guest. Walk to the left or right of the guest to serve or remove dishes.

○ Never allow your fingers to touch the food on a plate. If this happens by accident, apologize and get a fresh plate of food for the guest.
○ Never serve or remove a glass by grasping the drinking end. Hold the bottom or stem end of the glass.

STYLES OF SERVICE

Beyond the basics, the service team will also need to be able to execute any style of service that the client wishes. For a catered event, the most common styles include:

◼ AMERICAN

With this type of service, each course is individually plated in the kitchen. It is often used for sit-down banquets. The advantages of American service include an ability to present each portion consistently and serve the guests in less time than, for example, Russian service.

◼ BUFFET

The most common perception of a buffet is a long table consisting of a variety of hot and cold foods from which guests serve themselves. In the past, caterers often suggested the buffet model to their potential clients as a way to keep costs low, as buffet service requires fewer service personnel and no individual plating by the kitchen staff.

This is no longer the case, as the interactive buffet has all but replaced the traditional model. An interactive buffet consists of separate action stations, such as a carving station, an omelet station, a stir-fry station, a sushi bar, a mashed potato bar, and so on. Although the aspect of self-service

At **standard buffets,** chafing dishes are placed on tables so guests can serve themselves.

still remains, there are kitchen or dining room employees at each station, either serving or preparing foods for the guests.

There are many advantages to interactive buffet service for both the caterer and the customer. For the caterer, the interactive buffet is a premium service and profits are usually higher. In addition, as it is much more difficult to forecast the amount of food to prepare for a buffet than a sit-down plated banquet, food is usually prepared in smaller batches, making it possible to resell foods that have not gone through their final preparation. For the client, an interactive buffet is a source of entertainment and gives the guests the opportunity to talk to the chefs and food handlers about the menu items, their experience, or any other related topic. Due to the popularity of cooking and food programs on television, the interactive buffet has become one of the most popular kinds of service for caterers to offer their clients.

Standard Buffet

At standard buffet, platters or chafing dishes of food are placed on centralized tables and guests serve themselves. Servers will usually bring beverages to guests and clear their place settings between courses or trips to the buffet. Coffee service is also usually handled by servers.

Some buffets incorporate other service styles. For example, many hotels feature a Sunday brunch at which many foods are served buffet style, but main courses still come plated from the kitchen via American service. All buffets should be maintained by employees whose main function is to replenish foods and keep the buffet looking neat and tidy. Some

A huge banquet room set up with unusual triangular tables; smiling service staff stand at the ready.

caterers still offer their customers the standard buffet model as a way to cut costs by reducing service staff. Other caterers use the standard buffet model as a way to offer their clients a varied menu with many choices and have service personnel attending to each item on the buffet.

Interactive Buffet

An interactive buffet features action stations at which food handlers, typically kitchen or dining room employees, prepare, assemble, and plate food items in view of the guests. Buffet stations are usually set up separately, according to the style or ethnicity of the food being served at each. Guests visit these stations in any order and sample the food at each. Most caterers use smaller plates (six to eight inches in diameter) to encourage

Chefs at an **interactive buffet** are like food television come to life as they chat with guests about what they are preparing.

The Christmas lights on the trees in this outdoor plaza add a festive holiday touch to this outdoor banquet setup.

guests to graze (rather than gorge) and sample all of the foods. Coordinating decorations with the type of food being served will give guests an idea of the type of food being served at each.

The interactive buffet has emerged as a very popular model of service due to the public's ever-growing knowledge of food, cooking, and ingredients. While most caterers place small signs by each food item at a standard buffet, many caterers do not provide signage for items served at an interactive buffet in order to encourage guests and food handlers to engage in a brief conversation about the menu items.

◼ BUTLER

Butler or passed service is similar to Russian service. At a sit-down dinner, guests serve themselves from the platter of food a server offers to them. At a reception or cocktail hour, standing guests select hors d'oeuvre or finger foods from a server's platter or tray.

This self-service raw bar is all ready for holiday party revelers.

■ ENGLISH

English service is similar to family-style service: The food is served on large platters, each containing enough portions for the guests at each table. However, the platters are placed on each table in front of a designated host; the food is then plated by each table's host and the assembled plate passed to each guest, much like a traditional Thanksgiving dinner. Although this service style is rarely used, it may be suitable for a celebratory corporate event at which each department head is seated with his or her respective subordinates.

■ FAMILY

Family-style service is somewhat informal and may require less staff. All food is arranged on platters big enough to serve the guests at each table. The platters are then placed on the table and the guests are encouraged to help themselves to the food. This style of service is appropriate for a catered Thanksgiving or holiday dinner because it promotes a feeling of warmth and togetherness among the diners. Foods that cool quickly (steak) or are hard to handle (spaghetti and meatballs) should not be served family style. All platters should be warmed or chilled prior to service to help retain food temperature.

▣ FRENCH

French service consists of teams of service personnel—most commonly a captain, front waiter, and back waiter. Menu items come from the kitchen partially prepared. The captain or front waiter cooks and plates the dishes tableside in front of the guests. The front or back waiter serves the dishes to each guest. A cart called a *guéridon* (a small, round table in French) equipped with a gas cylinder and burners is customarily used to assemble the plates. Traditional French dishes such as duck *à l'orange,* Dover sole *à la meunière*, and flaming crêpes suzettes are commonly served in this fashion.

Servers' uniforms should always be clean and pressed; their hair should be pulled back; their makeup and jewelry should be understated. And they should always be polite—and smiling.

Landmarks like museums, estates, and even train stations, with their beautiful architectural details, can make lovely locations for banquets.

For a catered event larger than twenty or thirty guests, this style of service is difficult—and pricy. However, many caterers use the inspiration of French service and style a component of their service after it. A sit-down banquet can have just one simple course, such as a mixed salad or soup, served French style, for example. Tableside desserts, such as bananas Foster or cherries jubilee, which are flambéed, are also manageable French style for large banquets. Although additional servers are required, profits are usually increased because caterers who offer an element of French service can charge more than they do for similar menu items served American style.

◻ RUSSIAN

With Russian service, food comes from the kitchen on platters, each large enough to serve a complete table or more. Some operations have the waitpersons carry all course components on one platter, while others have each waitperson serve a different plate component in succession.

With some preplanning to guard against wind and rain—and the weather's cooperation—outdoor events can be memorable affairs.

Because this type of service is considered formal, waitpersons usually wear white gloves. Finer establishments train their servers to use a fork and spoon to handle the food, while less upscale operations may require them to use tongs of some type. The servers place heated or chilled plates (depending on the menu choice) in front of each guest prior to serving. The chef selects foods that retain their temperature well and designs, portions, and arranges the food so it is easy to serve.

STAND-UP COCKTAIL PARTY

Many banquets, whether sit-down or buffet style, are preceded by a cock-tail hour or reception. The food items served during this period usually consist of finger foods or hors d'oeuvre that are passed by servers, and

At a **sit-down banquet,** servers bring food and beverages to guests as they sit at tables. If the seating is assigned, tables will be numbered, as they are here.

Clients often request special decorations for **theme or holiday parties.**

possibly some additional self-service stationary items. Occasionally, this model of service is used for an entire event. In this case, guests are encouraged to "graze" or consume a larger variety of foods in smaller amounts. Although considered less formal, stand-up cocktail parties encourage guests to mingle and are often more fun than traditional, more structured banquets.

■ SYNCHRONIZED

Synchronized service involves multiple servers surrounding a table of guests and setting down plates of food in front of them simultaneously. The menu items come out of the kitchen with decorative covers, or cloches, which are also removed in unison after the plates are set on the table. This type of choreographed service requires proper training and practice to make it effective. However, synchronized service may greatly enhance the atmosphere of a banquet and justify higher service charges.

COORDINATING SERVICE FOR A SIT-DOWN BANQUET

At a sit-down banquet, servers bring food and beverages to guests as they sit at tables, usually in seats assigned by the event's hosts. Caterers may use a variety of choreographed service techniques to distribute the food and beverages to the guests. Each course should ideally be served within a twenty-minute period. Many caterers use a multistation model—multiple banquet assembly lines strategically located behind the scenes in order to serve each course to the entire room in a reasonable amount of time. Each assembly line usually accommodates between 100 and 150 guests; if they are double-sided, their capacity expands to approximately 175 to 200 guests within that twenty-minute window. Each banquet assembly line is equipped with food-holding units for either hot or cold foods, such as hot boxes, rolling refrigerators, steam tables, or chafing dishes; serving utensils; plate wipes; and any special equipment needed for the plating of specific menu items.

Here is how the service team works together for this type of catered event:

- **Up to one day before:** The event planner refers to the banquet event order and confers with the chef to troubleshoot and confirm details. Off-premise location details such as setting up tents or a dance floor are completed under the supervision of the event planner.
- **Hours before the event:** The setup crew lays out the correct linens, tableware, china, glassware, floral arrangements, and so on as directed by the event planner. It also sets up the servers' pantry and banquet assembly areas. In addition, the florist, musical enter-

tainment, wedding cake baker, bartender, photographer, and so on, come in to do their own setup.

○ **An hour or two before dinner is served:** The bartender serves drinks. Appetizers may be served buffet style or passed butler style by waitpersons, usually in a different area than the one in which the sit-down dinner will be held. At a formal dinner or gala, a reception at which waitpersons pass chilled glasses of champagne among the guests replaces the cocktail hour.

Interactive buffets are presently the most popular buffet service model.

- **Thirty minutes before dinner is served:** The first course, having been inspected by the expediter, arrives at the behind-the-scenes banquet assembly lines. At the dinner hour, the event planner, host, or maître d'hôtel gives a signal for the guests to enter the dining room.
- **During dinner:** The flow of the food and beverage service is now the job of the maître d'hôtel, banquet manager, or captain. The service of each course during a banquet should take no longer than twenty minutes, regardless of the number of guests attending. Good organization and proper setup will help the caterer meet this objective. The maître d'hôtel sends food handlers or runners to the kitchen to alert the chefs that guests are ready for each course; the courses are usually served in twenty-minute intervals. The expediter or food checker makes sure each dish or platter of food passes inspection. Food handlers or runners bring out the food to the banquet assembly stations, which are hidden behind the dining area. The waitpersons serve the food to the guests, then remove plates and tableware to the banquet assembly area to get ready for the next course. Buspersons take the used plates and tableware back to the kitchen for the dishwashers to clean. The sommelier oversees the wine service. Between the entrée and dessert, the event planner asks the client for the final payment.
- **After dinner:** Buspersons continue to take items back to the kitchen to be cleaned. Soiled table linens are collected. The setup crew dismantles the room. The kitchen crew cleans up the kitchen.

COORDINATING SERVICE FOR A BUFFET

Buffet-style banquets usually feature multiple, identical food stations in order to avoid long lines and congestion in the dining area. While the number of items at each station will affect the time each guest spends on the buffet line, fifty to seventy-five persons can usually be accommodated per line.

Here is how the service team works together on a catered buffet:

○ **Up to one day before:** The event planner refers to the banquet event order and confers with the chef to troubleshoot and confirm details. Off-premise location details such as setting up tents or a dance floor are completed under the supervision of the event planner.

○ **Hours before the event:** The setup crew lays out the correct linens, tableware, china, glassware, floral arrangements, and so on, as directed by the event planner. It also sets up the servers' pantry and banquet assembly areas. In addition, the florist, musical entertainment, wedding cake baker, bartender, photographer, and so on do their own setup.

○ **An hour before dinner is served:** The bartender serves drinks. Appetizers may be served buffet style or passed butler style by waitpersons, usually in a different area from the one in which the buffet dinner will be held. Cold and hot foods begin to arrive at the appropriate stations.

○ **At the dinner hour:** The event planner, host, or maître d'hôtel gives a signal for the guests to enter the dining room.

○ **During dinner:** The flow of food and beverage service is now the job of the maître d'hôtel, banquet manager, or captain. The expediter or food checker makes sure all food passes inspection. Food handlers or runners bring the food out to the buffet. The maître d'hôtel sends food handlers or runners to the kitchen to alert the chefs when menu items need to be replenished. The waitpersons serve beverages to the guests, then remove plates and tableware as needed.

Buspersons take the used plates and tableware back to the kitchen for the dishwashers to clean. Toward the end of the meal, the event planner asks the client for the final payment.

- ○ **After dinner:** Buspersons continue to take items back to the kitchen to be cleaned. Soiled table linens are collected. The setup crew dismantles the room. The kitchen crew cleans up the kitchen.

UNIFORMS

Successful caterers require both their front- and back-of-the-house staff to wear uniforms in order to promote teamwork and professionalism. Uniforms also provide a professional identity for a catering staff, branding the company and distinguishing it from its competition. The caterer's logo embroidered on the uniforms of wait staff, bartenders, valets, coat checkers, and chefs can promote the catering business in a quiet yet effective way. (Of course, front-of-the-house staff in direct contact with guests should also be well groomed, and always have clean hair and nails.)

Some caterers supply and launder complete uniforms for all of their employees. While this benefit can be costly, it ensures that all personnel will show up to work with clean, well-maintained uniforms. Other caterers mandate that a certain uniform be worn but make their employees responsible for the purchase and maintenance of them. This option is less expensive for the caterer but may lead to some inconsistencies in appearance. Whichever option is implemented, strict penalties must be in place for those employees who do not comply with uniform requirements as a way to minimize the amount of management needed in this area.

The following are sample checklists for front-of-the-house staff, breaking down their various duties.

General Maintenance To-Do List

- ❑ Walk grounds, checking for debris and garbage.
- ❑ Use power blower to sweep curbsides and parking lots clean.
- ❑ Turn on air-conditioning and lighting in the ballrooms, bathrooms, ceremony areas, and administration areas. Check lamps, bulbs, and lighting fixtures.
- ❑ Perform inventory and maintenance of facility equipment and stock.
- ❑ Paint and patch areas throughout the facility where needed.
- ❑ Check maintenance list issued by the operations department for repairs. Perform upkeep, improvements, and refinements to ensure proper running conditions.

General Maintenance Seasonal Building Schedule

- ❑ Install and remove window air-conditioning units.
- ❑ Check and clean or replace air-conditioning filters.
- ❑ Start up and shut down pavilion fountain.
- ❑ Hook up and disconnect Hudson Pavilion ceremony audiovisual equipment.
- ❑ Start up and shut down landscape irrigation system.
- ❑ Start up and shut down the water feed to River Room.
- ❑ Check and test the heater units for the steam boiler and garage.
- ❑ Performance test the steam radiators.
- ❑ Check all gutters and leaders.
- ❑ Create storage space for the winterizing of all equipment.

ROTUNDA

These functions are to be performed daily:

- ❏ Sweep floor
- ❏ Mop floor
- ❏ Dust and polish tables
- ❏ Dust and polish concierge desk
- ❏ Clean light fixture by desk
- ❏ Clean and check lighting
- ❏ Empty and reline ashtrays
- ❏ Empty and reline garbage cans
- ❏ Clean and polish main entry doors
- ❏ Dust all chairs
- ❏ Clean mirrors above doors and main foyer
- ❏ Clean and polish all brass signage and fixtures
- ❏ Dust and clean fireplace
- ❏ Make sure storage closet has been properly maintained
- ❏ Dust and water plants

SALES PARLOR

These functions are to be performed daily:

- ❏ Vacuum carpet
- ❏ Dust shelves
- ❏ Dust pictures
- ❏ Clean and dust furniture

- ❑ Keep cabinets organized
- ❑ Polish brass fixtures
- ❑ Clean and dust light fixtures
- ❑ Clean windows
- ❑ Check all lights
- ❑ Turn on air-conditioning and house music

Make sure the room is set up and ready every day by 9 A.M. with the following: ice water, hot water, decaffeinated coffee, cream, sugar, sugar substitute, tea bags, napkins, and snacks (e.g., cookies, fruit, and so on).

PHONE ROOM

These functions are to be performed daily:

- ❑ Dust
- ❑ Wipe down phones
- ❑ Empty garbage cans
- ❑ Vacuum and sweep
- ❑ Organize phone books

UPSTAIRS BALCONY AREA

These functions are to be performed daily:

- ❑ Dust woodwork
- ❑ Dust light fixtures
- ❑ Vacuum stairs and balcony
- ❑ Dust and polish brass fixtures
- ❑ Dust and polish wall sconces

SUITES AND OFFICES

These functions are to be performed daily:

- ❏ Vacuum carpet
- ❏ Empty garbage
- ❏ Wipe down doors
- ❏ Pull out and clean the cabinet desks
- ❏ Arrange other furniture accordingly
- ❏ Clean bathrooms
- ❏ Check heating and air-conditioning equipment
- ❏ Dust pictures
- ❏ Clean windows*

* Weekly

ADMINISTRATION OFFICES:
SECOND AND THIRD LEVELS

Most of these functions are to be performed daily:

- ❏ Vacuum carpet
- ❏ Empty trash baskets
- ❏ Wipe down doors
- ❏ Turn on lights
- ❏ Turn on air-conditioning or heating
- ❏ Wipe down desk tops
- ❏ Clean or wipe down all additional furniture
- ❏ Clean or wipe down windowsills
- ❏ Clean or wipe down shelves
- ❏ Clean or wipe down pictures
- ❏ Clean or wipe down office equipment

EMPLOYEE AND CLIENTELE BATHROOMS

These functions are to be performed daily:

- ❑ Sweep and mop
- ❑ Clean sinks
- ❑ Clean toilets
- ❑ Clean urinals
- ❑ Clean mirrors
- ❑ Dust and clean vanity lights
- ❑ Wipe stall doors
- ❑ Wipe down bathroom walls
- ❑ Wipe down handicap bars
- ❑ Dust and clean windows inside and out*
- ❑ Empty garbage
- ❑ Empty sanitary napkin receptacles
- ❑ Polish all brass fixtures
- ❑ Check air deodorizer units
- ❑ Make sure there is a full complement of toilet paper, tissue boxes, sanitary napkins, and guest towels

* Weekly

RIVER AND PAVILION FOYERS

These functions are to be performed daily:

- ❑ Vacuum carpet
- ❑ Dust woodwork
- ❑ Dust and polish furniture
- ❑ Dust lighting fixtures
- ❑ Polish all brass fittings
- ❑ Empty garbage cans
- ❑ Check doors and walls for any type of markings

- ❑ Dust and water plants and planter boxes
- ❑ Clean and maintain fireplaces*

* Seasonal

HUDSON PAVILION COAT CHECK ROOMS

These functions are to be performed daily:

- ❑ Vacuum carpet
- ❑ Empty garbage
- ❑ Wipe down ceilings
- ❑ Dust shelves
- ❑ Wipe down coatracks
- ❑ Stock rooms with white shopping bags, tape, coat check numbers, baskets, and a sufficient amount of hangers

SKYLINE SUITES

These functions are to be performed daily:

- ❑ Vacuum carpet
- ❑ Check lights
- ❑ Check and clean windows
- ❑ Clean vents
- ❑ Dust windowsills
- ❑ Clean fireplace when needed
- ❑ Set the room accordingly

HUDSON RIVER ROOM

These functions are to be performed daily:

- ❑ Vacuum carpet
- ❑ Check and clean mirrors and windows

- ❏ Straighten curtains and tassels
- ❏ Check and dust ceiling tiles
- ❏ Check pin spot fixtures
- ❏ Clean and dust window ledges
- ❏ Clean vents
- ❏ Set room accordingly (showcase)

PAVILION ROOM

These functions are to be performed daily:

- ❏ Vacuum carpet
- ❏ Vacuum behind the stone railing (bartender's station)
- ❏ Check and clean windows
- ❏ Check wall-lighting fixtures
- ❏ Clean vents
- ❏ Set room accordingly (showcase)

PAVILION PROMENADE

These functions are to be performed daily:

- ❏ Sweep floors
- ❏ Remove trash and debris
- ❏ Check lighting fixtures, including timer switch
- ❏ Check and clean windows*
- ❏ Straighten trees and planter boxes
- ❏ Check kitchen thoroughly
- ❏ Check outside lights and door locks

* A complete cleaning of ceilings and windows is conducted upon notification by Operations Department.

OUTSIDE GROUNDS

These functions are to be performed daily:

- ❏ Pick up trash and debris beginning at main circle and moving down to lower front of entranceway
- ❏ Power blow circle, parking lot, ceremony areas and surrounding areas
- ❏ Turn on pavilion ceremony sprinkler system for forty minutes, then shut it down
- ❏ Check landscaping lights
- ❏ Straighten up woodshed
- ❏ Trim the ivy on River Room ceremony steps
- ❏ Arrange ceremony chairs in line or store them properly
- ❏ Clear ceremony fountain of any debris
- ❏ Clean windows*
- ❏ Salt and shovel**

* Weekly
** Seasonal

These functions are to be performed during events, every twenty minutes without hampering employee or guest movement. When doing rounds, removing empty glasses and cleaning ashtrays are the most important things aside from the bathrooms.

1. Upper Gallery
- ❏ Check skyline and pantry doors for fingerprints
- ❏ Spot sweep carpet down to rotunda

2. Skyline (Ladies' Room)
- ❏ Check mirrors and sinks
- ❏ Check level of soap and paper supplies

- ❑ Check stalls and toilets
- ❑ Remove garbage
- ❑ Sweep floor

3. Rotunda (Ladies' Room)
- ❑ Check mirrors and sinks
- ❑ Check level of soap and paper supplies
- ❑ Check stalls and toilets
- ❑ Remove garbage
- ❑ Sweep floor

4. Pavilion (Ladies' Room)
- ❑ Check mirrors and sinks
- ❑ Check level of soap and paper supplies
- ❑ Check stalls and toilets
- ❑ Remove garbage
- ❑ Sweep floor

5. Rotunda
- ❑ Check ash urns
- ❑ Check marble tables
- ❑ Check fireplace*
- ❑ Clean glass and mirrors on front doors
- ❑ Spot sweep rotunda floor
- ❑ Check gray floor mat**

* Seasonal
** Foul weather only

6. Front Entrance
- ❑ Empty ash urn

- ❏ Spot sweep cement
- ❏ Empty valet room garbage

7. Phone Room
- ❏ Clean phones
- ❏ Wipe down chairs
- ❏ Empty ash urn
- ❏ Spot sweep carpet

8. Sales Parlor
- ❏ Clear empty cups and any garbage
- ❏ Replenish coffee break
- ❏ Clean glass on table
- ❏ Sweep carpet

9. Pavilion Foyer
- ❏ Check Baldwin door glass and brass
- ❏ Dust off and align furniture
- ❏ Check ash urns
- ❏ Spot sweep carpet

10. River Foyer
- ❏ Check elevator walls and glass for fingerprints
- ❏ Check ash urns
- ❏ Check fireplace*
- ❏ Sweep elevator and hallway
- ❏ Spot sweep foyer carpet, especially by service doors

* Seasonal

Food-Service Staff Checklists

COCKTAIL RECEPTION CAPTAIN'S CHECKLIST

■ SETUP

❑ **Meeting with maître d'hôtel:** Thirty minutes before staff arrival, review the banquet event order with the maître d'hôtel, focusing on bistro and bar arrangements; set place cards.

❑ **Cocktail reception inspection:** Make sure there are the correct number of tables and the proper number of chairs at each, that the linen color is correct, and that all equipment is in place.

❑ **Setup:** Make sure the bars, bistros, café tables, bussing area, and pantry are equipped as necessary and that back-up food and place cards table are in place.

❑ **Final setup:** All staff should be ready and in position thirty minutes before invitation time. Call all butlers to the pantry to review the cocktail reception menu. Call the bartenders to the bar, and get the front door person, card table person, bistro carver, and runners in place.

❑ **Final inspection:** Make sure the lighting and room temperature are correct, all beverages are at the bars, all food is at the bistro and stations, all candles are lit, and all staff are in position.

■ COCKTAIL RECEPTION

❑ **Position butlers:** Assign them to cover all areas with hors d'oeuvre, drinks, and bussing.

❑ **Bars:** Open one bar to start, then open the second bar.

- ☐ **Bistro:** Check that carvers and servers are preplanning their tasks properly.
- ☐ **Client:** Assign a butler to pay special attention to the client during the cocktail reception.
- ☐ **Reassign staff as needed:** Shift butlers to new areas or tasks to troubleshoot any problems.
- ☐ **Kitchen:** Contact the kitchen if food quantities get dangerously low.
- ☐ **Closing cocktail reception:** Upon the signal from the maître d'hôtel, send the staff (except bartenders) to their dining room positions ten minutes before the end of the cocktail reception.
- ☐ **End of cocktail reception:** Send bartenders to their dining room positions; direct the guests to the dining room.

DINING ROOM CAPTAIN'S CHECKLIST

■ **SETUP**
- ☐ **Meeting with maître d'hôtel:** Thirty minutes before the staff arrives, review the banquet event order with the maître d'hôtel, focusing on table setting; get the sign-in sheet, assignment sheets, table numbers, and number slips.
- ☐ **Dining room location inspection:** Make sure there are the proper number of tables and chairs, that the linen color is correct, and all equipment is in place.
- ☐ **Setup:** Set up the sample setting, guest tables, service bar, service area, kitchen prep area, coffee reset area, cake and challah tables, bread baskets, and napkins (for both guests and service).
- ☐ **Final setup:** Set up the ice water glasses. Preset the appetizers and bread. Light the candles. Wipe down the wine bottles.

◼ DINING ROOM

❑ **Wait staff positions:** Make sure all wait staff are at their tables with wine and service napkins; check room lighting and temperature.

❑ **Greet guests:** The captain at the entrance to the dining room should direct the guests to their tables.

❑ **Maître d'hôtel signals:** Help relay signals to the rest of the staff.

❑ **Cake:** Assemble toasting and cake-cutting equipment and assist the maître d'hôtel during the toast and cake cutting.

❑ **Gifts:** Collect all personal belongings from the ceremony, client gifts, the top of the cake, and so on, in coat check room.

❑ **Breakdown:** Collect dirty linen and get it to off-premise storage; clear the service bar, service area, bride's room, sales office, and photo location.

❑ **Sign-out:** Sign out all staff and give the sign-out sheet and bar tab consumption to the maître d'hôtel.

Checklist for Continental Breakfast Setup

❑ Make sure the room setup is correct.

❑ Start brewing coffee.

❑ Check that breakfast buffet preset is complete: cups and saucers, teaspoons, all-purpose glasses, juice pitchers, samovars and coffee pourers, cream and sugar trays, risers and overlays, bread-and-butter liners for butter and preserves, service silver, paper cocktail napkins, and tea and hot chocolate trays.

❑ Check that meeting table presets are complete: water glasses, water pitchers on liners with a service napkin nest, hard candies, blotters, pads, and pens or pencils.

❑ Confirm that the kitchen staff has arrived and is putting together the breakfast items.

- ❑ Pour juices in juice pitchers and half-and-half in creamers, and put out lemon wedges on bread-and-butter plates for tea.
- ❑ Fill a coffee pourer with hot water for tea and hot chocolate.
- ❑ Fill samovars with coffee.
- ❑ Pick up breakfast items from the kitchen and arrange them on buffet risers.
- ❑ Place appropriate service silver with each breakfast item (butter knives for butter, teaspoons for preserves, dessert spoons for berries, forks for cut fruit, and so on).
- ❑ Put signs in place to indicate coffee, decaffeinated coffee, and hot water.
- ❑ Go back over the menu to make sure every item is in place.
- ❑ Let the client contact know that breakfast is ready and ask if he or she needs anything.
- ❑ Check the buffet every five minutes until the meeting begins; replenish any breakfast foods, beverages, coffee cups, glasses, half-and-half, and so on.
- ❑ When the meeting begins, leave the room; return when the meeting is over to clear the buffet and all tables.

WAITPERSONS' DOS AND DON'TS

▪ DOS

Appearance

1. You must be clean and well-groomed at all times, and wear a clean and pressed uniform and shined shoes.
2. Keep your hair neat and pulled back; all accessories (if worn) must be black.
3. Makeup must be understated.
4. The only earrings permitted are studs.
5. The complete uniform must be worn beginning at setup time.

Manners

1. Always be cordial and polite with guests. Smile.
2. Always know what you are serving and how to pronounce it.
3. Greet guests confidently but respectfully.

Service

1. Always pour wine and champagne using a service napkin.
2. Fill white wine and champagne glasses half full; red wine glasses, one-third full.
3. Put down plates from the left, using your left hand.
4. Always serve from the guest's left and continue clockwise around the table.
5. Always clear from the guest's right using your right hand, three plates at a time.
6. Watch for signals from the maître d'hôtel.

◼ DON'TS

1. Do not smoke or chew gum in the building; eat and drink in the employee area only.
2. Never enter or exit through the front entrance.
3. Never use guest rest rooms.
4. Never leave the kitchen area without a jacket and tie on.
5. Never say "no" to a guest; when unsure of an answer, excuse yourself and get the maître d'hôtel.
6. Don't behave casually in guest areas; never lean against walls, put your hands in your pockets, or chat in groups.
7. Never rush in guest areas.
8. Keep all personal opinions to yourself.
9. Do not refuse coffee at any time once a party has begun.
10. Do not refuse a guest's request during a cocktail reception even if that guest is out of your assigned area.

9.

food preparation
and service

The centerpiece of any catered function is, of course, the food. The food you serve must not only look and taste great, it must also be priced right so you can make a profit (see Chapter 3, "Pricing for Profit"). The food must also be served appropriately (see Chapter 8, "How Can We Serve You?"). The quality and creativity of your food should be your calling card and your best marketing tool. It should distinguish your events from those of the competition, bringing you repeat business from existing clients and referrals from word-of-mouth buzz. That's a tall order, especially for a new business searching for an identity.

The centerpiece of any catering event is, of course, the food.

Some caterers will develop menus based on what their competitors are offering. Others will try to design menus that completely set them apart. Either way, the demographic information about a caterer's customer base should have a profound influence on menu selections. For example, most caterers will include popular regional fare in their repertoire. Most caterers in the Cape Cod area feature fresh seafood items and clam chowder; in New Orleans, caterers offer items such as jambalaya and gumbo; and in Kansas City, slow-smoked foods like brisket and ribs make their way onto catering menus.

Mainstream caterers, however, offer eclectic menus that appeal to a majority of people. Although it is important for a catering menu to reflect modern trends in cooking and eating, it is equally important to include recognizable cultural favorites. Menu items should correlate with the seasons and climate and include as many indigenous, locally grown ingredients as possible.

Because catering for a series of events without repeating any menu items can increase labor costs and create chaos, caterers typically have multiple event-driven menus. They also develop all-season and all-occasion menus. Most important, a caterer should develop menus that reflect the core nature of his or her business, with foods that the kitchen crew loves to produce.

The Recipe Manual

All of this starts with recipes you've created, gathered, modified, tested, and used successfully in the past. Caterers organize their recipes to make them both comprehensive and accessible—very important when everyone from the event planner to the sous-chef needs access to them.

Whether the recipes are kept in a computer file or arranged in a printed manual, a recipe compilation will help maintain the consistency and efficiency of menu production. All recipes should:

○ Use only standard measurements
○ Be written with instructions that are easy to understand
○ List ingredients in the order in which they are used
○ Include the number of servings or another form of yield
○ Include notations on ingredient substitutions, quirks in preparation, serving tips, and cost of ingredients
○ Include instructions on recipe conversion

Before new recipes are added to the manual, they should all be tested and proven feasible. Proven recipes, however, are often subject to revision based on availability of ingredients, brainstorming among cooks, and ongoing food trends. Recipes should therefore be regarded as living documents or blueprints.

STANDARDIZED RECIPES

All food-service operations rely on the consistency of their food products for continued success. If clients hire you for an event next month because they love the baked brie appetizer they tasted at one of your events, then that appetizer should taste and look the same as it did when they tasted it last month. The kitchen staff should be vigilant about preparing all menu items in a consistent manner. Caterers cultivate customers who return time and time again—hopefully for each event-worthy occasion. Most returning clients will request one or more menu items that they have especially liked in the past and will expect it to look and taste as they remember it. The overall quality of the food should remain excellent for much of the same reasons. A client who has a great experience with a caterer's food during an initial event but is disappointed during a second event with the same caterer will probably not return for a third try—and the likelihood of that client referring other potential customers will be greatly diminished.

To ensure consistency:

○ Secure reputable purveyors for ingredients and pay their bills promptly.
○ Implement procedures for receiving and storing food products.
○ Develop and test all recipes.
○ Compile recipes in a manual.
○ Use ingredients that are readily available.
○ Purchase and maintain the proper equipment to prepare the recipes.
○ Supervise food handlers.
○ Taste all products prior to service.
○ Educate front-of-house staff on all menu items.
○ Include recipe conversion increments in recipes, if possible.

RECIPE CONVERSION

Having designed a recipe to serve fifty people, you might then be asked to decrease that recipe to serve twenty people or increase it to serve 150 or even 1,500 people. How would you go about this?

Let's say you want to increase Greenfields Catering's apple pie recipe, originally for eight, to serve fifty. Begin by converting all recipe measurements to weight, either ounces or pounds.

There are many software programs designed specifically for catering companies that link together recipes, inventory, purchasing, and production needs. These programs allow you to:

- Input a base recipe with notes on food safety and an implied hazard analysis and critical control (HACCP) system
- Scale the recipe up or down
- Include photos that show the finished product
- Give step-by-step instructions for the recipe
- Determine inventory requirements for each individual ingredient
- Compile an order sheet for purchasing based on the desired amount of production
- Compute the cost of the recipe based on the actual price of each ingredient

GREENFIELDS CATERING APPLE PIE

YIELD: 8 SERVINGS

Flour, 8 oz

Butter, 8 oz

Apples, Granny Smith, 8—about
   8 oz per apple or 64 oz total

Sugar, 4 oz

Ground cinnamon, 1 tsp

Now, divide the desired recipe yield by the original recipe yield:

$$\frac{50}{8} = 6.25$$

In this case, since you cannot bake part of a pie, round up to the nearest whole number. Then, multiply each ingredient (except the spice, see below) by the resulting factor—in this case, 7.

GREENFIELDS CATERING APPLE PIE

YIELD: 7 PIES/56 SERVINGS

Flour   8 oz x 7 = 56 oz = 3 lbs 8 oz
Butter   8 oz x 7 = 56 oz = 3 lbs 8 oz
Apples   8 Granny Smith @ 8 oz = 64 oz x 7 = 448 oz = 28 lbs
Sugar   4 oz x 7 = 28 oz = 1 lb 12 oz
Ground cinnamon as needed

It is helpful to have a recipe conversion chart in your recipe manual. Whenever a recipe is converted, however, your kitchen staff must make sure that it looks and tastes as close to the original as possible.

■ SEASONING ADJUSTMENTS FOR CONVERTED RECIPES

Recipes that are multiplied do not, however, always yield the same results as the originals. Salt, pepper, dried herbs and spices, and intense flavoring agents such as hot pepper sauces and fresh herbs do not multiply exactly, so these ingredients should be always added in small increments until the desired flavor is reached.

The Production Plan

A catering chef will not order the food for an event until a week or less before the event takes place in order to guarantee a fresh product. (Nonperishable inventory or frozen products may be ordered farther in advance.) There are, however, certain menu components, such as soups, sauces, and some hors d'oeuvre, that can be prepared in advance or frozen. In any case, most of the food production will occur one to two days before the event. A reputable catering chef will compile a weekly production plan or prep list. This plan will be based on the banquet event orders (BEOs) that are passed along from the catering sales department. Most BEOs will be in the chef's hands at least two weeks before the event to allow for proper planning. The guest count, however, will not be final until one week before, with possible additions coming in up until a day before the event (see Chapter 7, "Event Planning").

The production plan should be based on the guaranteed count. Purchasing more products in anticipation of the client adding more guests is not recommended unless they might be used for other events or preparations. Any food products that have a one-time or specific use and are purchased to preclude the possibility of running out may never be used and will decrease net profits.

WORKING WITH PURVEYORS

Before you order those twenty-eight pounds of Granny Smith apples to make your apple pies for fifty, you'll need to develop relationships with companies supplying them—and the other food products, beverages, paper goods, equipment, office supplies, and many other items you need to run a business. Although you certainly want the best price for these products, you must also consider service and quality when you select your vendors.

Certain products, such as liquor, do not change in name brand or quality from purveyor to purveyor, and service and price become the main criteria for evaluating the source. The quality of food, on the other hand, vacillates much more widely, and you'll need to have several suppliers on hand. Over time, most caterers get to know the strengths and weaknesses of all of their suppliers and order accordingly.

For example, you may use a full-service produce supplier for the majority of your fruits and vegetables, but use a smaller produce company for its lettuce because it is of superior quality and less expensive than the full-service company's. Another reason to use multiple suppliers is their delivery frequencies: A seafood purveyor that can make daily deliveries might be preferable to another that delivers three times per week, even if its prices are slightly higher.

In order to maintain a good relationship with suppliers, order products as far in advance as possible and pay their bills in a timely fashion. Last-minute ordering can greatly inconvenience suppliers of food products as they try to manage their inventory efficiently and not overstock. In addition, items that they do not normally stock and have to special order may not be available on short notice. Suppliers will change their payment policies to COD (cash on delivery) after a caterer has been repeatedly late paying its bills. Although unethical, some suppliers will also try to pass off substandard products to their customers who do not pay on time.

SEASONAL MENUS

A caterer who designs menus around fresh, locally grown, readily available foods will develop a competitive edge. Locally grown products in season are at their best quality—and at their lowest price. Perishable food items imported from distant areas often lose quality during transport. Because many clients are used to buying off-season fruits and vegetables at the grocery store and may not be aware of their actual growing seasons, event planners should be educated on the seasonality of fresh food products.

Theme-, Event-, and Venue-Driven Menus

Although most caterers design a variety of menus, many of which are occasion- or event-specific, very few will be executed without some modification: Most clients will request deviations from any suggested menu. A good event planner will provide constructive feedback as to the feasibility of such requests, and know whether they deviate too far from the theme of the event. Plus, caterers should always be ready to offer production-proven menu items outside of any preconceived event or theme menu they suggest originally.

EASE IN PREPARING, HOLDING, AND SERVING

Preparing food for catered events is very different from food prepared *à la minute* or order by order, as in most restaurants. All restaurant chefs and catering chefs do the initial preparation (or *mise en place*) of their menu items in advance. The main differences are that catered food is normally prepared in larger volumes, and only to the extent that it needs only final cooking, reheating, or assembly prior to service.

Some popular restaurant menu items therefore require modification when brought into the catering arena. In a restaurant, the thin slices of veal scaloppine are sautéed and then served quickly to prevent the meat from overcooking and drying out. If a catering client requests veal scaloppine for a party of 150, the caterer or event planner will either have to try to recommend a substitute or modify the item to ensure quality. Thicker-cut pieces of veal, such as medallions or chops, can be seared off in bulk and reheated in an oven just prior to serving without too much moisture loss. If the caterer is still pressured to use scaloppine due to cost or customer preference, a thicker coating of breading applied to the veal may extend its holding ability. A well-trained event planner will be able to guide the client into making choices that are practical simply by explaining any challenges associated with a menu item.

Ease of serving is another important consideration in menu planning. Beef Wellington, a popular catering entrée for more formal events, is traditionally trimmed whole beef tenderloin that is seared, spread with a cooked mushroom purée (duxelles), wrapped in puff pastry, and then baked. Most caterers modify this dish slightly, first cutting the beef into portion-size slices, searing them off, and then proceeding in the traditional way. At service time, the portions, which are much smaller than a whole beef Wellington, can be then baked in much less time. In addition, the individual Wellingtons do not require slicing, which would release the meat's juices and make the pastry soggy.

Foods practical for a sit-down banquet may not be practical for buffet service, and vice versa. Fresh asparagus can successfully be served hot at a sit-down banquet by reheating it right before plating. However, asparagus placed in a chafing dish on a buffet will overcook and deteriorate rapidly. A client who requests asparagus on a buffet should be guided into serving it cold or at room temperature, possibly with a sauce or vinaigrette on the side. Although catering clients may have specific food requests, their main priority is that the food be wonderful, and they will take a credible event planner's suggestions seriously. (And of course, food served impractically can damage the caterer's reputation as well.)

MATCHING MENU ITEMS TO AN EVENT

A catering venue's atmosphere, be it beachfront, mountain meadow, estate garden, sporting event, or formal dining room, will also influence the menu. Certain foods are just not appropriate for certain events, occasions, or venues. One common mistake is serving mayonnaise at an outdoor buffet. Whether in a bowl by itself or as an ingredient in a salad, mayonnaise becomes translucent and unappealing quickly outdoors—it also becomes unsafe to eat if kept unrefrigerated for too long.

The time of an event also has impact on its menu design. The menu for a wedding on a Sunday afternoon may include fresh fruits, light pastries, egg dishes, and composed salads—items that would not work as well for the same wedding on a Saturday evening, when a fancier, heartier menu is expected. A caterer who accommodates any menu request without considering its impact on production, service, or atmosphere may encounter problems or challenges that lead to substandard performance.

To help you avoid the "veal scaloppine mistake" and choose the best foods for catering menus, here are several comprehensive lists.

■ PRACTICAL FRESH INGREDIENTS

Meats for Roasting

Roasts are especially practical for catered events. Most are large and serve from ten to twenty people each. (The following lists of suggested meats, fish, and seafood are all arranged from most expensive to least costly.)

- Veal rack, veal loin, veal top round
- Beef rib, beef loin, beef tenderloin
- Lamb leg, rack of lamb

- Pork loin, ham
- Venison rack or loin
- Turkey breast

Meats for Pan Searing, Pan Frying, Deep-Frying, or Sautéing

These portion-size items cook individually. Although portion-size items are easier to serve from a banquet assembly line, they have less holding ability.

- Veal medallions cut from the loin or leg
- Veal rib chops
- Rack of lamb or lamb loin chops
- Beef loin, rib, or tenderloin cut into medallions or steaks
- French-style chicken or pheasant breasts
- Duck breast with skin
- Pork cutlets from the loin

Meats for Braising or Stewing

Braised meats are not often served at banquets because they are perceived as inexpensive, lesser-grade cuts. All of these items are available several different ways, including bone out or in, fresh or frozen, and domestic or imported. Any meat purveyor will be able to help you choose a market form that best suits your needs. The following items, if prepared properly, can be delicious—and practical—for fall or winter events or when trying to cut menu costs.

- Beef chuck, cubed or as Swiss steaks
- Bone-in chicken
- Lamb shanks
- Veal shank (osso buco)

Fish and Shellfish

Fish and shellfish are more costly and have a shorter shelf life than meat. In addition, they do not hold well after cooking unless cooled quickly and served chilled. When planning a banquet with fish on the menu, suggest thicker cuts of oily fish, such as salmon, tuna, or swordfish. These are usually available year-round and have widespread popularity. Popular shellfish items such as shrimp, crab, and lobster can also be prepared and served successfully if cooked right and especially if served chilled, which ensures success and protects product quality.

- Lobster salads
- Steamed or boiled lobster
- Chilled crabmeat cocktail
- Crab cakes
- Poached and chilled shrimp
- Stuffed and baked shrimp
- Grilled or seared tuna or swordfish steaks
- Tuna carpaccio or *tartare*
- Pan-seared salmon fillets
- Smoked or cured salmon
- Baked or stuffed clams
- Steamed and chilled mussels

Vegetables

As a general rule, green vegetables are the least stable but the most popular. Root vegetables, including carrots, parsnips, turnips, and sunchokes, are stable and simple to cook but may require innovative preparations in order to sell them to a client. Vegetable stews or casseroles, such as ratatouille, are the easiest to hold and can be prepared ahead of time.

Most catering chefs prepare their vegetable dishes well in advance of an event. Green vegetables are typically parcooked in boiling water or a convection steamer and then shocked, drained, and reheated in batches close to service time. Other, more stable vegetable dishes can be reheated in hotel pans using a steaming unit, oven, or hot box. Caterers who cold plate and reheat plated food in a hot box must choose vegetables that retain their integrity through this process.

Vegetables appropriate for batch cookery can be cooked or reheated in increments during service. They include:

- Asparagus
- Broccoli
- Green beans
- Sautéed spinach and other soft greens

Vegetables and preparations with long holding ability include:

- Braising greens, including collard and kale
- Custards
- Grilled and marinated vegetables served room temperature or chilled
- Purées made without green vegetables
- Ratatouille
- Roasted root vegetables
- Salads
- Shell bean ragouts
- Zucchini, squash, or eggplant casseroles

Starch and Farinaceous Products

Most starchy products, such as rice, potatoes, pasta, and grains, can be served successfully at any banquet if proper handling is exercised. For example, french fries are difficult to keep hot and crisp during a typical banquet service. By cooking them in small batches, table by table, however, you will achieve success. But a more practical approach might be to serve waffle-cut potato chips (*gaufrettes*) or straw potatoes, both of which are cut much more thinly than standard french fries and cooked to a point of almost complete dehydration, which maintains their crispness even while they are kept warm under heat lamps or in an oven.

Rice dishes reheat poorly in an oven or on top of the stove but do well when placed in hotel pans, fully wrapped with plastic, and reheated in a steaming unit. The same holds true for wild rice and grain dishes. Pasta dishes are difficult to execute consistently; batch cookery is the best way to avoid overcooking them, and baked pasta dishes such as lasagna or baked ziti are the easiest to execute. Most potato dishes, with the exception of deep-fried choices, can be prepared and held easily.

Some suggested preparations of potatoes, rice, pasta, and other dishes include:

POTATOES
- Potatoes gratin
- Small potatoes, roasted with their skin on
- Mashed or puréed potatoes
- Baked potatoes
- Twice-baked or stuffed potatoes

RICE
- Rice pilaf
- Steamed rice
- Risotto (parcooked)
- Stir-fried rice

PASTA
- Cannelloni

- Baked ziti or penne
- Lasagna
- Gnocchi gratinée

OTHER DISHES
- Boiled wild rice
- Boiled wheat berries
- Couscous
- Bulgur wheat (tabbouleh)

Techniques for Successfully Holding Foods

There are creative ways to prepare some foods that traditionally do not hold up well. Brining, dry-curing, and batch cooking can all extend a caterer's repertoire.

BRINING

Brining or curing meat or seafood increases its shelf life and holding ability while enhancing its flavor, and many meat and seafood menu items can be improved through these techniques. Typical brine—or wet-cure—is made from salt, liquid (usually water), sugar, and spices. Salt is the most important ingredient for both dry- and wet-curing. The salt initially draws moisture out of the product and then creates an osmotic effect that causes the product to reabsorb more liquid than it initially lost. The flavor of that liquid is enhanced by the salt, sugar, and spices, which in turn preserve the product, keep it moist during cooking, and make it taste better. Roasts, whole turkeys and chickens, large fish fillets, and steaks all respond well to brining.

Submerge the meat or seafood in the brine and refrigerate it. In general, larger products with more fat must brine longer (fat hinders osmosis), but ultimately your taste preference will determine how long to allow them to brine. You can also inject brine into larger products by using a brine pump to ensure even curing. After brining, the product should be rinsed in cold water, dried, and refrigerated overnight so it can form a tight, skinlike surface known as a pellicle. The pellicle will allow the item to be cooked or smoked properly without dehydrating.

DRY-CURING

A dry-cure contains all of the same ingredients as brine with the exception of the liquid. Although the effect is similar to brining, dry-curing is better for smaller, thinner, leaner cuts of meat or seafood, like beef, pork, and salmon—think beef Bresaola, homemade salami or sausage, prosciutto made from the leg of a pig or duck, or gravlax.

Seafood meant for dry-curing, such as salmon, scallops, and trout, is sometimes packed in a mixture of salt, sugar, and spices for a predetermined time as they would be if brined. They are then rinsed, dried, refrigerated, and allowed to form a pellicle.

Sodium nitrite or sodium nitrate, in the form of "pink salt" or tinted curing mixture (TCM), is sometimes added to a brine or cure. Used properly, these chemicals promote pink coloration in meat products, enhance the color of seafood, increase shelf life, and prevent botulism. It is paramount to follow recipe guidelines or ratios exactly when using these products: Add too much, and those consuming the cured or brined products can become ill.

BATCH COOKERY

Many menu items that do not have sufficient holding ability can be prepared in small, consecutive batches throughout the service period of an interactive buffet. Fully cooked broccoli held in a hot box for fifteen minutes or longer will lose its bright green color and become mushy; but par-cooked broccoli reheated in either boiling water, a steamer, or a sauté pan in batches and served French style does not.

Batch cookery can also involve staggering the firing of delicate proteins, such as portions of salmon, by placing them in the oven sequentially. The portions will then finish cooking incrementally, making it possible to plate them in a table-to-table manner. Batch cookery may not always be possible, however, especially for off-premise caterers—sometimes kitchens are not large enough to support the technique.

Transporting Food

Full-service, off-premise caterers always transport food, beverages, equipment, and personnel to their events. Other caterers, such as the neighborhood delicatessen, either deliver food or package it for pickup by the client. In all cases, proper care and forethought are needed when packing food products for transport. Some prepared foods do not transport well and are best prepped on-site. These include fruits and vegetables that oxidize quickly (bananas, pears, avocados, celeriac, etc.) and airy foods like whipped cream or meringue, which can deflate.

a

A **catering truck** ready to be loaded (a), the **truck's interior,** fully loaded (b), and a **worker** packing catering equipment(c).

THE CATERING VEHICLE

Purchase a station wagon, a sports utility vehicle, a van, or optimally, a refrigerated truck. Any catering vehicle should have an automatic transmission so anyone can drive it. Whatever you purchase, register it as a commercial vehicle so you can display signs and access parking areas reserved for commercial vehicles. Driving with food for more than two hours requires a refrigerated vehicle. If you must rent one, this cost is normally passed on to the client.

Fit your vehicle with bracing devices to hold thermo-insulated containers, speed racks, coolers, crates, and boxes to prevent them from moving while driving. Straps and bungee cords also help. Always keep the vehicle well maintained and clean. An unsanitary catering vehicle can lead to health department violations. And *always* drive responsibly.

b

c

◼ PACKING FOR TRANSPORT

Pack food in thermo-insulated containers and coolers, which can also be used at the venue to keep food hot or cold. Liquid foods, such as sauces, soups, and beverages, should be packed in containers with tight-fitting lids.

Square containers will save space. Use sturdy sheet and hotel pans to lay out portioned food; wrap them completely with plastic film whenever possible. Similarly, rolling racks of food should be wrapped entirely in plastic film or covered with a thermo-insulated canvas.

Encourage all employees to lift catering products and equipment safely and properly: by bending their knees and using their leg muscles to raise the items upward. The use of ramps or hydraulic lifts helps with loading or unloading trucks. Hand trucks and dollies are essential for avoiding employee injury. Larger deliveries should never be made by one person in case of injury. More safety-related information and tips can be found online at www.osha.gov.

The Environment

Climate and overall environment can greatly affect the outcome of a recipe or cooking technique. The most commonly known example concerns the boiling point of water, which falls as the altitude rises.

High Altitude
- Artificial and natural leavening works more slowly, so an additional amount of leavening may be needed.
- More time is required to aerate cream or egg whites.

Higher Humidity
- Products leavened by yeast may proof faster and require retarding.
- Crisp foods, such as cookies, chips, and crackers, may become soggy.
- Desserts may sweat and become unappealing.

- Cheese may develop surface mold.
- Colored decorations may run.
- Raw meat and fish will deteriorate more quickly.

Temperature

Extremely High Temperature
- Food deteriorates rapidly.
- Most fats soften or melt at temperatures over 80 °F.
- Chocolate does not congeal.
- Gelatin will not set.

Extremely Low Temperature
- Fats harden or congeal.
- Freezing rapidly deteriorates fresh fruits and vegetables.

Convenience Products

Food products designed to cut down on labor and preparation time vary greatly, and caterers should only use them if they do not affect the quality of the finished product in any measurable way. For example, garlic can be purchased whole, peeled, or chopped and packed in vegetable oil. While using whole garlic and peeling it just prior to use is best, using prepeeled garlic from a plastic jar is not likely to make a difference in the taste of the final dish. Prechopped garlic packed in oil, however, has a somewhat artificial, chemical flavor that makes it a poor choice for use in commercial cooking.

Recommended Convenience Products

- Prewashed lettuce mixes (mesclun, field greens, and so on)
- Prewashed spinach
- Peeled raw potatoes in Cryovac
- Prepeeled garlic and shallots
- Natural demi-glace and other meat sauces not made from base
- High-quality canned tomatoes, artichokes, and roasted peppers
- Peeled, fresh-cut raw root vegetables in Cryovac
- Mayonnaise
- Puff pastry products such as dough, sheets, or parbaked shells
- Chocolate dessert shells
- Decorations for cakes and other desserts
- Phyllo dough products
- Frozen and pasteurized egg products
- Some individually quick-frozen seafood products such as king crab, snow crab, and cooked green-lipped mussels
- Fresh pasta products (usually sold frozen)

Dried products designed to be reconstituted, such as baking mixes, sauce mixes, and instant potatoes, are generally inferior in quality (dried fruits and vegetables are exceptions). Avoid most frozen and canned vegetables except for frozen corn and peas, individually quick-frozen fruits for some uses, and canned tomatoes when fresh ones are not in season. The following is a list of convenience products that should be avoided for quality reasons:

Convenience Products to Avoid

- Chopped garlic or shallots in oil
- Most premade salad dressings
- Meat and seafood bases

With proper planning, leftover food from a catered event can be minimized. But if the actual attendance of an event falls considerably short of the guaranteed count, leftovers will abound. A caterer may want to give the leftover food to the client who paid for it, but may not be able to do so depending on local health department regulations. If the client does not refrigerate the leftover food until hours after the event, it may become contaminated and cause illness when consumed. These circumstances may also increase a caterer's liability because of the difficulty to prove when and where the contamination occurred. It is best to remove leftover food from the event staging area and store it properly for possible future use.

As a general rule, food that has been prepared in advance, cooled or stored correctly, and has not gone through its final preparatory cooking stage, may be used again. Leftover food that has been fully prepared and held at an unsafe temperature or placed on a buffet should be discarded (see Chapter 4, "Setting Up the Catering Kitchen").

- Premade potato salad, macaroni salad, and coleslaw
- Frozen hors d'oeuvre

SUBCONTRACTED PREPARED INGREDIENTS

Many caterers purchase freshly made products, especially wedding cakes, specialty breads and cakes, and individual pastries, from other food businesses. Some caterers find it easier to purchase menu items such as sushi for their events instead of hiring someone proficient in making them. (Of course, it's much easier to justify having a sushi chef on the payroll if selling sushi becomes a common thread in most of your events.) Caterers also often purchase ice carvings and edible decorations for their events.

PURCHASING FULLY PREPARED MENU ITEMS

Caterers set themselves apart from their competitors by featuring freshly prepared, creative menu items. The production process is a complex one, from facilitating the kitchen with the proper equipment and workspace, hiring an effective kitchen staff, purchasing quality products, to eventually turning those products into delicious and safe food. This "manufacturing" aspect of the catering business is the most complex and creates the most stress for caterers and their employees. Over the last decade, there has been measurable growth for companies, often started by former caterers and hotel chefs, that produce and sell innovative, ready-to-serve menu items. Rising labor costs for kitchen employees coupled with better quality products available have led some caterers away from preparing their menu items from scratch and toward purchasing them from one or more of these reputable companies. A big change has come from the technology used to produce and package these products. Sous vide technology is arguably the best process for producing fully cooked and frozen food items. The steps for this process are as follows:

- Fresh, raw ingredients are placed in a sterile, sealed plastic bag.
- The food is cooked at a low, consistent temperature, usually in water.
- When the food is fully cooked, it is quick chilled and flash frozen.

The benefits of sous vide cooking are that the food retains all of its flavor and nutritional value. In addition, the food becomes pasteurized and free of virtually all of its vegetative bacteria. The plastic package also protects the food from freezer burn while stored for future use. While this process seems simple and safe, there are some potentially dangerous problems that can result if not done correctly. Bacteria flourish at temperatures between 70° and 140°F. This type of environment can be created if the food is not cooked thoroughly or cooled properly. Most health officials are leery of permitting sous vide cooking on a commercial level, and even if they do, they require a detailed HACCP plan for each menu item produced.

Cuisine Solutions (cuisinesolutions.com) is one of the best choices for purchasing ready-to-serve menu items produced with the sous vide method. Although these items do not come cheap, their cost will be offset by savings in labor and equipment costs. Cuisine Solutions offers high-end seafood, poultry, and meat entrées as well as side dishes and desserts. As always, any fundamental decision that a caterer makes, such as the one to purchase ready-to-serve food instead of preparing it in-house, requires much careful deliberation.

In Chapter 10, we will look at how to set up the dining room and the bar area for a catered event.

10.

dining room and beverage management

Once you have a banquet event order (BEO) for an event, your staff will need to set up the dining room for serving food and beverages. In this chapter, we'll look at how to organize the physical layout for an event—from the cocktail hour through the meal to after-dinner coffee and dessert. We'll start with the dining room.

Dining Room Management

Along with the event worksheet or BEO (discussed in Chapter 7), you'll need a master list of dinnerware and serving ware, a list of any party rentals, an off-premise event packing list (if it's an off-premise event), and a floor plan showing how the banquet or catered event will be set up.

DINNERWARE

Most caterers buy or rent basic, medium-weight white china for dinnerware. A five-piece place setting includes two 7-inch plates for salad and dessert, a 9- or 10-inch dinner plate, and a coffee cup and saucer. These are purchased or rented by the piece in quantities (e.g., twelve dozen 10-inch plates), not by place setting.

If the largest number of guests your catering operation can accommodate is 100, then you should buy plates, cups, dishes, glasses, and silverware for 150 to allow for breakage and loss. If you're renting, 120 place settings will be enough.

You might also need bread and butter plates, soup cups or bowls with their accompanying plates, parfait glasses, and other dinner pieces. Catering businesses with a more casual approach to breakfast, brunch, or lunch affairs will want coffee mugs, too.

For a catered interactive or stationary buffet-type cocktail or dessert party, you can be more creative, perhaps using smaller, geometrically shaped plates or different colors; you will also need three to four 5-inch plates per person. For a casual lunch, you could use inexpensive glass dinnerware. For an outdoor barbecue at a sporting event, you would most likely employ sturdy, disposable dishes; for a formal event, bone china.

Each place setting also includes five pieces of silverware: salad fork, entrée fork, knife, teaspoon, and soupspoon. Depending on what your menu offers, you might also need to include butter knives, oyster forks, fish knives, dessert forks and spoons, or demitasse spoons. A water goblet should also be part of each place setting, whether or not wine or other beverages are served.

The event planner and maître d'hôtel will supervise the laying of each table in accordance with the type of meal and service planned for the event.

SERVING WARE

At a catered event, the food is assembled and brought to the guests or served buffet-style, requiring special serving ware. Wait staff will usually serve with basic ware, including large round or oval trays and platters, bread trays or baskets, silver water pitchers, iced tea carafes, coffeepots, creamers and sugar bowls, serving ladles, serving forks, and tongs. At a stationary buffet table, food is usually served in chafing dishes, large mahogany salad bowls, silver trays and platters, compotes, and vegetable dishes. Coffee service usually means coffee urns and hot water urns for tea, pitchers of iced tea, plus accoutrements for lemon wedges, cream, sugar, artificial sugar packets, and so on.

Service style impacts the serving equipment needed. For synchronized service, you need a cloche for each plate; for Russian service, more elaborate silver trays; for French service, a *guéridon* (rolling cart), a *réchaud* (portable gas burner), and a chafing pan. Similarly, the venue will also dictate how much and what kind of dinnerware and serving ware you'll need. If dishwashing is available, then you can figure on less; if there is no dishwashing and limited water, you'll need multiple plates, cups, and water goblets on hand.

The list of dinnerware and serving ware will be unique for each catering business. Just as you would detail the list of kitchen equipment necessary to prepare, cook, and assemble each menu item, you should also detail a list of dinnerware and serving ware and have enough on hand.

The banquet manager or event planner should consult with the client to determine table size and overall layout; clients often want to provide other items for the tabletop design, such as candelabra, candles, floral arrangements, menu cards, and place cards, and these items must be accommodated. Discussing them during the initial consultation may yield opportunities for the caterer to help arrange for these items and earn additional revenue.

LINENS

Along with the place settings, you need to plan for table linens. In addition to tablecloths to fit each table, you will also have napkins, table skirts for each buffet or service table, and draping fabric on top. A head table might have special adornment, such as a gold lamé front skirt and napkins.

A set table should look generous, never skimpy in any way. The tablecloth should drape adequately, and the napkin should be wide enough to cover the lap. The fabric should have a good feel and should launder well.

If you use a laundry or linen service, it probably also launders your chefs' coats and kitchen staff's aprons. Such services also often offer standard 72-inch square tablecloths suitable for 48- and 54-inch round tables. But using rental linens can be problematic: They don't give your catering business a unique look, and you can wind up with torn, stained, or otherwise unattractive linens from time to time. Owning a washing machine and dryer large enough to handle the volume you need can be a good idea.

LINEN AND TABLE SIZES	
Cloth Size	**Table Size**
54-in square	Bridge table or 30-in round
72-in square	48-in to 54-in round or square
90-in round	30-in round cocktail table
108-in round	54-in round or square
114-in round	54-in round or square
120-in round	60-in to 72-in round
120 x 60-in rectangle	96 x 30-in banquet table

DISPOSABLE LINENS

At cocktail parties with passed appetizers or at an outdoor barbecue, disposable paper goods are sometimes used in place of linens. Paper plates, napkins, tablecloths, and place mats can be pleasing and functional if used in the proper setting, such as a casual lunch, a casual business cocktail party, or an outdoor event. Using disposable paper goods in place of china can also be efficient if dishwashers are not available. They can also eliminate party rentals, thus saving money for the client.

OFF-PREMISE EVENT PACKING LIST

It's essential to have an accurate event packing list so you don't forget anything for an off-premise event. Go through the menu one line at a time. For each line on the menu, list each dinner and serving piece required, and the number of each. For example, if the first course is plated poached

ITEM NAME	AMOUNT
KITCHEN NEEDS	
PLASTIC SPOON	BUCKET
CARVING KNIVES	
TOOTHPICKS	2
SQUIRT BOTTLES	4
HALF SHEET PANS	30
METAL SPATULA	2
RUBBER SPATULA	2
KITCHEN SPOONS	5
TONGS	2
METAL SCOOPS	2
SPIDER	1
PASTRY BAGS	8
SQUARE CUTTING BOARD	3
PARCHMENT PAPER	12
PEPPER BLACK/WHITE/SALT	1 EACH
BAR MOPS	12
GLOVES: SMALL/MEDIUM/LARGE	1 EACH
FRYING OIL	1
HAND SINK SOAP/PAPER TOWELS	FILL
COLANDER	1
PAM SPRAY	1
ARGO CORN STARCH	1
ALUMINUM FOIL	1
SARAN WRAP	1
STERNO: SMALL/LARGE	12
GARBAGE CANS	2
CASSETTE FUEL (PER STOVE)	6
SKYLINE PANTRY SMALL PARTY ITEMS	
ROASTING PANS/HOTEL PANS (SHALLOW)	2 EACH
HOTEL PAN DEEP WIRE STAND	1
BAINS-MARIE (ASSORTED SIZES)	6
LADLES ASSORTED	4
LARGE PASTA POT/W/STRAINER BASKET	1
HORS D'OEUVRE TRAY	
HAMMER COPPER OVALS	2
COPPER TRAY SQUARE	2
BLACK OCTAGONAL ROUND	2
SQUARE SILVER TRAY	2
BLACK LACQUER TRAY	2
NEW SQUARE YELLOW TRAY	2
FROSTED GLASS PLATTER	2
GLASS CONFETTI	2
SLEIGH WICKER TRAY	2
COPPER PANS ROUND	2
PURPLE OVAL TRAY	2
GREEN FLOWER GLASS TRAY	2
GOLD DOT GLASS TRAY	2
RECTANGULAR TURQUOISE CHINA	2
CLEAR GLASSES	2
SHOT GLASSES	0
PORCELAIN SPOONS	0
FLAT WICKER TRAY	2
BAMBOO TRAY	2
STEAMER BASKET	4
GLASS PEBBLE BOWL	2
PIZZA PADDLE	2
10" SILVER REVERE BOWL	2
8" SILVER REVERE BOWL	2
5" SILVER REVERE BOWL	6
4" SILVER REVERE BOWL	2
4" GLASS V BOWL	8
5" GLASS V BOWL	6
SMALL SQUARE CHINA BOWL	4
BAMBOO BOX	4
TERRA COTTA BOWL SMALL	4
TRUFFLE BOXES	
BLACK CONE BASKET	2
CHILDRENS STATION	
3-QUART CHAFER	5
3-QUART LINERS	8
COPPER RÉCHAUD STOVE	2
COPPER CRÊPE PANS	8
Candy Jars/Bushel Basket/Bicycle/ Paper Bags	6/6/1/50
SEAFOOD STATION	
GLOW TRAY/GLOW TRAY BASE	
CLEAR GLASS CURVED BOWL	1
LARGE SHELLS/STAR FISH	3
LOBSTER TRAP/BUOY/NETTING	8
	2

ITEM NAME	SINGLE STATION	DOUBLE STATION	TRIPLE STATION
MEDITERRANEAN PASTA STATION			
COPPER CRÊPE PANS	4	8	12
DEEP COPPER PANS W/LIDS	2	4	6
HAMMER RED COPPER OVALS	2	4	6
TERRA COTTA SALAD BOWLS	6	10	14
TERRA COTTA POT W/HANDLE AND LID	4	6	8
TERRA COTTA BOWLS MEDIUM	2	4	6
5" GLASS V BOWLS	2	4	6
GLASS PEBBLE BOWLS	2	4	6
SMALL ROUND SPECKLE BOWLS	4	8	12
BRICKS	6	12	18
SMALL PEDESTAL RISERS	1	2	3
BLACK RÉCHAUD BASE	4	8	12
BLACK STOVES	2	4	6
WOOD WINE CRATES	1	2	3
IRON WINE STANDS	1	2	3
CHIANTI BOTTLES/RED WINE BOTTLES	5	10	15
PEPPER MILLS TALL	1	2	3
PASTA JARS	2	4	6
PEDESTAL URNS	1	2	3
CARVING STATION			
OVAL WOOD CARVING BOARD W/NAILS	2	4	6
LARGE SILVER OVAL TRAY	1	2	3
OVAL WOOD CARVING BOARD AND TRAY	1	2	3
RECTANGULAR MARBLE SLABS	1	4	6
GREEN SPECKLE BOWLS	2	4	6
COPPER CRÊPE PANS	2	4	6
TERRA COTTA BOWLS MEDIUM	4	8	12
BLACK RÉCHAUD BASE	1	2	3
BRICKS	4	10	16
BUSHEL BASKET LARGE/SMALL	2 EACH	3 EACH	4 EACH
BUSHEL BASKET MEDIUM	3	6	8
BUSHEL LIDS	3	6	9
COW TRAYS	2	4	6
ROOSTER	1	2	3
STEEPLE CANDLE OR RED CANDLE	2	4	6
THE BISTRO BUFFET			
SILVER PAELLA PAN	2	4	6
COPPER CRÊPE PANS	2	6	10
WHITE RECTANGULAR CHINA PLATTER	2	4	6
TERRA COTTA BOWLS MEDIUM	2	4	6
WHITE OVAL CHINA PLATTER	4	8	12
RECTANGULAR MARBLE SLABS	2	4	6
BLACK RÉCHAUD BASE	2	4	6
TWIG RUNNERS	4	8	12
3 TIERED OVAL IRON STAND	1	2	3
RECTANGULAR BASKET W/IRON HANDLES	2	4	6
RECTANGULAR IRON STAND	1	2	3
WOOD COLUMNS LARGE & MEDIUM	1 EACH	2 EACH	3 EACH
CHILI PEPPER DISPLAY JARS ASSORTED	3	6	9
SMALL PEDESTAL RISERS	1	2	3
PEPPER BRAIDS	1	2	3
GARLIC BRAIDS	1	2	3
DOME CANDLES	2	4	6
BEAN JARS	2	4	6
ASIAN STATION			
RINGS	1	2	3
WOKS	3	6	9
TURNERS	2	4	6
SILVER BURNER STOVES	1	2	3
BLACK RÉCHAUD BASE	2	4	6
WHITE SQUARE CHINA BOWL DEEP	4	6	9
WHITE SQUARE CHINA BOWL MEDIUM	6	10	14
CLEAR RIDGE BOTTLES	2	4	6
BLACK GRIDDLE	3	5	8
METAL BANANA LEAF PLATTER	2	4	6
GREEN BOWLS	5	8	12
PORCELAIN SPOONS	5	8	12
STEAMER BASKET AND ONE LID	5	8	12
SILVER RIM BAMBOO BASKETS	4	8	12
BLACK CONE BASKET	1	2	3
ASIAN SCREEN	1	2	3
BLACK LANTERN SET	3	6	9
CHOP STICKS	50	100	150
BAMBOO PLACE MATS	5	10	15
CHINESE NEWSPAPERS	4	8	12
GLASS BLOCKS	4	8	12
BLACK OCTAGONAL OVAL TRAY (OPTIONAL)	6	10	14
WHITE SQUARE BOWL SMALL (OPTIONAL)	3	6	9

salmon accompanied by a white wine, you'll need a white wineglass, dinner plate, and fish knife, in addition to the standard five-piece place settings of dinnerware and silverware per person. If the first course is appetizers passed butler-style, you'll need cocktail napkins, two or three small plates per person, and a serving tray for each server.

Dinnerware and serving ware are usually packed in racks, bags, cases, or boxes that hold a certain quantity of items. After you know the total for each piece, figure out how that translates into the appropriate packing method. The less you and your staff handle the dinnerware and serving ware, the less chance there is for breakage. Your glasses and coffee cups, for example, should be transported to the site in the same racks in which they're washed, dried, and stored; plates are usually stacked twenty high; more than that is difficult for chefs and servers to reach and use.

Suppose you have to pack for an event of one hundred guests at twelve tables. You need a 200-count box of paper cocktail napkins; three racks each (thirty-six per rack) of white wineglasses and water goblets; 18 dozen 5-inch plates (packed in stacks of twenty); 9 dozen dinner plates (packed in stacks of twenty); ten 12-count bags each of salad and dinner forks, knives, and teaspoons; twelve tablecloths; 120 napkins; one case of brandy ponies; and one 12-count box of salt and pepper shakers.

The packing list will also include barware and setups, as such ginger ale, tonic water, cola, orange juice, lemon and lime wedges, cherries, and so on.

DINING ROOM LAYOUT

The event planner, chef, client, and maître d'hôtel will probably all have a hand in deciding how the dining room will be laid out for the event. The event planner will have a diagram of the layout based on discussions with the client; however, it is not uncommon to change things around a bit at the last minute, due to an addition to the guest count, the direction of the wind (at outside events), or the space needs of the entertainers: Everyone should remain flexible. As a basic rule, the tables and chairs should focus on the head table and allow for ease of movement and serving.

Beverage Management

The service of beverages, especially alcoholic beverages, can be one of the most lucrative arenas for a catering business.

ALCOHOLIC BEVERAGES

A major question for a new catering business is whether it needs a liquor license: Navigating the bureaucratic hurdles involved in applying and being approved for a liquor license in some locations can be both expensive and time-consuming.

Most on-premise catering operations have a liquor license and sell alcoholic beverages. Usually, the gross profit earned on alcohol is 60 to 80 percent, which represents a much larger overall gross profit than on the sale of food items. In addition, alcoholic beverages, with the exception of open bottles of wine and beer, are not perishable, and with good controls in place there is minimal waste.

Many off-premise caterers do not bother to get licensed because they do not serve liquor in one location but transport alcoholic beverages to a variety of locations for their events. Whether or not the caterer has a license to sell alcoholic beverages, most state laws permit alcoholic beverages to be served if provided by the host of the event or another licensed source. Some arrange for the delivery of alcoholic beverages to a catering venue from a licensed retail source, such as a liquor store. The clients pay the liquor store directly for the product and also pay the caterer a fee for the arrangement.

Off-premise caterers can also find other ways to earn profits on beverage service. For example, a per person bar setup fee can be charged if the caterer supplies everything for the bar except the alcohol. These items may include all soft drinks, mixers, garnishes, paper goods, and ice.

■ LIABILITY ISSUES

Either way, if alcoholic beverages are served at a catered event, the caterer can be held liable for any problems caused by intoxicated guests. A guest who leaves the event intoxicated and causes an automobile accident may share liability with anyone who has served him or her alcohol prior to the accident. This includes the host of the event, the caterer, and especially the server or bartender who served the drinks. All caterers must have substantial liability insurance policies in place in case they are sued for causing intoxication in persons who then injure or kill themselves or others.

Anyone who will be serving alcohol should also go through a formal training program. Caterers can get most of this training information through local or regional liquor authorities. The maître d'hôtel, sommelier, or catering owner can conduct this training, which should cover the following:

○ **Legal limits:** Blood alcohol–level tests are used to determine whether a person is legally intoxicated; the legal limit for blood alcohol levels while driving differ from state to state. The differences between driving while intoxicated, driving under the influence, and passing such a test can be very small—usually in the range of .01 to .02 percent; the penalties, however, can differ drastically.

- ○ **Signs of intoxication:** Slurred speech, swaying from side to side, a glazed look in the eyes, and tripping or stumbling are all signs of intoxication.
- ○ **Alcohol tolerance:** Weight affects a person's tolerance for alcohol. Larger, heavier people have a greater tolerance for alcohol, as do people who drink often.
- ○ **Variance in products:** The alcohol percentages, or proofs, of different alcoholic products, vary widely. Wines range from 12 to 14 percent alcohol content. Beers run from 3 to 8 percent alcohol content depending on brand. Hard liquors vary the most. With hard liquor, check the proof on the bottle. An alcoholic beverage that is 100 proof is 50 percent alcohol (% = proof/2).
- ○ **Drinking age:** Be sure to avoid serving alcoholic drinks to minors.

How to Handle Someone Who Is Drunk

- Try to ignore or stall a drunk person waiting to order another drink.
- Offer him or her a glass of water or something to eat instead. (This will dilute the alcohol in his or her bloodstream.)
- Kindly refuse to serve him or her.
- Notify a supervisor and the host of the event so that safe transportation can be provided for the drunk person.

There are many state-run training and certification programs that offer the best of this type of education. Check the Web site of your jurisdiction's authority governing alcohol sales and distribution for the type of program available. This Web site should also furnish information on the penalties incurred for serving alcohol to minors and any days and hours when alcohol is not permitted to be served or purchased in certain towns or counties. (Many counties in the United States—referred to as "dry" counties—prohibit the sale of alcohol altogether.)

Some jurisdictions will require a special off-site permit for each individual event and may ask the caterer to provide detailed information about the site, including a diagram with lineation of the area where alcohol will be served. This permit may be required regardless of whether the caterer is licensed. An off-premise caterer must be aware of the liquor laws for every location at which it provides service to avoid breaking any of these laws unintentionally.

◼ BASIC BAR EQUIPMENT

The bartender is in charge of making sure that the bar area has the appropriate equipment, which includes bar strainer, bar towels, bottle and can openers, corkscrews, plenty of ice with tongs or scoops for serving, large pitchers, measuring spoons, mixing glasses or shakers, mixing or stirring spoons, 1-ounce jiggers, paring knives and zesters, and wastebaskets. The bartender also organizes the mixers, garnishes, napkins, and barware.

Glassware for bar and wine service includes:

- Narrow tulips or flute glasses for sparkling wine and champagne
- 8- or 10-ounce tall or wide tulips for white or blush wines
- 8- or 10-ounce wide-bowl glasses or goblets for red wine
- Small wineglasses or ponies for fortified wines like port

- Pilsner glasses or sleeves for beer
- 10-ounce highball glasses
- Martini glasses
- Rocks or footed rock glasses
- Snifters for brandy or cognac

You might also want to have a special glass for a signature drink—your own margarita or martini glasses, for example, for your house concoctions.

◼ PORTION CONTROL

Just as with food service, you must implement portion control in your alcohol service if you want to make a profit. The regular size for a bottle of wine or spirits is 750 ml, or about 25 ounces. Most wine portions are 4- to 5-ounce pours, with five to six pours per bottle. The portion size for spirits is $1^1/_2$ ounces, with sixteen pours per bottle. Fit your wine and spirits bottles with the appropriately sized pouring spouts, and portioning will be automatic.

◼ TYPES OF BAR SERVICE

Cash Bar

At a cash bar, all the guests pay the bartender for their drinks. In some cases, drink vouchers can be purchased at a centralized location, which makes it easier on the bartenders—and controls the collection of money. Some caterers permit the display of tip cups, while others do not but instead charge a separate bartenders' gratuity. Cash bars are mostly found at business-oriented events or where the consumption of alcohol is subtly discouraged: People paying for their drinks tend to drink considerably less.

Caterers usually reduce the inventory for cash bars compared to amounts associated with an open bar.

Open Bar

An open bar means that guests do not pay for any beverages they drink during the event. The charge for an open bar is usually a set figure per person. A service charge or gratuity is often added to the final bill based on this charge. The price for an open bar usually depends on the specific beverages that are offered. An open bar offering top-shelf beverages, for example, will be more costly than one serving only well drinks—those of inferior brands and quality. Because the drinks are free, more diligence is required in making sure that no guests become intoxicated at an open bar event. Most caterers do not permit the display of a tip cup at an open bar.

By Consumption

The host can also be charged for the actual amount of drinks consumed at the event. Each type of drink (mixed well drinks, mixed top-shelf drinks, wine, beer, and soft drinks) is priced individually, and the bartenders keep a tally of how many of each are collectively consumed by the guests. At the conclusion of the event, the caterer hands the customer an itemized bill for the beverages and collects payment.

ANCILLARY PERSONNEL

A variety of arrangements can be made regarding the service of beverages to ancillary personnel at an event. Some clients may request that band members, photographers, DJs, and so on, be served alcoholic beverages, while other clients may not permit it or require them to pay separately for the drinks that they consume. In any of these cases, the same precautions should be taken to prevent anyone from becoming intoxicated.

◼ WINE

Wine is often considered the most food-friendly alcoholic beverage. Most caterers have someone on staff who is knowledgeable about wine and who can assist the client in choosing appropriate wines and pairing them with menu items. It is important for this individual to respect the price range and tastes of the client and not to behave snobbishly or intimidate the client in any way. The sommelier or wine steward should also be on hand at the event to make sure the wines are opened and served at the appropriate times.

Wine should be stored properly, in a climate-controlled environment; upon service, it should already be at the correct temperature. The recommended temperatures for wine are as follows:

Wine	Range	Ideal
Light-bodied reds	50–55°F	53°F
Dry whites and rosés	44–54°F	48°F
Medium- to full-bodied reds	55–65°F	60°F
Sparkling	41–47°F	44°F
Sweet and dessert	41–47°F	44°F
Ports	Room temperature	

Handling and Pouring Wine

Servers must be trained to handle and pour wine properly, and different wines require different types of handling. Older, full-bodied red wines often contain sediment that collects at the bottom of the bottle. While the sediment is not harmful if consumed, it doesn't taste good—or look nice floating around in a wineglass. Servers must be taught how to decant this type of wine before serving it. Sparkling wines must be opened carefully, away from guests, in case the server loses control of the cork.

There are preferred glasses for each type of wine. Red wines need the most area to breathe, or oxidize, and are usually served in a wider-rimmed glass than white wines. Sparkling wines are often served in flutes, which have very narrow rims that prevent excessive loss of carbonation. Caterers should choose wineglasses that are attractive and allow enough surface area for the wine to release its bouquet. Any restaurant supply house or rental company can recommend the proper glasses for the caterer to use. Extremely fragile glasses should be avoided for larger banquets whenever possible.

Most caterers ask their servers to pour four to five ounces of wine per glass. This amount usually fills the average glass between one-third and one-half full. The server must use common sense, however, and determine the number of glasses needed to serve all of the guests before deciding on the portion size.

Corkage Fees

Some clients will want to provide their own wine for a catered event. In such cases, it is customary for the caterer to charge the client for handling and pouring the wine, a fee that offsets the loss of the profit the caterer would have made from selling wine to the client. The customary corkage fee ranges from $5 to $15 per bottle.

◼ THOUGHTS ON CHAMPAGNE

Many social events include a champagne toast as part of the festivities. Typically, servers pass around prefilled glasses that contain between three and four ounces each. A bottle of sparkling wine contains approximately eight servings poured in this manner. Therefore, an event of one hundred guests requires twelve bottles, or one case, of sparkling wine for the toast alone.

The sale of the sparkling wine produces additional profit for the caterer over and above what is generated by the sale of other beverages for the event. If, however, a client needs to trim the budget, a caterer may suggest eliminating the sparkling wine; guests can always use whatever beverage they are drinking at the time of the toast.

◼ ALCOHOLIC BEVERAGE CONTROL

While alcoholic beverages are the most lucrative menu item for the caterer, serving them can mean a loss rather than a profit if bottles disappear before, during, or after an event. Many caterers use an alcoholic beverage control system to deter theft.

Such a system involves making the bartender responsible for taking inventory before and after the event using a worksheet that the client is asked to sign at the end of the event, especially if there has been an open bar. Such a worksheet lists each type of wine or spirits offered at the event and the count for each. Here is an example of what such a worksheet might look like after a party at which Greenfields Chianti was served:

Total bottles at the start of the event	100
Total empty bottles at the end of the event	85
Partially used or open bottles at the end of the event	5
Unopened bottles at the end of the event	9
Total number of all bottles at the end of the event	**99**

Such a form will immediately disclose any missing bottles. In this example, one bottle has gone unaccounted for.

◼ DEALING WITH LEFTOVER ALCOHOLIC BEVERAGES

Licensed on-premise caterers, like bars or restaurants, will take a liquor and wine inventory after each event, ensure each bottle is closed properly, and lock up all alcoholic beverages for future use. Off-premise caterers should not transport partially used bottles of alcoholic beverages—most states have laws prohibiting their transport. An off-premise caterer with a liquor license should leave the open bottles with the client and charge accordingly. This arrangement is best discussed during the planning stages for the event and should be included in the contract.

HOW TO ESTIMATE BEVERAGE CONSUMPTION

It is difficult to estimate the amount of alcoholic and nonalcoholic beverages required for an event. The majority of commonly served beverages are not perishable, and a small amount of overbuying will not matter. The following considerations may help in planning:

○ Most people consume an average of two beverages per hour.
○ People drink more at an open bar.
○ People drink more alcoholic beverages in cooler weather and more nonalcoholic beverages in warmer weather.
○ More alcohol is consumed during evening events.
○ More alcohol is consumed during weekend events.
○ More alcoholic beverages are consumed at social events; more non-alcoholic beverages, during corporate events.
○ More alcohol is needed if bartenders are free pouring rather than using measuring devices.
○ The most popular hard liquors are vodka, gin, scotch, and bourbon.

CUSTOMER-TO-BARTENDER RATIO

When planning bar service for an event, most caterers use the ratio of one bartender for every fifty guests. Two or three bartenders can work out of a single bar if the area is large enough and set up correctly. Most caterers also assign additional service personnel to serve drinks butler style during the reception portion of an event. This reduces congestion at the actual bar area and enhances service overall.

■ STANDARD BEVERAGE SERVICE

At the minimum, a full bar should include:

Alcoholic Beverages

Regular and lite beer

White, red, and sparkling wine

Vodka

Gin

American or Canadian whiskey (rye)

Bourbon

Scotch

Rum

Tequila

Vermouth (sweet and dry)

Kahlúa

Grand Marnier

Campari

Jägermeister

Brandy

Nonalcoholic Beverages

Regular and diet cola

Lemon-lime soda

Tonic water

Club soda or seltzer

Ginger ale

Water

Orange, grapefruit, pineapple, and cranberry juices

Bloody Mary, margarita, daiquiri, and sour mixes

Basic Garnishes

Lemon and lime wedges and twists

Orange slices

Maraschino cherries

Pitted green olives

Cocktail onions

Salt (for rimming glasses)

■ PREMIUM BEVERAGE SERVICE

Most caterers offer their clients premium services that enhance the overall atmosphere of an event and create a more memorable experience. Some of the premium beverages options most in demand are discussed below.

Vodka Bars

Vodka is the most popular hard liquor in the United States, and it is drunk worldwide as well. Many vodka manufacturers have enhanced their line of products with flavored or infused vodkas. Some caterers offer a special bar set up with a variety of vodkas, some infused with signature flavors they prepare themselves. Many of the ingredients for these house-prepared concoctions will be displayed in the bottle or even served out of special decanters. Vodka bottles can be stored and displayed in drilled out blocks of ice, which not only keeps the vodka chilled, but creates a dramatic effect as well. Caviar is often served alongside vodka, taking an already premium service further upscale.

Martini Bars

Gin, vodka, and sake martinis and their many variations are popular cocktails. Many caterers offer a martini bar in addition to their regular bar setup.

Typically, a martini is a blend of gin or vodka and dry vermouth. The cosmopolitan adds cranberry and lime juice to the standard ingredients; the dirty martini, a few drops of olive brine. Books on martini making (as well as on general bartending), such as Kim Haasarud's *101 Martinis,* are available at most bookstores.

Rolling Bars and Flaming Drinks

For many years, caterers have used portable bars on rolling carts to serve beverages to guests seated at a banquet. This service can be further enhanced by some showy preparations such as flaming coffee drinks, drinks made in a blender, or layered drinks in decorative glassware.

Theme Beverages

Pairing specific beverages with food is a way to upsell the customer. Specific wines may be paired with each course of a banquet. A sommelier or another staff member can introduce the wine just before pouring it, adding an educational touch to the experience. At an interactive buffet, a sushi station can offer sake in traditional decorative cups; a Mexican station, beer or shots of tequila; a caviar station, iced vodkas (as discussed above).

NONALCOHOLIC BEVERAGES

Serving nonalcoholic beverages does not require a license; they can be charged to the client in the same manner as alcoholic beverages.

WATER SERVICE

Water is often preset during catered affairs. Glasses are placed on the tables and filled with ice and water shortly before the guests arrive. The glasses are replenished many times during the meal and are usually not cleared until the guests depart. A water analysis should be done for any catered venue to prevent the service of distasteful water or ice. Water softeners and filters can usually rectify any problem; however, if an unpalatable taste persists, the caterer should train event planners to sell bottled water to all of its clients at a minimal cost.

Ice

Caterers should never run out of ice during an event. High-volume on-premise caterers purchase or lease high-output ice machines that can replenish ice quickly. The ice machine manufacturer or commercial equipment dealer can recommend the right machine for your operation based on the number of guests you serve per hour.

Before an ice machine is purchased or rented, a caterer must decide on the size and shape of the ice cube, which will determine how much ice will fit in a glass and how much liquid it will displace. Thin, disc-shaped cubes displace the most liquid; large, square cubes displace the least. Squares also melt more slowly than disc shapes and may be preferable to caterers who preset iced beverages prior to their events. A reputable equipment dealer will provide samples of each type of cube to assist with decision making.

Most off-premise caterers have arrangements with ice manufacturing companies that deliver to their event sites. Most of these companies have round-the-clock emergency service to assist eating establishments when their own machines break down. The cost of ice and its delivery must be figured into every proposal and passed on to the customer. Most off-premise caterers have ice machines at their production facility in order to shock vegetables, store seafood correctly, and control the temperature of food being transported. Due to the volume required, transporting ice to each event for beverage service is not as practical as purchasing it from an ice manufacturer and having it delivered to the site.

■ COFFEE SERVICE

Coffee can be served from a glass pot or from a preheated, metal or ceramic pot, depending on the style of service. A metal or ceramic pot should be carried on an underliner plate with a napkin, with the underliner held as a splash guard while the coffee is being poured, although good service techniques and well-designed coffeepots with long, low spouts will minimize splashes.

When pouring coffee, the cup should be left on the table and filled fairly close to the top, leaving enough room for cream and to stir it without spilling. By filling the cups adequately, the server will need to make fewer return trips to the table for refills. (For the same reason, when pouring for one guest, servers should always ask the other guests at the table if they would like coffee as well.)

Coffee Service Basics

1. Always set sugars and creamers before serving the hot beverages.
2. One sugar bowl and creamer is needed for every four guests. If guests are just having espresso, serve sugar only; do not serve lemon twists unless they are requested.
3. Set warm coffee cups to the right of guests with the handles at four o'clock. The coffee spoon may be preset next to the dessert flatware or on the saucer with its handle at four o'clock.
4. If guests order cappuccino or espresso, ask if they would like it before, with, or after dessert.

Besides the basic coffees, a caterer might also want to provide popular dessert drinks made with coffee, from Irish coffee to flaming extravaganzas that show off the tableside artistry of a caterer.

◼ TEA SERVICE

Tea—Chinese, Indian, and herbal—has become very popular, and people who love tea are very particular about how it is brewed. Always use freshly boiled water: Start with cold water to avoid impurities that may be associated with water coming directly from a hot water heater.

Whether you offer loose tea (which most tea aficionados prefer) or tea bags (which are easier for the caterer), it can brew in either a large or an individual-size teapot, or in the teacup itself. Most green teas are best brewed at water temperatures between 160° and 180°F; most black teas, between 190° and 210°F. Black tea should steep for a maximum of five minutes, and green tea for a maximum of three.

To serve tea in a formal, classic manner, use two preheated ceramic teapots with a capacity of about 12 ounces each. (Preheating takes the chill off the pots, ensuring a better infusion and helping the tea stay hot longer.) One pot is used for the infusion. The second, for additional hot water, should be served at the end of the infusion time. Both pots are presented on underliners with a lemon wedge garnish. Sometimes the lemon is wrapped in cheesecloth to prevent seeds from falling into the cup and juice from squirting in unwanted places. A heated cup is served on a saucer.

Guests always pour their own tea: brewed tea first, then hot water if necessary to achieve the desired strength. Since the richness of cream would mask the delicate flavor of tea, a choice of milk or lemon should be offered. In proper tea service, sugar cubes are served with tea, though honey may be preferred with herbals. If only one pot is served, the hot water should be poured over the tea bag to allow it to steep before the pot is served to the guest. An extra underliner should be served for the used tea bag, which should be removed from the table immediately after it is used.

Tea Service Basics

1. Recite the teas that are available.

2. Ask the guest if he or she would like milk or lemon.

3. Place the teapot to the right of the guest above his or her cup and saucer.

4. Explain the recommended steeping time for that particular tea.

A BASIC BAR GUIDE AND CHECKLIST

1. THE BASIC BAR
Every basic bar consists of:

❏ **Liquor**
13 bottles:
Vodka
Gin
Scotch
Whiskey/bourbon
Rye
Rum
Sweet vermouth
Dry vermouth
Triple sec
Tequila
Campari

❏ **Other Alcohol**
White Zinfandel
White wine:
    Chardonnay
Red wine: Cabernet
    Sauvignon or Merlot
Champagne
Beer
Lite beer
Nonalcoholic beer

❏ **Juice/Misc.**
Orange
Cranberry
Grapefruit
Pineapple
Bottled lime juice

Tomato (for Bloody
    Mary mix)
Sour mix
Water

❏ **Soda**
7 kinds:
Cola
Diet cola
Lemon-lime
Ginger ale
Club soda
Tonic water
Sparkling water

☐ **Garnishes**	☐ **Glasses**	Scoops
7 kinds:	All-purpose glasses	Pourers
Lime wedges	Champagne flutes	Cocktail napkins
Lemon wedges	Martini glasses	Service towels
Orange slices		Tubs (and appropriate
Lemon twists	☐ **Other Items**	linens)
Olives	Stirrers	Garbage pail
Onions	Shakers	Ice
Maraschino cherries	Strainers	

2. SETTING UP

Before setting up, the lead bartender should meet with the maître d'hôtel or captain to discuss:

☐ The guest count

☐ The number of toasts expected, and when

☐ The number of bars in the cocktail area, and the type of each (single, double, and so on)

☐ If there is a visible bar in the dining room

☐ If ceremony wine is needed

☐ Keys

☐ If any special beer, wine, liquor, or cordials are needed

(If so, the lead bartender should get the keys to the inner liquor room, get the necessary bottles, lock the door, and return the keys when done.)

Bartenders have three areas to set up:

1. Cocktail area

2. Service bar

3. Wait staff's service area

Set-up duties include, but are not limited to:

THE COCKTAIL AREA

Each bar in the cocktail area must contain:

Glassware
- All-purpose glasses arranged in a honeycomb pattern, with triangles created toward the front of the bar
- Champagne glasses arranged in diamonds among the triangles
- Martini glasses arranged in diamonds among the triangles

Liquor and Other Alcohol
- Check liquor against the issue form to verify quantities, retaining this form until the end of the event.
- Place three speed-rack liquors—vodka, scotch, and gin.
- Line up the eight other liquor bottles—whiskey, bourbon, rum, Campari, sweet vermouth, dry vermouth, triple sec, tequila, and a bottle of lime juice—toward the front of the bar in a cutout created between the glasses.
- Arrange any special liquors alongside the ten regular liquor bottles, unless told to keep them under the bar.
- Place the red wine alongside the final liquor bottle on each side of the cutout—two bottles for each bartender (six total per bar).

Keep one chilled tub behind each bar containing white wine, champagne, and beer (regular and lite).

Soda

- Place two cans or bottles of each on top of each bar, and appropriate stock underneath.

Juice

- Pour the five kinds of juice, sour mix, and water into pitchers; stock appropriate backup underneath the bar.

Garnish

- Give each bartender his or her own glass of lemon and lime wedges. Stock each bar with one glass of each of the other five garnishes.
- Bartenders cut their own fruit; if they are too busy, the lead bartender should tell the captain, who can assign someone to cut the fruit for them.

Other Items

- Stock each bar with the other listed items: stirrers (two glasses), cocktail napkins, scoops, shakers, strainers, pourers, service towels, garbage pails, tubs, and ice.

THE SERVICE BAR

The behind-the-scenes service bar is where the wait staff gets its mixed drinks. It must contain all the liquor, other alcohol, soda, juice, garnishes, and other items that are found at the cocktail bar. In addition, the service bar must be stocked with an ample supply of all-purpose glasses, a large garbage can on wheels, and silver trays.

THE SERVICE AREA

Bartenders are responsible for delivering, opening, and icing all wine in the service area. If they are too busy, the lead bartender should tell the captain, who can assign someone to assist.

SETUP TIPS AND TRICKS

Don't forget less popular drinks when getting liquor from the liquor room—white Zinfandel, nonalcoholic beer, sparkling water, etc. And remember to bring sparkling water and limes for butlering during the cocktail reception.

When setting glasses, use the all-purpose racks as a spacing guide:

1. Place a row of all-purpose racks along the table edge closest to the guest side.
2. Line up one row of glasses along the inside edge of the all-purpose racks on the bartender's side of the table.
3. Remove the racks.
4. Place two more complete lines of glasses on the table (a total of three complete lines).
5. For the fourth line, place four glasses in a row, then skip a space, then place another four glasses and skip a space, and so on, until you reach the end of the table.
6. Fill in the three glasses in front of the four in the next row and two glasses in front in the next row. The final row should only have one glass (this will create a triangle).

3. THE COCKTAIL RECEPTION

Bartenders should be the first people in place. They should be fully dressed and ready to open forty-five minutes before invitation time—bars will likely be the only thing open for guests who arrive early.

A bartender is often the first person a guest sees, and a guest's first impression is often formed within fifteen minutes of his or her arrival. Bartenders must smile and be cheerful and polite when they greet guests and serve drinks to set the proper mood for the party.

During the cocktail reception, bartenders are responsible for serving drinks and keeping the bars stocked and neat; bartenders are not, however, glued to the bar. They can and will be asked to perform other tasks by the captain when needed.

4. DURING THE PARTY
During the party itself, bartenders should:

- Assist the wait staff in preparing drinks at the service bar.
- Keep the service bar stocked with supplies.
- Save all empty liquor bottles (to be placed back in their issue containers at the end of the party).
- Remove all liquor and soda from the cocktail area during lulls in activity.
- Keep an ample supply of wine in the service area.
- Act in a responsible manner, discouraging staff from hanging around, drinking, or fooling around in the service bar area.

- Lead by example and never engage in the aforementioned activities
- Report any improper activities in the service bar area to the maître d'hôtel or captain.
- Help out the rest of the staff in whatever way possible (serving out, working on the kitchen line, pouring wine on the floor) during lulls in activity.

5. BREAKING DOWN THE PARTY
After the party, bartenders must help with its breakdown:

- Remove all liquor, soda, and other alcohol from the service bar, service area, and cocktail area, and return them to their proper places.
- Clean the service bar, removing all tubs or leaving them on a cart for staff to remove.
- Cover all leftover fruit and other garnishes and put them in the refrigerator.
- Fill out consumption reports, being sure to add any special liquors and wines, and put all full, partial, and empty bottles back in their bins.
- Reseal open bottles with new seals.
- Return unused liquor to the liquor room.
- Lock the door and return the keys to the maître d'hôtel.

6. GUIDE TO COMMONLY SERVED COCKTAILS

The following is a list of the most commonly requested cocktails and instructions on how to mix them. Remember, when serving drinks:

- Always hold a glass by its base.
- Fill all glasses with ice completely unless a guest requests otherwise.
- Keep the bar neat.

Bay Breeze
1 part vodka
1 part cranberry juice
1 part pineapple juice

Bloody Mary
1 part vodka
1 part Bloody Mary mix
Garnish with lime

Campari and Orange
1 part Campari
1 part orange juice
Garnish with orange slice

Cosmopolitan
1 part vodka
1 part triple sec
1 part lime juice
Splash cranberry juice
Garnish with lime or twist
Serve straight up in martini glass

Cuba Libre
1 part rum
1 part cola
Garnish with lime

Daquiri
2 parts white rum
½ part lime juice
1 teaspoon sugar syrup
Garnish with lime slice or cherry

Gibson
1 part gin
Splash dry vermouth
Garnish with onions
Serve straight up in martini glass

Gimlet
2 parts gin
1 part lime juice
Garnish with lime

Gin and Tonic
1 part gin
1 part tonic
Garnish with lime

Greyhound
1 part vodka
1 part grapefruit juice

Jack and Coke
1 part whiskey
1 part cola
Garnish with lime

Kamikaze
1 part vodka
1 part triple sec
1 part lime juice

Kir Royale
1 part crème de cassis
5 parts champagne
Pour crème de cassis into a glass
Pour champagne on top

Long Island Iced Tea
1 part tequila
1 part rum
1 part vodka
1 part gin

1 part triple sec
Splash sour mix
Splash cola

Madras
1 part vodka
1 part cranberry juice
1 part orange juice

Malibu Bay Breeze
1 part Malibu rum
1 part pineapple juice
1 part cranberry juice

Malibu Pineapple
1 part Malibu rum
1 part pineapple juice

Manhattan
2 parts rye
1 part sweet vermouth
Garnish with cherry

Margarita
2 parts tequila
1 part triple sec
1 part lime juice
1 part sour mix

Martini

1 part gin
Splash dry vermouth
Garnish with olives or twist
Serve straight up

Mimosa

1 part champagne
1 part orange juice
Serve in champagne flute

Mojito

1 part rum
3 parts club soda
12 mint leaves
½ lime
½ part sugar
Mash mint leaves, sugar, and lime juice together
Add rum and top with club soda
Garnish with mint sprigs

Negroni

1 part gin
1 part Campari
1 part sweet vermouth
Garnish with twist

Old Fashioned

2 parts whiskey
2 dashes Angostura bitters
1 dash soda water
1 teaspoon sugar
Dissolve sugar with bitters and soda water
Add ice cubes and whiskey

Perfect Manhattan

2 parts rye
1 part sweet vermouth
1 part dry vermouth
Garnish with cherry

Rob Roy

2 parts scotch
1 part sweet vermouth
Garnish with cherry

Rye Presbyterian

1 part rye
1 part ginger ale
1 part club soda

Scotch Sour
1 part scotch
1 part sour mix
Garnish with cherry and orange

Screwdriver
1 part vodka
1 part orange juice

Sea Breeze
1 part vodka
1 part grapefruit juice
1 part cranberry juice

Seven and Seven
1 part Canadian Club
1 part lemon-lime

Shirley Temple
1 part lemon-lime or ginger ale
Splash grenadine
Garnish with cherry

Sidecar
1 part brandy
1 part Curaçao
2 parts lime juice

Spritzer
1 part white wine
1 part club soda
Serve on the rocks

Tequila Sunrise
1 part tequila
1 part orange juice
Splash grenadine

Tom Collins
1 part gin
1 part sour mix
Shake
Add splash club soda

Vodka Gimlet
2 parts vodka
1 part lime juice
Garnish with lime wedge

Vodka Martini
1 part vodka
Splash dry vermouth
*Serve straight up in
 martini glass*
Garnish with olive(s) or twist

Vodka Sour
1 part vodka
1 part sour mix
Garnish with cherry and orange

Whiskey Sour
1 part whiskey
1 part sour mix
Garnish with cherry and orange

Vodka Tonic
1 part vodka
1 part tonic
Garnish with lime

- *On the rocks* means served over ice.
- *Straight up* means served chilled and strained, but without ice.
- *Neat* means served straight from the bottle—unchilled and without ice.

7. AND DON'T FORGET. . .

Bartenders represent the caterer and must live up to its reputation.
Keep the following in mind:

Arrive neatly dressed; keep your tuxedo in excellent shape.

All guests are potentially future clients; treat them with the utmost respect and always give them the right of way.

Always ask the maître d'hôtel or captain if there are any specials.

Don't open too many bottles of special wine.

Chill enough beer if a large beer-drinking crowd is anticipated.

Unless you are a lead bartender, wear your tuxedo to work but carry your shirt, and change into it after you arrive.

Don't disappear during a ceremony; bartenders must help out with ceremony activities.

The liquor room is not a hangout.

The food, of course, is the centerpiece of any catered event. In Chapter 11, you'll learn about sample menus appropriate for various functions.

11.
sample menus
and service

For caterers, creating new dishes and menus in response to their clients' needs is an ongoing process. To get those creative juices flowing, this chapter offers sample menus for the most common catered events. Each event presents a different challenge in terms of both food and service. These are our recommendations for the types of catered foods that prepare, hold, assemble, and serve well at each—and the creative spin that a catering chef or owner can put on them.

Brunch Buffet

Brunch buffets, typically on a Saturday or Sunday, are perfect for christenings, confirmations, bar and bat mitzvahs, and baby or bridal showers, especially if they can be held outdoors in nice weather. When inviting guests from out of town for an evening event, many catering clients will also host a brunch buffet the next day before saying good-bye.

A brunch buffet consists of both breakfast and lunch menu items. While this leaves caterers with many menu items from which to choose, it's better to serve lighter items than more filling ones. Progressive caterers are steering away from typical breakfast meats such as pork sausage and bacon, replacing them with poultry and vegetarian items that also go well with eggs, such as chicken sausage and vegetable hash.

This brunch is served as an interactive buffet. Bread baskets containing the morning pastries, butter, honey, and fruit preserves are placed on each table. One interactive station serves the Bloody Marys and mimosas; another, signature juice drinks; a third, Belgian waffles. Two other buffet areas are also set up to serve a selection of breakfast entrées and desserts.

On Each Table

- Croissants, scones, muffins, and breads
- Cream scones, morning glory muffins, and strawberry rhubarb streusel muffins
- Fruit preserves, honey, and whipped butter

Station One

- Pepper vodka Bloody Marys
- Mimosa

Station Two: Juice Bar

- Peach smoothies
- Citrus coolers
- Mediterranean juice blend
- Veggie drink

Station Three

- Belgian waffles with fruit sauces and syrups
- Gravlax with black bread and mustard dill sauce

Grand Buffet

- Frittatas with bacon, onions, and potatoes
- Grilled vegetables
- Eggplant and prosciutto *panini*
- Couscous with curried vegetables
- Sliced turkey breast with apricot chutney
- Mozzarella and prosciutto roulade

Dessert Buffet

- Grand Marnier–infused strawberries
- Citrus crisps
- Sand cookies

Corporate or Social Casual Lunch

Corporate luncheons are most often scheduled in order to get employees and associates together at a specific time for speeches and presentations, which then take place periodically during the meal. Because of the business setting, lunch must be served quickly. You should therefore recommend menu items that hold their temperature well and have universal appeal. Have multiple corporate casual lunch menus designed to fit a wide spectrum of budgets.

The style of service for a typical corporate or casual lunch is American, with wait staff serving each person. This lunch also works well for community and social groups.

On Each Table
○ White and red table wines

Amuse-Gueule
○ Cucumber-avocado rolls

First Course: Appetizer
○ Crab cakes with mango avocado salsa

Entrée
○ Breast of chicken with duxelles stuffing

○ Brown rice pilaf with pecans and green onions

○ Summer squash noodles

Dessert
○ Buttermilk *panna cotta* with seasonal fruits

Outdoor Lunch Buffet or Barbecue

Outdoor events are challenging because the weather can greatly affect the event's success. Most outdoor events take place under a tent or other sheltering structure, such as a pavilion. It's best not to commit to cater an outdoor event at a venue unprotected from the weather.

The most common weather culprits are rain and wind. If you're catering an off-premise event outdoors, bring along plenty of tie-downs for tablecloths, tent walls, curtains, or raised flooring. Tent heaters or fans are available for events that take place at times when the outdoor temperature is unpredictable. On the positive side, an outdoor event is usually memorable, especially at a standout location. Caterers have great success producing events at zoos, botanical gardens, beaches, amusement parks, and the grounds of private mansions and estates.

Unless your client wants the typical hamburger and hot dog repertoire, why not grill more unusual, upscale foods? Some caterers specialize in barbecues, pig roasts, or clambakes, while others rent grills, smokers, and other equipment necessary for outdoor catering on an event-by-event basis.

The style of service for this menu is interactive buffet, and the main station is the grill. You can be sure that guests will have lots of questions for the barbecue chef.

At the Bar
- Wheat beer
- Mojitos
- Tangerine margaritas

On Each Table

○ Crostini with white bean dip, marinated tomatoes, and tapenade

Grill Station

○ Herb-crusted steak

○ Fish kebob

○ Portobello steaks

○ Grilled chicken breasts with fennel

Salad Buffet

○ Orzo salad

○ Tomato and mozzarella salad

○ Japanese-style cucumber and wakame salad

○ Mediterranean potato salad

○ Tabbouleh

Additional Interactive Items

○ Eggplant *panini*

○ Vietnamese salad rolls

Dessert Buffet

○ Ambrosia

○ Assorted cookies

○ Strawberry-rhubarb crisp

Cocktail Parties

STANDARD COCKTAIL PARTY

Stand-up cocktail parties encourage attendees to socialize and mingle; they work best for events such as open houses, art exhibits, corporate milestone celebrations, and retirements, and are sometimes even appropriate for weddings and anniversaries. Most cocktail parties are scheduled for less time than full-service sit-down banquets or buffets.

Typically, servers pass finger foods and canapés that can be eaten easily by guests as they mingle and imbibe. There is usually some seating available. Menu items served at these events are usually eclectic and reflect a variety of ethnic and cultural influences.

The type of service for a stand-up cocktail party is butler style.

At the Bar

- Martini bar
- Champagne with infusions

Passed Hot Hors d'Oeuvre

- Beef *negimaki*
- Bacon-wrapped shrimp
- Chicken *saté* with peanut sauce
- Spanakopita
- Pancetta-risotto cakes with sun-dried tomato pesto
- Shrimp and avocado quesadillas

Passed Cold Hors d'Oeuvre

- Cucumber cups with scallop seviche
- Potato blini with smoked salmon and caviar

- ○ Crostini with white bean spread
- ○ Tartlet with foie gras mousse
- ○ Sushi

Passed Dessert
- ○ *Mignardises* (miniature petits fours and pastries)
- ○ Chocolate-dipped berries
- ○ Bubble tea

PROGRESSIVE COCKTAIL PARTY

Progressive cocktail parties are usually scheduled for a longer time than standard cocktail parties and may feature stationary or interactive food areas. Menu items should be designed so the guests eat them either standing or sitting down. At any kind of cocktail party, standard or progressive, the food and beverages should be interesting enough to encourage conversation but not so overbearing in spice or temperature as to create discomfort among the guests.

This menu includes some of the same items as the menu for the standard cocktail party, but uses interactive stations. The service is butler style for the champagne and cold and hot appetizers, interactive buffet for the sushi and blini stations, and stationary buffet for the main courses and desserts.

At the Bar
- ○ Martini bar
- ○ *Sangria* with lime and premium tequila

Passed Butler Style
- ○ Champagne

Passed Cold Hors d'Oeuvre
- Cucumber cups with scallop seviche
- Tartlet with foie gras mousse
- Crostini with white bean spread

Passed Hot Hors d'Oeuvre
- Prosciutto-wrapped shrimp
- Phyllo pockets with goat cheese, spinach, and sun-dried tomatoes
- Pancetta-risotto cakes
- Chicken *saté*

Station One
- Sushi

Station Two
- Blini with caviar

Grand Buffet
- Grilled vegetables and aïoli
- Indian grilled lamb with mango chutney
- Poached salmon with dill butter

Dessert Buffet
- Citrus tartlets
- *Palmiers*
- Chocolate truffles
- Linzer cookies

International Interactive Buffet

At interactive buffets, the food is served at individual "action stations" where trained personnel prepare, finish, or assemble menu items in front of the guests. Each station often reflects a specific ethnicity or style of food: pasta, sushi, and so on. The interactive model of buffet has gained immensely in popularity due to the public's increased knowledge of food and cooking and its desire for events that encourage mingling (formal meals tend to inhibit it).

This type of buffet is ideal for large corporate events or social occasions for which a sit-down dinner is deemed too formal. In this buffet, there is something for everyone. The menu demonstrates the tremendous variety that can make an interactive buffet an exciting event for all.

The servers bring coffee and tea to each guest at the table and clear plates, but guests help themselves to offerings from the various stations and buffet areas.

At Each Table

- Water glasses
- Coffee and tea service

Italian Station

- Artichoke and fennel salad (stationary)
- Focaccia and ciabatta (stationary)
- Pasta carbonara (interactive)
- Gnocchi Piedmontese with duck confit (interactive)

American Regional Station

- Sliced barbecued beef brisket (interactive)

- ○ Chopped salad (interactive)
- ○ Parker House rolls (stationary)
- ○ New England clam chowder (interactive)
- ○ Mini crab cakes (interactive)

Asian Station

- ○ Sushi (interactive)
- ○ Vietnamese salad rolls (interactive)
- ○ Soba noodle salad (stationary)
- ○ Chinese skewered bites (stationary)

Mexican Station

- ○ Black beans with peppers and chorizo (stationary)
- ○ *Arroz blanco* (stationary)
- ○ Barbecued lamb tamales (stationary)
- ○ Tortilla soup (interactive)
- ○ Jicama salad (stationary)
- ○ Taco sauce (stationary)
- ○ Guacamole (interactive)
- ○ Pork *picadillo* empanadas (stationary)

International Desserts Buffet

- ○ Crème caramel
- ○ Italian pastries
- ○ Fruit strudels
- ○ Green tea ice cream (interactive)
- ○ Blood orange sorbet (interactive)

Dinners

FORMAL DINNER

Formal dinners consist of from five to eight courses, each of which is usually paired with the appropriate wine. The menu items should be upscale, in keeping with the more formal service. For the proper effect, the tabletop design should be elaborate: use fine china, crystal glassware, and silver flatware, not regular party rental china, glasses, and silverware. Fresh floral arrangements often grace a formal dinner table if the budget allows. Musical entertainment might also be part of the festivities.

A formal dinner can begin with a champagne toast and reception, followed by hors d'oeuvre passed butler style. The event itself, appropriate for a wedding reception, gala, special awards banquet, anniversary, or celebratory business event, is always a sit-down dinner. The menu below features wow-factor items such as lobster, smoked salmon, lamb chops, and premium cheeses.

The style of service for the dinner itself could be American (each person is served an assembled plate), English (the host at each table serves the food Thanksgiving style), or Russian (guests are served from platters by white-gloved wait staff). For a very important formal dinner, the service style might also be synchronized, with each guest at a table presented with a dish simultaneously. Caterers should enlist their best-trained servers for this type of event (see Chapter 8, "How Can We Serve You?").

Amuse-Gueule
- Smoked salmon barquettes

Appetizer or First Course
- Lobster salad with mangoes

Entrée
- ○ Grilled lamb chops with rosemary-roasted artichokes and cipollini
- ○ Roasted Tuscan-style tomatoes

Cheese Course
- ○ Stilton, tallegio, and fresh chèvre with walnut raisin bread

Dessert
- ○ Ganache–blood orange torte
- ○ *Mignardise* (petits fours and pastries)

WINE-PAIRING DINNER

Wine-pairing dinners have long been popular at restaurants; now they've become popular for catered events, too. Wine producers or merchants sometimes hire a caterer to produce an event that showcases their wines. Wine aficionados also cater wine-pairing dinners at their residence—for fewer people, but with higher-quality food and beverages.

This example follows some very general rules in wine pairing, such as serving a dry sparkling wine with an eclectic array of hors d'oeuvre, an herbaceous white wine with mild seafood, a big red wine with beef, and a fruity dessert wine to cap off the dinner. Wine-and-food pairings are always a matter of opinion; however, most experts agree that matching the basic taste of the food to a wine with a similar quality (an acidic wine with an acidic food, for example) makes the most sense.

The service styles for this event include a butler-style reception with sparkling wine and a formal American-style presentation of plated dishes to each diner with wine poured by the wait staff, sommelier, or host. Make sure you have enough of each type of wineglass.

Reception/Cocktail Hour

- **Passed sparkling wines:** Prosecco, Champagne

Hot and Cold Passed Hors d'Oeuvre

- Potato crêpes with caviar
- Beef tartare canapés
- Barbecued shrimp with bacon
- Risotto cakes

First Course

- **Wines:** Sauvignon Blanc or Côte du Rhône
- Cod *à la nage* with fresh vegetables, herbs, and olive oil

Second Course

- **Wines:** Pinot Noir or Burgundy
- Duck confit with fava bean purée

Third Course

- **Wines:** Cabernet Sauvignon or Bordeaux
- Sirloin of beef with truffle sauce
- Green beans with walnuts

Dessert

- Muscat or Sauternes
- Pineapple tartes tatins with vanilla sorbet

Outdoor Wedding

Every caterer should be able to handle a wedding, but to distinguish yourself from every other caterer in town, you'll need to offer exciting, affordable menu items with a twist. In this case, it's a seafood bar with raw and steamed items accompanied by interesting sauces, a lobster quesadilla hors d'oeuvre, and the beautiful colors in the crab and avocado salad.

The food at a wedding reception needs to please both families. This can present a challenge when the two families come from very different cultures. What do you serve when a wedding will unite a family of Hindu vegetarians who regard cows as sacred and a family of steak-loving Christians? A creative caterer will suggest several stationary buffet stations, some serving vegetarian Indian fare, and others serving more traditional American fare, with one exception—instead of beef prime rib, you will serve bison. This type of savvy compromise can solve potentially disastrous problems—and greatly elevate your reputation.

Passed hors d'oeuvre and buffet appetizers, probably accompanied by champagne, are followed by a sit-down dinner of two courses and finally, the traditional cutting of the wedding cake.

There should be a separate table for the wedding cake, beautifully arranged, perhaps with a silver wedding-cake stand and fresh rose petals as a garnish. Sometimes the caterer is in charge of making and serving the wedding cake; in other instances the bride's family arranges for a wedding cake to be made and delivered to the event. Either way, you should be ready to showcase the cake to its best effect.

In addition to the cake, brides often want the caterer to provide miniature desserts as well—small glasses of tiramisù, ramekins of crème brûlée, elegantly decorated cupcakes—to which guests then help themselves from a dessert buffet. Coffee and tea can be served by the wait staff.

Champagne Toast

Passed Hors d'Oeuvre
- Lobster quesadillas
- Beef *negimaki*
- Creamed wild mushroom tartlets
- Cucumber cups with scallop seviche
- Prosciutto and melon canapés
- Fontina bruschettas with oven-roasted tomatoes

Stationary Seafood Bar
- Oysters with dipping sauces
- Steamed crab claws, mussels, and shrimp
- Exotic vegetable *crudités* with hummus
- Hazelnut romesco sauce

Appetizer
- Crab and avocado salad

Entrée
- Standing rib roast au jus
- Macédoine of vegetables
- Duchess potatoes

Dessert
- Wedding cake

Corporate or Community Black-Tie Fund-Raiser Gala

Fund-raising events are held in hopes of collecting enough money from guests to cover the cost of the event and make a substantial donation to a specific cause. Tickets to catered fund-raisers are usually quite expensive. Although attendees know that they are making a contribution, they also expect some value for their money.

This is the type of event at which showmanship like synchronized service, "sabering" off the top of a champagne bottle, or pouring champagne down a "fountain" of fluted glasses can really make the evening memorable.

This menu selection is tasteful, and although their perceived value is high, the menu items' costs are actually quite moderate—which is necessary to maximize the donations' value. Caterers who take on fund-raising events rarely donate their services, although they may discount them in exchange for promotional opportunities that are often available through this type of event (see Chapter 6, "Marketing").

Black-tie fund-raiser galas are a mix of butler-style service for passed hors d'oeuvre and American service for the sit-down, three-course dinner that follows. Coffee, tea, and wines are also served by the wait staff.

Assorted Passed Hot and Cold Hors d'Oeuvre

First Course or Appetizer
   ○ Tuna carpaccio with shiitake salad

Entrée
   ○ Grilled rib-eye steak with *marchands de vin*

- *Galettes de pommes de terres*
- Seasonal vegetables

Dessert

- Flourless warm chocolate cake with raspberry coulis

Late-Night Dessert Buffet

Social or corporate group events after the customary dinner hour, such as orchestral or theater performances, retirement parties, and so on, often culminate in a dessert buffet. The guests will usually have eaten dinner prior to the event and not desire a full meal so close to bedtime. A dessert buffet with an elegant coffee and tea service—decaffeinated choices are important here—ends the evening on a graceful and colorful note.

The menu provided has choices for everyone, from serious chocoholics to people who prefer lighter, fruitier desserts. For a more stylish presentation, use individual- or bite-size items, as a whole sliced cake starts to look less than ideal after the first slice is gone. It's also easier for guests to serve themselves and enjoy more variety with smaller desserts.

The style of service for this event is traditional buffet from which guests help themselves, with one interactive station. Guests can help themselves to coffee and herbal teas—with garnishes like rock candy swizzle sticks, whipped cream, fresh mint sprigs, and lemon slices.

Dessert Buffet

- Crème brûlée
- Chocolate mousse in chocolate cups
- Citrus tarts

- Linzer cookies
- Chocolate and praline éclairs
- Soufflé glacé
- Petits fours
- Fruit jellies
- Poached Forelle pears
- Tiramisù in glasses
- Pecan diamonds

Station One

- Bananas Foster
- Chocolate fondue
- Crêpes suzettes

Station Two

- Elegant coffee and tea service

appendix:
basic banquet
kitchen layout

This appendix displays a layout of a basic banquet kitchen including the necessary general equipment and space for volume cooking in a banquet setting. This plan should be altered depending on the complexity and volume of the menus it is going to serve.

Walk-in Refrigerator and Walk-in Freezer

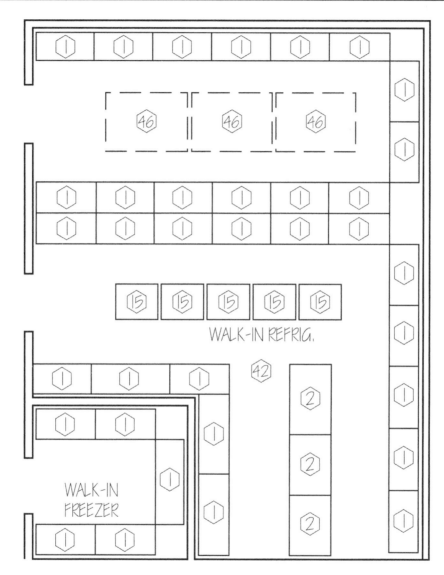

There is adequate **walk-in refrigerator and freezer space,** with doors that are accessible to each prep area in the kitchen. The walk-ins are level with the floor, making it easy to roll in speed racks full of product.

The **walk-in refrigerators** and **freezers** are located away from heat sources.

ITEM #	QTY	MFR MODEL # DESCRIPTION	DIMENSIONS			ELECTRICAL				BTUH	REMARKS
			W	D	H	V	PH	A	kW		
1	35	InterMetro Storage shelving	36	18	84						
2	3	InterMetro Storage shelving	36	24	84						
15	5	Seco # OR 1820 Heavy-duty rack	20½	26	68						
42	1	Combination walk-in refrigerator and freezer	312	240	84						See spec sheet
46	3	Carter-Hoffman # PHB-650A Mobile refrigerator	50	35	73	120	1	8.5			

EQUIPMENT SCHEDULE

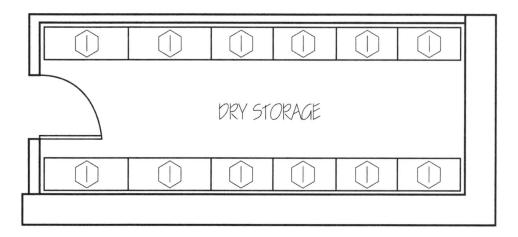

DRY STORAGE

EQUIPMENT SCHEDULE											
ITEM #	QTY	MFR MODEL # DESCRIPTION	DIMENSIONS			ELECTRICAL				BTUH	REMARKS
			W	D	H	V	PH	A	kW		
1	12	InterMetro Storage shelving	36	18	84						

Dry storage is away from food preparation areas that may affect temperature and humidity adversely.

The **dry storage** can be arranged so that the items used most often are the most accessible.

These **prep areas** (opposite page) are located away from heat sources and have access to refrigeration without requiring workers to go to the hot side of the kitchen. The kitchen is equipped with a tilt skillet, steam kettles, and a convection steamer for volume preparation. A centralized **steam line** powers multiple pieces of equipment.

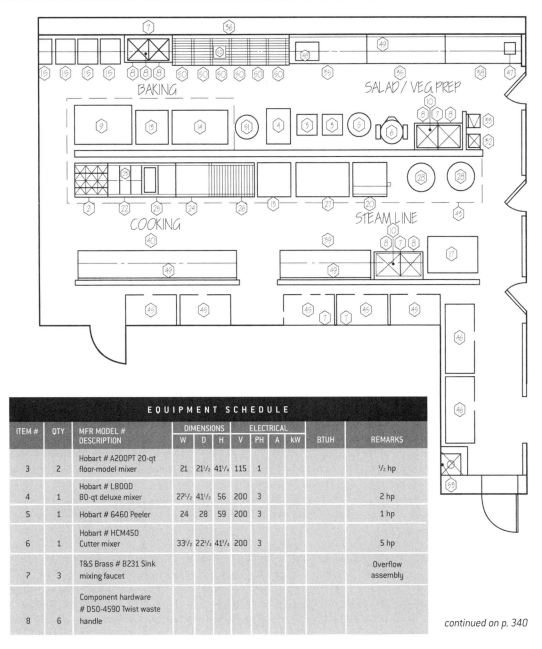

EQUIPMENT SCHEDULE

ITEM #	QTY	MFR MODEL # DESCRIPTION	DIMENSIONS			ELECTRICAL				BTUH	REMARKS
			W	D	H	V	PH	A	kW		
3	2	Hobart # A200PT 20-qt floor-model mixer	21	21½	41¼	115	1				½ hp
4	1	Hobart # L800D 80-qt deluxe mixer	27½	41½	56	200	3				2 hp
5	1	Hobart # 6460 Peeler	24	28	59	200	3				1 hp
6	1	Hobart # HCM450 Cutter mixer	33½	22¼	41¾	200	3				5 hp
7	3	T&S Brass # B231 Sink mixing faucet									Overflow assembly
8	6	Component hardware # D50-4590 Twist waste handle									

continued on p. 340

ITEM #	QTY	MFR MODEL # DESCRIPTION	DIMENSIONS			ELECTRICAL				BTUH	REMARKS
			W	D	H	V	PH	A	kW		
9	1	Blodgett # 961 Double-deck gas oven	60	40	60					74K	Steam jets, cordierite deck
10	3	Custom two-bay stainless steel vegetable sink	51	27½	35						
13	2	Blodgett # DFG-102 Gas-fired double convection oven	38	37	70	115	1	9		110K	
14	1	Baker's Aid # BAP-2-RI Two-rack proof box	60	36	89½	208 110	1 1	34.6 4.6	7.2 5		
15	4	Seco # OR 1820 Heavy-duty rack	20½	26	68						
17	1	Scotsman # CM1400 Modular contour cuber with BH 1000 bin	52/52	24/31½	27/44	208	1	246			1292 # CAP 3.25 hp
20	1	Cleveland # PGM-300-2 Pressure steamer—2	36	37	64	115	1		.1	300K	Gas-fired steam generator
21	1	Wolfe # KFS-6-27 Six burner with convection oven	36	38	66	115	1	4		150K	Double-high shelf, stainless steel left shelf
22	1	Wolfe # KFS-0-27-3HT Hot top with convection oven	36	38	48½	115	1	4		135K	
23	1	Wolfe # FS-RB-36A Salamander broiler	36	19	17½					66K	
24	1	Wolfe # FS-HB-27-1 Broiler, range, and finishing oven	36	38	72					140K	
25	1	Wolfe # FS-WTF-42S and FS-FM Gas fryer	36	38	66					120K	High riser
26	1	Wolfe # FS-SCB-47 Charbroiler	47	38	66					116K	Double-high shelf
27	1	Market Forge 1300 40-gal ultraskillet	56	27	42	120	1	2		114K	
28	2	Groen AH/1 Gas-fired 60-gal steam kettle	41	44½	49	115	1	2		145K	
32	1	M&E MFG. # BH Base-mounted hand sink	17	14	43						Provide soap dispenser and paper towels above
33	1	Halsey Taylor # SW 4A Wall-mounted cooler	18	14	40	115	1	2.4	.2		⅙ hp
35	2	Custom stainless steel table with undershelf	84	30	35						*See drawing*

ITEM #	QTY	MFR MODEL # DESCRIPTION	DIMENSIONS			ELECTRICAL				BTUH	REMARKS
			W	D	H	V	PH	A	kW		
36	1	Maple-top table	126	30	35						*See drawing*
38	1	Corner stainless steel table with undershelf	72	30	35						
39	1	Stainless steel prep table with undershelf	96	30	35						
40	1	Stainless steel prep table with undershelf	168	30	35						
43	1	Gaylord Ventilator and exhaust/ makeup air unit									*See spec sheet*
45	5	Carter-Hoffman # BB-1300 HTD Banquet cart	55	32	74	120	1	13	1.5		
46	2	Carter-Hoffman # PHB-650A Mobile refrigerator	50	35	73	120	1	8.5			
47	1	Robot Coupe # R6N Food processor	13	14	25	208	3	2.8			
48	1	Hobart # 1612 Slicer	26	24	25	115	1	15			
49	3	Wall-mounted stainless steel double shelves	Varies	18	18						
50	6	Wilder # 217SW/P17NF Wooden bench table	18	27	22						
51	1	Duchess Dough divider	18	23	69						
52	1	Hobart # 1841 Load cell scale	14	15	8	115	1				
53	1	T&S Brass # B-665-BSTR Service sink faucet									

The centralized **steam line** allows any equipment requiring connections to the building's water or steam lines to be hooked up more easily.

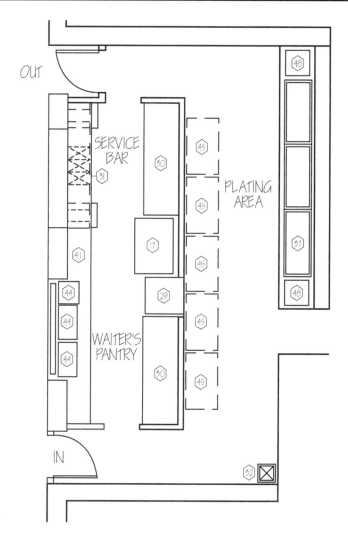

The **service bar** and **servers' pantry** are accessible from the banquet room through a counter area, which is supplied from the kitchen storage areas, making replenishing during an event invisible to guests. The **plating area** has heated banquet carts to hold product during service time. There is a double-sided assembly line for faster service, complete with a steam table, icing bins, and automatic slicers; its location prevents banquet service from interfering with any preparations in the kitchen for subsequent events.

The **service bar** and **plating area** are right near the door.

EQUIPMENT SCHEDULE

ITEM #	QTY	MFR MODEL # DESCRIPTION	DIMENSIONS			ELECTRICAL				BTUH	REMARKS
			W	D	H	V	PH	A	kW		
17	1	Scotsman # CM1400 Modular contour cuber w/ BH 1000 bin	52/52	24/31½	27/44	208	1	246			1292 lb capacity 3¼ hp
29	1	Traulsen # RIH-1-32 Roll-through heated cabinet	36	39	83	208	1	7.5	1.5		
30	2	Traulsen # RUC-3-32 WSC Three-section undercounter refrigerator	105	36	34	115	1	12.1			⅓ hp
31	2 1	(2) 24-in ice bins Three-bay sink w/ 18-in drain	120	21	29						Two-bottle troughs
32	1	M&E Manufacturing # BH Base-mounted hand sink	17	14	43						Provide soap dispenser and paper towels above
37	1	Chef's table w/ two food warmers, cold pan, and heat lamps	252	42	35						*See spec sheet*
41	1	Custom beverage and bar counter	309	24	35						
44	3	Blickman # AT-810E Twin-tank coffee urn	33½	17	30	208	3	39	15		
45	5	Carter-Hoffman # BB-1300 HTD Banquet carts	55	32	74	120	1	13	1.5		
48	2	Hobart # 1612 Slicers	26	24	25	115	1	15			

Dish and Pot Washing

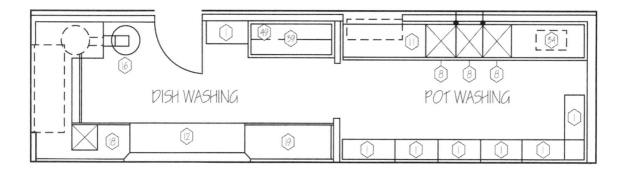

DISH WASHING

POT WASHING

The **dish and pot washing** areas are easily accessible to the service staff and kitchen staff, which can drop off cookware. **Dish and pot washing** functions are separated, reflecting the different equipment necessary to handle each efficaciously.

EQUIPMENT SCHEDULE											
ITEM #	QTY	MFR MODEL # DESCRIPTION	DIMENSIONS			ELECTRICAL				BTUH	REMARKS
			W	D	H	V	PH	A	kW		
1	7	InterMetro Storage shelving	36	18	84						
7	2	T&S Brass # B231 Sink mixing faucet									With overflow assembly
8	3	Component Hardware # D50-4590 Twist waste handle									
11	1	Custom three-bay pot sink	204	27½	35						
12	1	Hobart # CPW-100 Gas-fired dishwasher	100	22	58						
16	1	Somat # SPC-20SHT Close-coupled waste pulping system	24	31	64	208	3				With trough connection; 2 hp
18	1	Custom U-shaped soil table		30	35						
19	1	Custom clean table	75	30	35						
34	1	Zurn # z-1170-400 Grease intercepter	17	25	17						With high and low 2-in tapping and straight flow control
38	1	Corner stainless steel table with undershelf	72	30	35						
49	1	Wall-mounted stainless steel double shelves	Varies	18	18						

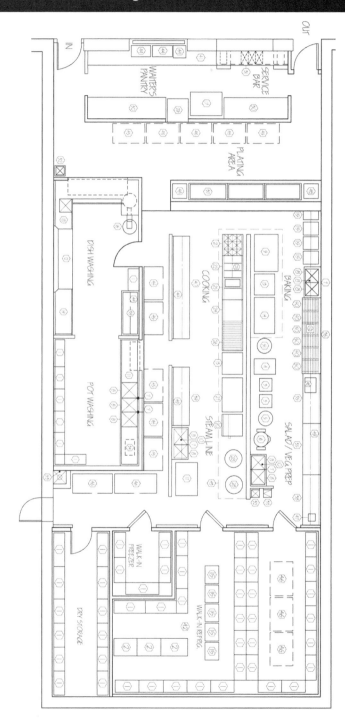

index